D1560186

How Do We Get Out of Here?

How Do We Get Out of Here?

Half a Century of Laughter and Mayhem
at The American Spectator—From Bobby
Kennedy to Donald J. Trump

R. EMMETT TYRRELL, JR.

POST HILL
PRESS

Published by Bombardier Books
An Imprint of Post Hill Press
ISBN: 978-1-63758-956-4
ISBN (eBook): 978-1-63758-957-1

How Do We Get Out of Here:
Half a Century of Laughter and Mayhem at *The American Spectator*—
From Bobby Kennedy to Donald J. Trump
© 2023 by R. Emmett Tyrrell Jr.
All Rights Reserved

Cover Design by Hampton Lamoureux

Post Hill Press
New York • Nashville
posthillpress.com

Published in the United States of America
1 2 3 4 5 6 7 8 9 10

To Jeanne
To P.D., Katy, and Annie

Contents

Whom the Gods would destroy, they first make famous.

Chapter I

HOW DO WE GET OUT OF HERE?

On April 24, 1968, a few weeks before Bobby Kennedy was shot dead as he walked without a security detail through the kitchen of Los Angeles's Ambassador Hotel, he addressed a full and rowdy house at Indiana University's auditorium. It was toward the end of Indiana's Democratic presidential primary in which he was competing with Senator Eugene McCarthy and Indiana's governor, the state's favorite son, Roger Branigin. Kennedy would win the race and head on to the next primary in California.

As surprising as it may sound, I was the only person standing on stage behind him, though I was then a very green editor of a new off-campus *conservative* magazine, *The Alternative*, which I edit to this day under the name *The American Spectator*. There were plenty of Kennedy supporters in the auditorium that day. There were even some campus radicals. Yet I was the solitary figure standing behind the massive black curtains that were his backdrop. I had walked over to the auditorium with my younger brother, Roger, but when we got there, we split up; he to the orchestra pit, I to the stage. There was no one else on stage, just me behind the curtains!

Sometimes, no matter how perceptive one fancies oneself, the significance of an event, even a very large event—say a presidential election, say an assassination—escapes one's notice. I quickly forgot the events of April 24, 1968. My life was about to speed up, and it has remained at high speed ever since.

Within months, I pretty much forgot my adventure with Bob Kennedy. It lay fallow in my mind for years. I was like Fabrizio, Stendhal's hero in *The Charterhouse of Parma*, riding my horse through the battle of Waterloo without a clue as to the meaning of it all. *Clop, clop, clop*, young Fabrizio rides on. *Clap, clap, clap*, throughout the great auditorium, the significance of that afternoon in Indiana would not be recognized by me for years to come.

All that was on my mind that day was how ironic it was that I, a stalwart of the New Right as it was then called, was within a few feet of the liberals' great hope for a reiteration of Camelot or of the New Frontier, Bob Kennedy! I was the lone figure standing behind him. Just me! Standing alone, peering out at the crowd from behind the curtain! There I stood as he mesmerized yet another audience in his increasingly frenzied campaign for the Democratic presidential nomination. No one else was with us! I was twenty-four years old.

And, the truth be known, in April 1968, I already had my candidate. I was supporting Governor Ronald Reagan in his brief run for the Republican presidential nomination. I even had a "Reagan for President" button in my pocket. It would be twenty years before the import of Kennedy's speech began to eke back into my mind, and perhaps twenty more years before the issues he raised that day became clear to me. Bob Kennedy was contagiously eloquent that afternoon. He was polished. He was au courant. He reached out to the throng with an infectious sense of urgency. Yet practically every word of that speech in the light of oncoming history was wrong. Moreover, the speech, as good as it seemed to be in 1968, quickly and unaccountably faded from my mind, and twenty years later its sense of urgency had vanished too.

Weeks later, when bullets announced the tragic denouement of his quest for the presidency, I had put—for the most part—his April speech out of my mind. Life then took off for me: The growth of my magazine and all the adventures that came with it crowded out other thoughts. Suddenly the years of student protests were upon us and the race riots and the assassinations and Watergate and all the hullabaloo that went with it, some transient, some still with us.

The Nixon years arrived in typical Republican sobriety but culminated in tragedy. Then there was the Ford interlude and more Republican sobriety, and then the delightful Carter years when I was given my first chance to bedevil a president and never missed an opportunity to do so. Years later, President Carter's aide, Robert Pastor, assured me during a junket to Mexico City for President Miguel de la Madrid's inauguration: "Carter *hated* you." Wow, my first presidential endorsement!

Then the years with Ronald Reagan in the White House, schmoozing with him, dining in the State Dining Room, and inviting him to my home for dinner, he and a security detail composed of hundreds plus his own bartender. He drank Screwdrivers—two! Then came the first Bush years: luncheon in the Rose Garden where I counseled him not to raise taxes. Bush was a gent, even if he ignored my counsel and that of Chief of Staff John Sununu and an advisor, Charlie Black. After President George H. W. Bush came the rollicking Clinton years, a descent from the Greatest Generation to the Phoniest Generation, that is to say, the coat-and-tie radicals of the 1960s generation. Bill never had me to dinner, though we shared a dining room once at the Jockey Club in Washington in 1995 where we chatted until I noticed that he was becoming agitated; his wife, too, was becoming agitated. I suggested he go over and sit down, *and he did*! The president of the United States sat down at my command! We never renewed the conversation.

Yet, I never stopped pursuing him and his lovely wife, Bruno, through the 1990s, through the next two decades, even through the #MeToo hysteria, when he was lying low.

Then came another Bush, George W., not quite the gent that his dad was, but he did have me into the White House for dinner with a prince. That would be Prince Charles, not the entertainer, Prince. Then the years of Barack H. Obama—a soigné cipher—and finally my 2016 pick for president, Donald Trump. I spotted him when he came to *The American Spectator*'s 2013 gala and picked him to win the presidency about the time he first came down the escalator at Trump Tower. I repeated my pick frequently right up to his election. "Happy Days Are Here Again"! Or were they?

On and on, for over fifty years, the world whirled and clanged. At times, it picked up speed. Occasionally, it slowed down. But usually, it whirled ever faster. There is a continuity from 1968 to the 2020s. It is a continuity of Episodic Chaos followed by Episodic Calm. One wonders what it all means.

The year nineteen sixty-eight would go down in history as a seminal year in American politics. With it, the whirl quickened. It was the year in which many moderate students became radicalized, at least temporarily, until they began facing the grim news from the Internal Revenue Service. In time, they would revert to the bourgeois grind, but for a while, they would experiment with drugs and sex and, what would become a fixture of society lasting for decades, rock 'n' roll: pontificating, sermonizing, at times seemingly sanctifying whatever it touched. It would take forty-eight years, but finally, rock 'n' roll received its apotheosis with the conferral of the Nobel Prize in Literature upon Bob Dylan. He skipped the ceremony. He already had skipped literature.

The race riots continued. The student protests continued. Innovative acts of criminality were dreamed up, beginning with the poisoning of foods on supermarket shelves so that their containers had to be sealed before being put out in the stores. Letters began being mailed containing dangerous substances. There were drive-by shootings. Soon the campus youth and certain youngish politicos of a forward-leaning disposition would be experimenting with what the sociologists call "lifestyles." Hollywood weighed in as the films with an expansive wholesome cowboy theme were dumped and replaced by angst and Deep Thoughts—something about Mrs. Robinson and Jesus. Jesus? What did He have to do with anything?

Moreover, there were those who experimented with Eastern mysticism. Maharishi something or other led a motely of middle-class Americans and some other drugged-up lunatics, many of whom within just a few years were living life on the streets. They were called the homeless! Today, they have been elevated almost to the estate of Native Americans. Most were the walking dead. In sum and in fine, America was on the hem of what would be a country bereft of authority: the authority to define a sentence, the authority to defend its borders, the authority to assert itself against what became a free-floating moralism, the American Left.

Robert Kennedy was himself a moderate with a mixed record. In his early years, he was very anti-Communist (he worked for Senator Joe McCarthy as an assistant counsel on the Permanent Subcommittee on Investigations and chose McCarthy as godfather to his first child), very Roman Catholic (he was given to making the sign of the cross when passing a Catholic church), and very patriotic (he treated the flag with reverence). Within a few days of my encounter with him, on April 28, to be exact, the *New York Times* ran an article about his campaign, chiding him with the headline: "Kennedy: Meet the Conservative."[1] The *Times* notwithstanding, in the swift currents of 1968, Bob Kennedy was, in fact, edging ever so steadily leftward. All Democrats driven by ambition would suffer this weakness for decades to come.

Addressing the crowd at the Indiana University auditorium that day, he sounded an anti-colonial theme, a theme that he may have learned from his father, though by 1968 it had taken on revisions. He

5

and his brothers were deeply influenced by their very opinionated father. Anti-colonialism had been part of his father's political credenda, along with such Irish-American prejudices as isolationism, opposition to the British crown, and fleeting admiration for Germany. Bob Kennedy's father, the fabulously wealthy conservative investor, Joseph P. Kennedy, had sounded such beliefs in the middle 1930s when he was chairman of the Securities and Exchange Commission, and in 1938 when he became the rambunctious American ambassador to the Court of St. James's. He clung to his brand of anti-colonialism for years thereafter.

Joseph Kennedy was, by today's standards, bipartisan. The former ambassador talked his ideas up with the former Republican president, Herbert Hoover, and other Republican acquaintances, such as the aviator, Charles A. Lindbergh, who was by now a figure in the right-wing America First Committee. He tested his ideas out on the conservative Senator Robert A. Taft, as in the postwar period he became still more isolationist. He was a man whose ideas had no future, though his progeny certainly did. In the 1930s, he had even taken a passing shine to Hitler, dictatorship being in those days viewed as vaguely progressive by certain forward-leaners. *The New Republic* even put in a good word for Mussolini.[2] As the decades passed, his views became increasingly controversial. By 2020, he would be yanked from television talk shows for some of the things he said in the 1930s. Anti-colonialism and even isolationism have had a long and respectable place in American history, tracing their roots back to the Founding Fathers, most notably to George Washington's "Farewell Address" with its admonitions against entangling "our peace and prosperity in the toils of European ambition…"[3]

Yet in the spring of 1968, Bob Kennedy put a different edge on the term "anti-colonialism" as it was used in the recent past. It was no longer the anti-colonialism that his anti-British father, and even President Franklin D. Roosevelt, inflicted on their World War II allies, Great Britain and France. They really were imperialists, and proud of it. Bob Kennedy's anti-colonialism was the anti-colonialism that in the 1960s, left-wing critics applied to the United States of America. The Left was still raving about American imperialism as we entered the twenty-first century. Supposedly we were meddling in countries where we ought not to meddle. This meddling was also known as "foreign aid," and often it was much appreciated by its recipients. In fact, in the years ahead it helped backward countries to develop. Though back in the late 1960s, for a Democratic presidential aspirant, it was keeping the downtrodden of the Third World—a term then coming into fashion—downtrodden.

In the flat, nasal accent of Massachusetts, Bob Kennedy declaimed:

> It is unlikely that whatever the outcome of the war in
> Vietnam, the dominoes will fall in either direction....
> Cambodia, under the leadership of Prince Sihanouk,
> has sought neutrality...but acted strongly and suc-
> cessfully against any internal Communist activity.
> Laos...has held back and even made progress against
> its domestic Communists, the Pathet Lao.... In Africa,
> the active anti-colonial movements, in Angola and
> Mozambique, are led by native nationalists, closer to
> the West than to Communism.[4]

Few skeptics were in the audience that day, and in the following years, as the dominoes fell and each of the above countries suffered the totalitarian lash, few liberals ever acknowledged how tragically wrong they had been.

On and on he went that afternoon, enthralling his audience. He kept mentioning the war in Vietnam, but in a curious way. He spoke as though it were winding down. So often, when we look back on public assessments tendered long ago, they seem to us oddly out of focus. Bob Kennedy's Vietnam War was to last seven more years. Anti-colonialism gave way too often to a local strongman claiming the heroic mantle of George Washington or Gandhi or Mao Zedong. The junior senator from New York spoke of the minatory Soviet Union and struggling China, betraying no hint that in twenty years the Soviet Union would be a corpse, and China would be not impoverished and struggling but growing and prospering though still a totalitarian regime.

Wearing a blue suit, as blue as the bluest sky, and rhythmically brushing a mop of brown hair from his brow, Kennedy employed his entire body, wiry and earnest, in a tireless performance. He was in top form there in Indiana! If his speech that day, which I have kept all these years, sounds invariably off-key today, in 1968 it was current to the utmost, and the applause cascaded down on him. He answered questions from the audience, clasped hands from the outstretched arms, then, suddenly, he stepped behind the curtain and, confronting me, he asked, "How do we get out of here?"

Uh, I had no idea how to get out of "here." I actually had no idea how I had gotten here. Earlier I had just edged sideways for about ten minutes, *slowly, slowly*, out of the range of the stagehands and the police. Then forward as the rows of curtain engulfing me slipped away, then—oh hell, by the time I got to center stage, I did not know how I had gotten there or how to get out. But Kennedy and I were all *alone*, and I had to figure out how we would exit. He obviously thought I was an advance man, possibly a security agent like those who could have been of assistance to him in a few weeks. Presumably, a car was waiting for him. My role as Bob Kennedy's newly appointed advance man was too good to pass up. It might be years before I was again with a politician of his stature. Possibly, I might never meet another world leader. After all, I was a graduate student at Indiana University, and Indiana was a long way from Washington or any other center of power.

So, I was very professional, even a bit assertive. Fortunately, no one was coming forward to help. But the pressure was on me—and I was *lost*. How does one maneuver through a vast maze of black curtains to Bob Kennedy's waiting car, which was waiting, well, where? I thought it had to be off to the left. There was a backstage exit over there. He followed me through the curtains to the left. Then I sheepishly strode back through the curtains to the right. Then to the left and then to the right, again. There seemed to be a light off to the left, an "Exit" light! A car with its engine running was just beyond the light, outside the auditorium's rear door. The crowd was forming as I led him out into the street. I had found the Kennedy car—at least I hoped it was the Kennedy car—and we hastened down the steps to it. He seated himself in the backseat and looked up at me, smiling. Then I suffered an inspiration. I took my "Reagan for President" button from my pocket and dropped it into his outstretched hand. He looked at it and laughed. Off his driver took him. I left Bob Kennedy laughing!

My next memory of Bob Kennedy was some seven weeks later on television. He was in the kitchen of the Ambassador Hotel lying on the floor dying. A busboy named Juan Romero had thrust a rosary into his hand (coincidentally his brother, too, had a rosary in his coat pocket when he was assassinated), and as he lay on his back on the kitchen floor, his eyes wide open, his head illuminated in what looked very much like a halo, he put me in mind of one of the martyred saints he so revered.[5] Later it occurred to me that the mortally wounded senator held the rosary in the same hand where I, seven weeks before, had placed a "Reagan for President" button, and he had laughed.

Supposedly he asked the busboy, "Is everybody all right?" Harry Benson, the British photographer who twenty-six years later did a spread on me when *Esquire* was covering my Clinton pursuits, believes he heard Kennedy say, "My head," and Benson thought he heard his wife, Ethel, tell him, "I'm with you, my baby." Someone else heard him whisper, "Jack…Jack."[6] Then he was taken to a nearby hospital. Ethel remained at his side. He died early the next day. Once again, in California as in Indiana, he had had no security except, of course, for me in Indiana. It seems that Bob Kennedy, like his older brother, had shunned security. It was, to my mind, a brave thing to do, a defiant thing to do, but it denied America a new, never-to-be-examined chapter in its history. A new Kennedy administration, the second in eight years, would almost certainly be out of the ordinary. Bob Kennedy's abruptly truncated campaign had made that much clear.

Over the next decades, America attempted to sort it all out: the drugs, the sex, the demonstrations for random causes—some noble, some not. Progressive values, as seen from the vantage point of the twenty-first century, look like one pell-mell flight from authority. Each authority that was abandoned was usually never replaced. The rules of grammar, the rules of deportment, the rules for citizenship, the rules of governance, all were abandoned. There were no replacements, except for, perhaps, a soft tyranny. The goal of the radicals in 1968 was the New Morality. Oddly, the goal of the radicals in 2020 was nothing more substantial than a burp about progress.

Though Bob Kennedy's run had been uphill, and he would have still faced formidable opponents in Vice President Hubert Humphrey and the Republican candidate, Richard Nixon, he might have reached the presidency. After vanquishing Humphrey, he would have treated America to a second Kennedy versus Nixon contest, and had he won that race, he would have given us a second Camelot or perhaps Something New. One thing is certain: Washington would have been much different.

A decade later, his old political aide Paul Corbin told me that by 1968 Kennedy was being widely misconstrued. Paul was now a confidant of my close friend and occasional lawyer, Bill Casey, Ronald Reagan's 1980 campaign manager and later his head of the Central Intelligence Agency. Paul thought that that *New York Times* headline from April 28, 1968, was onto something. Bob Kennedy may not have led America to Ronald Reagan's brand of conservatism, but he was not leading it into the quirky world of Jimmy Carter nor the jejune amorality of the New Morality.

His unwritten chapter of American history would have been, Paul believed, more conservative, though for conservatives it might not have been conservative enough. It would have been, Paul said, a mixture of concern for the very poor and the New Conservative values:

decentralization, local control, and federalism. Looking back on Bob Kennedy's 1968 campaign, there is something surprisingly prescient about it. Could Paul have been right? Kennedy spoke in Indiana about partnerships between private enterprises and community development groups in the inner city. He talked about what the columnist Jack Newfield called "radical ideas and somewhat conservative values."[7] So his speech of 1968 was not completely out of focus. In fact, it might have, at least on domestic matters, anticipated the future.

As for my candidate Ronald Reagan, his time would come years later. For now, he was merely the governor of California. The night after Sirhan B. Sirhan shot Kennedy in what some American historians have called the first act of terrorism against America, Governor Reagan made a public statement on Joey Bishop's nationally televised program. Reagan, the rising Cold Warrior, said something that has gone unnoticed by historians ever since. Sirhan, a Palestinian Christian, claimed to be angry with Kennedy for his support of Israel the year before in the Six-Day War. The night after Kennedy died, Reagan told Bishop that all of California was under a "pall," and that Kennedy had been struck down by a "senseless" and "savage act." Then the California governor linked his death to something more ominous. Yes, Sirhan was the immediate agent of Kennedy's death, but, said Reagan, "The enemy sits in Moscow." Reagan continued, "I call him an enemy because I believe he has proven this, by deed, in the Middle East. The actions of the enemy led to and precipitated the tragedy of last night."[8] Reagan recalled that exactly one year before Moscow had confected false intelligence about phony Israeli troop maneuvers and shared these fictions with Egypt and Egypt's Arab allies, goading them into action against Israel. The result was uncounted dead Arabs, Israelis, and now one American presidential aspirant, Bob Kennedy.

I did not hear Reagan that night, but I doubtless would have agreed with the emerging Cold Warrior. I was always anti-Communist. Even at a time of national mourning, the governor still had his eye on what he as president would call the "Evil Empire," an empire that in 1968 was worldwide. In twenty years, Ronald Reagan would personally expunge the evil. It might have sounded like a stretch at the time to link Moscow's propaganda with Sirhan's cowardly act, but it would not sound like a stretch years later when Reagan brought the Cold War to an end. By then, I think Reagan had earned his credentials as an expert on the Soviet Union. He knew evil when he saw it.

Reagan continued to link Moscow with the Kennedy brothers' assassinations eight days later, and like Woody Allen's fictional figure Zelig, I again made an appearance. On June 13, Reagan, having thought about similarities in the two Kennedys' assassinations, reminded an audience at the Indiana State Fairgrounds that Bob Kennedy's brother, John, also was a victim of Soviet Communism, even more directly. "Five years ago," Reagan said, "a president was murdered by one who renounced his American citizenship to embrace the godless philosophy of Communism, and it was Communist violence he brought to our land. The shattering sound of his shots were still ringing in our ears when a policy decision was made to play down his Communist attachment lest we provoke the Soviet Union."[9]

That day I led a group of students up to Indianapolis from Indiana University to support the governor during a press conference at the old Marott Hotel. He treated us to soft drinks and his legendary good cheer. So apparently my encounter with Bob Kennedy was not to be my last encounter with a politician of world stature, or at least potential world stature. Looking back on the whole rather astonishing interlude from April to June 1968, you will perhaps forgive me if I say that, for me, modern history is more engrossing than any modern novel.

As I say, it took more than twenty years for the full import of the Kennedy tragedy to hit me. By then I lived in Washington. I had invited Kathleen Kennedy Townsend and her husband David Townsend over for dinner at my McLean, Virginia, home, and as the evening progressed, it slowly dawned on me that I had been alone on stage with her father some two decades before and in a position not unlike that of Sirhan B. Sirhan. Yet I chose a button and a joke to express my disagreement, and Sirhan chose a gun and the cowardliness of an ambush.

Through my friendship in the 1980s with Paul Corbin I had been introduced to Ethel Kennedy's soirées at Hickory Hill, a few blocks away from my home in McLean. I became familiar with many of the Kennedy clan at gatherings large and small. One evening when I arrived for dinner, Ethel said to me something to the effect that: "I know why you get along so well with Kathleen. She is *soo* conservative." Well, her conservatism was somewhat debatable, at least in comparison to mine, but she is certainly elegant, sophisticated, and she has an unfailing sense of fun. We visited rather often until my reporting on the Clintons made our friendship—I guess the term would be "complicated."

That night at my home in McLean we had a grand time, made all the grander by my Grenadian housekeeper, Doreen Gibbs, who served dinner in the Grenadian style with a dish balanced perfectly on her head as she sashayed her 280-pound body around the dining room (she was a svelte 240 pounds when she arrived from Grenada). Kathleen remarked that I could not possibly be a racist, my conservatism notwithstanding. Kathleen noted that Doreen and I and her daughter, Nikki, got along so well. We talked a lot about public policy that night and other things, and slowly, slowly, the long-dormant memory of that faraway afternoon in Hoosierland so many years ago came to life. I woke up the next morning and thought of things that I had not thought about in many years. I had encountered many figures whom I did not plan on encountering back in 1968: figures in politics, business, sports, and the arts, abroad and at home; some common criminals; some uncommon Soviet dissidents.

Of all those I had encountered, only one man was about to be assassinated. What is more, Bob Kennedy was the leader of his party. The thought occurred as I took my morning coffee and it has continued to intrigue me: how his party has changed from 1968 to 1992, and how it has changed even more as we have departed the Obama era and entered the era of Donald Trump and then Joe Biden.

And what of Ronald Reagan, the other national figure whom I had met in the spring of 1968 amid the rolling hills of Indiana? His party has changed, too, but has it changed as much as the Democrats? By the 2020s, most of the Republicans' changes were made mainly in response to the Democrats' changes, or should I say their leaps to the left? Certainly, by the Obama administration, their leaps to the left made them the party of the Left. The liberals were liberals no more. Liberalism had died by 2011 when I wrote *The Death of Liberalism*. It took the political class a long time to note its passing. Some still talk of being liberals.

Republicans were to change all right, but they remained the party of small government, the rule of law, and strong foreign policy. Barry Goldwater, the Republicans' first conservative candidate in modern times, would at least recognize what his party has evolved into were he to see it in the 2020s. I am not sure that Bob Kennedy, or for that matter John Kennedy, would recognize the present-day Democrats. And one more thing, that faraway evening in my McLean, Virginia, home, Kathleen had revealed that she—proper Democrat that she was—believed that all Republicans, except for me, were self-proclaimed racists. Three decades after the passage (the *bipartisan* passage!) of the civil rights laws, most Democrats deeply believed that Republicans were self-proclaimed racists. Racism had not been an issue with me or with any of my associates for at least fifty years.

Chapter II

THE SIDEWALKS OF CHICAGO

O n December 14, 1943, my twenty-three-year-old mother-to-be and my sixty-three-year-old grandfather-to-be went careening down the snowy streets of Chicago to St. Anne's Hospital with me aboard, though I had no idea what was going on. All was dark around me, though I felt no discomfort and even gave a kick or two with my tiny legs. I later found out that I was in my mother's womb and resting, except for an occasional bump from my grandfather's lurching Cadillac. Truth be known, I would have been perfectly happy to remain in repose a while longer. But it was all out of my hands. Mother was uncomfortable and growing more so, and Grandfather had work to do at the factory. My father was miles away, for I was born in the midst of World War II.

Thus, began my life, and I have often wondered: "How did I get here?" And, "How do I get out of here?" I never asked to be born, after all.

Mother has always called December 14, 1943, the happiest day of her life. Though, she *would* say that. After all, she was my mother, and besides, she would be making two more trips to St. Anne's Hospital for my sister and my brother. Printing this chapter in gray ink would be appropriate because that is how I remember the early stages of my life. I remember my early years in gray with no memory of why I did the things I did when young. I suppose it was out of fear, a vague fear, and excitement, a sudden excitement, and a sense of fun. Those last two motivations have remained with me all my life.

I will always be thankful to have been born an American and to have enjoyed the freedoms inherited from our Founding Fathers. I hope we can pass those freedoms on to the generations that follow us. Not everyone has such a youth, certainly not if one is born beyond our shores, and then there is adulthood.

My grandfather on my mother's side was named J. Clarence Rogers, and he went by the name Clarence. His family was Irish, though they left the British Isles from Scotland. He pretty much built the Crown Stove Works, then a small shop that he inherited from his father. He would have taken an amazed exception to President Barack Obama's 2012 utterance that he "didn't build" the gas range company that bore the name Crown. Well, he did. There were no government subsidies around when he took the company over. Nor were there government grants or set-asides or any preferential policies whatsoever. He and the members of his generation never imagined the huge web of government programs, regulations, and policies, such as affirmative action, that encumber industry today.

When he would take me down to visit the factory in Cicero, Illinois—also the seat of operations for Al Capone and his Mafia— Grandfather Rogers was the master of his domain. The place was greasy, noisy, and dangerous, with huge steel presses crashing down to shape the steel and other noisy machines finishing the job. Yet his workers, mostly Irish and Italian, often from the Old World, loved him. Years later, a factory foreman told me proudly that my grandfather had resolutely resisted the Mafia's attempts to exact some sort of protection money or unionization from the Crown Stove Works. The Communist faction of the local union bombed the factory. A team of thugs jumped my grandfather, and he had to be hospitalized. Reputedly at the height of these confrontations, a Capone enforcer paid a visit to my grandfather, who got up from his desk, walked around to where Capone's enforcer was sitting, and told him to tell Capone that he could have my grandfather killed, but my grandfather would go to heaven. When a mafioso dies, my grandfather declared, he goes to hell. With that, my grandfather bid his tormentor adieu. Capone's consigliere was never heard from again.

When I heard the story as a young adult, it put me in mind of de Gaulle's meeting with the Russian ambassador to France during the Cuban missile crisis. Moscow's representative got nowhere with de Gaulle, and Capone's representative got nowhere with my grandfather.

My grandfather died in 1948 of prostate cancer when I was five. Every afternoon, as his life slowly ebbed away, I would climb onto his bed and try to comfort him. How, I do not recall. All I recall is that he disappeared for a short period of time, and my sister and I stayed with his nurse, Mrs. Christianson. One afternoon, the doorbell rang. We looked down the staircase and saw my mother with tears streaming down her cheeks. We knew none of us would ever see her father alive again. I assume I burst into tears. I know that for decades thereafter, whenever I have thought of him, I have been overcome with grief. He was my first encounter with a great man.

My family's money came from my mother's side. The entrepreneurship was supplied by my grandfather. The husbanding of his fortune after his death was left to my much younger grandmother, Bernadette, a strong moral force in the years after his death—and proudly and devotedly Irish Catholic, as were both sides of my family. My grandmother never understood what the feminists were so angry about. She saw that we children had all that we needed and were educated in private schools, so when I chose Indiana University over

Notre Dame, she was dubious. My family's sense of history came from my father's side. The Tyrrells go back many centuries. They were a Norman family.

William the Conqueror was a cousin and Walter Tyrrell marched with him. William arrived in England from Normandy rather spectacularly in 1066, as you might recollect. My family arrived more discreetly about 1076, though in less stressful circumstances. The Tyrrells eventually settled in Ireland in the late twelfth century, establishing a string of Norman castles across Ireland's midsection, only one of which remains. It stands guard over a road that slices through the nearly impenetrable peat bogs of Tyrrellspass in County Westmeath. The castle was strategically located. It was probably an ancient tollbooth. Surprisingly, Tyrrellspass Castle is only a few miles south of the Longfords' much larger Tullynally Castle, which is over 350 years old. Tyrrellspass Castle dates from 1411 and has always left a much smaller carbon footprint. I say surprisingly because when I visited with the Longfords at the home of Kitty and Malcolm Muggeridge in Sussex, England, in the 1970s and 1980s, I never realized that when they spoke of their Irish properties, they were talking about properties just up the road from Tyrrellspass Castle, and the Longfords were perhaps too polite to enquire as to my origins.

The Longfords had been friends with the Muggeridges since their early days when they were all on the left. Now the Muggeridges had forsaken the Left's promises of paradise on earth, but they remained close to the Longfords. I often visited the Muggeridges because Malcolm was one of the great characters of his day who wrote often and brilliantly for *The American Spectator* and because Kitty was a charming wit. She famously said of a vacuous television personality widely celebrated in the British Isles but endowed with a really cheap mind that "he rose without a trace." Somehow the Longfords often showed up when I was around despite being staunch Labourites, often on the far-out edge of reform. Possibly the Tyrrells owed the Longfords some act of fealty from medieval times, and Lord Longford was trying to figure out how to collect from me.

Still, our conversations were always cordial. On one occasion, I recall holding forth with gusto on my theory that a free society strengthens the virtues of its citizens. "Good heavens," Lady Longford erupted, "I had heard there were Americans like you." To which Kitty Muggeridge pronounced augustly, "I agree with Baub." Somehow, I think in centuries long past when the Tyrrells fought the English in such battles as the bloody Battle of Tyrrellspass, I would have been glaring down upon his lordship, though now he was a very agreeable pacifist.

At any rate, there were two strains of Tyrrells toward the end of the Middle Ages. Historians note that one strain was surprisingly peaceful and lived irenically, despite the English presence in Ireland. The other was more warlike and withdrew for a period to Spain, where they served as bodyguards to Philip II before returning to Ireland. I like to think that I would have ended up with the friendly Tyrrells. When the warlike Richard Tyrrell returned to Ireland late in the sixteenth century, he took up his aggressive ways and killed a plenitude of Englishmen before relative calm beset him. Slowly, things quieted down, though the English remained for centuries to the impoverishment of the Irish.

When John F. Tyrrell led his infant son P. D. Tyrrell to America from Dublin in the mid-1830s, it was difficult to say just which strain of Tyrrell was on the boat. I do know that P. D. Tyrrell eventually became a policeman in America and a very distinguished one. As the head of the Secret Service in Chicago, he broke the plot to steal Abraham Lincoln's body from its crypt in Springfield, Illinois, in 1876. He was recommended by Lincoln's son, Robert Todd Lincoln, to head the Secret Service nationally after the events in Springfield but was passed over. P. D.'s son, my great-grandfather Frank, whom I met before he died, was also a cop and for some years the sole survivor of the Haymarket riot of 1886.

I still have the huge picture of our sixteenth president that Lincoln's son, Robert, gave to P. D., according to its bronze plaque: "For Loyalty and Service To His Father, Abraham Lincoln." It hangs in my library in Alexandria, Virginia's Old Town district. We call the room the Lincoln Library, and Abe peers out toward the Confederate memorial on Washington Street. At least he once peered out toward the Confederate memorial. Now he peers out at a mysteriously cemented-over hole, which contemporary Americans are more comfortable with. Today, Abe's struggles for the Union are remembered by a cemented-over hole. What side of the hole was your family on? There was never any doubt in my family whose side we supported in the Civil War, and that our cause was just.

P. D.'s death was the occasion for one of my most personal encounters with "Fake News." When he died on April 3, 1920 (the *New York Times* reported that he died on April 4) the newspaper in its obituary claimed he had died at age ninety-nine and that he had served as "one of the guards about President Lincoln when the Chief Executive was assassinated." Now that is Fake News! P. D. was born circa 1831 in Dublin and died in Illinois in 1920. That would make him not ninety-nine but eighty-nine, and if anyone was guarding Lincoln at the time when "the Chief Executive was assassinated," it was not P. D. but a Washington policeman who was probably drunk after drinking at the same bar where John Wilkes Booth gathered his courage for one last act. Incidentally, at *The American Spectator*, we always remember John Wilkes Booth as the first idealistic actor in a long line of idealistic actors leading up to the likes of Jane Fonda and Alec Baldwin.

As for P. D.'s son, Frank, he, too, lived to a great old age, eighty-eight, and he, too, managed to attain distinction as a cop. The Haymarket riot has addled radical Leftists' imaginations for years. In fact, the Weathermen faction of the Students for a Democratic Society (SDS) bombed the Haymarket Memorial twice in 1969 and 1970, until the Chicago Police Department had to relocate the memorial inside of a police station. Barack Obama's old buddy Bill Ayers was behind the 1969 bombing and probably played a role in the 1970 attack. Years before, I, as a little boy, had appeared at a ceremony commemorating the riot and put a wreath on the memorial. Fittingly enough, the SDS attack missed me by twenty-two years.

So, I began life with my grandfather Rogers' money and the Tyrrells' relish for combat. I was well prepared for the life that lay ahead.

I grew up shadowed by the Cold War, though I did not recognize it until the Dominican priests at my high school, Fenwick High School, in Oak Park, Illinois, began to remind us students of the significance of domestic Communism, the Soviet invasion of Hungary, and Cuba's fall to Fidel Castro. Anti-Communism was still taught in high schools when I was young, and from civics class, I learned the principles of a democratic society. I understand that today the young are taught sex education and something about sex changes, but in the late 1950s, we could figure such things out for ourselves if we were so inclined.

At first, I lived in my grandparents' house on Euclid Avenue in Oak Park and later in a house that my grandfather built for my parents in the neighboring River Forest. Both municipalities are suburbs of Chicago, and Chicago was a bustling place in those days. Oak Park was famous for the previous generation's Ernest Hemingway and Frank Lloyd Wright, the architect, and because it was dry. River Forest was dry, too, and famous for its industrialists, its Mafia dons, and Chicago's budding population of television personalities. One, Paul Harvey, lived on our street, Park Avenue. He was a conservative with a nationwide following until his death in 2009. He was also a jogger, trudging by our house practically every day in the 1950s and 1960s. Chicago was then called the Second City, but with television programming drifting to the coasts, its industry slowing down, and the Mafia increasingly on the run from the authorities, its Second City status was fading.

If I were to revisit the Oak Park and River Forest of those days, I would expect them to be depicted in black and white. All my dreams from that time were in black and white. Moreover, everything would

21

move in slow motion and very quietly. Such are my memories of my childhood.

My first memory was gazing across the floor of my grandparents' sunroom into a forest of tall legs. There was animated talking in the heights above me and glasses tinkling and the smell of cigarettes and cigars. The adults were having a cocktail party, and it seems today that I eavesdropped on the adults' cocktail parties for years to come. A couple of years later, when I was four or five years old, I often sat on our spacious front porch with my mother and grandmother and watched the world pass by. I remember a very old lady from a huge mansion up the street who would bounce down Euclid Avenue in an ancient electric car that had survived World War I and World II, or so my mother told me. I think the electric car was called a Baker Victoria, and it looked like a black rectangle on wheels, not like today's sleek electric Teslas. There were students from nearby Oak Park High School who seemed very old to me. And there was a man with a limp, wearing a woolen cap and smoking a pipe, who hobbled along Euclid Avenue every day. He fascinated me, and when my mother saw him limp along, she was very relieved. I, too, had been walking with a limp of late, and she was about to take me to her doctor.

At the end of our block, a few doors down, there stood some sort of municipal building which was of little interest to me, but behind it, there was a stable with enormous horses. Were they Clydesdales? How were they employed? I never knew for sure, but I thought they had something to do with snowplows. There was a lot of snow in Chicago, and there still is. As I approached five years of age, my mother loosened the leash on my sister and me and gave us considerable freedom, which we did not always use prudently. On one occasion, we raided a neighbor's enormous vegetable garden. We picked tomatoes and corn and cucumbers and took them home. We were quite proud of ourselves: The produce grew right out of the ground, and it was free! At least until my mother and the neighbor discovered our larcenous act, and then came our first lesson in private property.

I began my formal education earlier than I might have expected. The reason was not because I was precocious but because our parish priest, Father Bianko was his name, feared that if I did not enter kindergarten at four years of age, my mother would perish. She was excitable, and I was combustible. It was Father Bianko's view that I was out of control, always out of control, and so off I went to the gothic spires of our beautiful parish church and school known as St. Edmund's. Thus, I began an exceedingly mediocre career as a student, not only in kindergarten but also in grammar school and even in high school and much of college. Frankly, I often found education baffling and boring. Fortunately, I never exactly failed anything, but I rarely excelled, though I found history and government increasingly absorbing.

At any rate, after a year at St. Edmund's, my family left Euclid Avenue for the nearby suburb of River Forest, where my grandfather had seen to it that a house was built for us on Park Avenue. It was on a block that was almost devoid of homes. There were a few homes there that had been built before World War II, but not many, and now in the early 1950s, a housing boom was underway as earthmovers dug into the virgin soil, or at least the prairie soil, which may have once been farmland but nothing more. With all the disruption, the land was alive with garter snakes, rabbits, chipmunks, and with what must be one of the most stupid animals on the Illinois prairie: gophers.

Within a year, there were at least four young families on Park Avenue, which, with my brother and me, composed a gang of six boys. We terrorized the neighborhood, collecting lightning bugs in jars in the evening and putting jars to even grislier use during the daylight hours. We learned to run down gophers and trap them in their dens by putting a gallon jug of water over the dens' entrance. The poor animals clamored into the bottles soaking wet, and then we did what with them? I know we kept them for a while, but what we eventually did with them, I have no idea. I recall what we did with the snakes we captured. We brought them to the home of the Birmingham boys, whose mother did not mind them at all. My mother always thought she was odd. At one time, the Birminghams had some forty of the black and yellow serpents slithering in cages on their back porch. Did Mrs. Birmingham sauté them? I can only tell you that I was never invited to dinner at the Birminghams.

Our gang played other games in the early 1950s. As houses went up, there were mountains of dirt piled high from digging their foundations. On them, we would play King of the Mountain and would have "mud ball" fights. One of our most dangerous endeavors was to build underground clubhouses or "forts" at the new construction sites. Luckily, the neighborhood construction ended before any of us were swallowed alive by a cave-in. In the open fields, we played baseball all day in the summer and flew kites in the spring. In autumn, we played football. My father had played in the 1939 College All-Star Game on Chicago's Soldier Field against the New York Giants. I usually wore his leather red, white, and blue helmet in our games until it could be worn no more and it just disappeared. As did my father. He was probably the most successful man I ever met. He never wanted to do anything, and he never did. We were never what you would call close.

The Tyrrells were the first non-Protestants to raise a new house on the block. The other new homes were inhabited by Methodists, Presbyterians, and Lutherans. This was a cause for friction, particularly with the Tyrrell children who were outnumbered five to two, and my younger brother, being some three years younger than the rest of us, was not much help in a fight. The neighborhood continued to expand and what we now approvingly call "diversity" increased. In the 1950s, along with diversity came animosity among ethnic groups, and with that came a rich and colorful lexicon of ethnic slurs, which only encouraged fighting. The Protestants were now outnumbered by the Irish, the Italians, the Germans, and the Eastern Europeans—even a few Jews. Slurs, such as "mick," "dago," "turkey," and "kike" followed, but not the n-word. There were no targets for the n-word in River Forest. Curiously, too, there was no slur for the Protestants. Was this an oversight or a manifestation of the Protestants' lingering hegemony over us? I still do not know, but today's experts on hate crimes should attend to this oversight.

With all the contemporary attention that today's advocates of diversity apply to society, they have still not repaired this longtime omission in our lexicon of ethnic slurs. We need to slur Protestants with the same ease that we slur the more recent arrivals. No, "old white men" will not do. Nor will "honky" do. For one thing, its origins are too obscure, and WASP is almost an honorific. They have all been tried, and they have failed.

Yet as year chased year, and the animosities borne of diversity disappeared, all the boys began to get along, and the girls, too. By the time we reached high school—Oak Park High School for the Protestants, Fenwick High School and Trinity High School for the Catholics—we seemed actually to like each other. The diversity practiced in the 1950s was apparently a more effective cure for divisiveness than today's version, given the present intensity of racial and religious friction. We even inter-married in the 1960s and, of course, inter-divorced.

By now, I was enrolled in St. Vincent Ferrer grammar school, from which I would graduate in 1957. Though the nuns were kind and solicitous, I cannot say that my performance improved. Actually, I have no idea what kind of grades I got. All I remember is that I had not a clue as to why I was going to St. Vincent's, and for most of my time there, I was hopelessly bored, but not all of the time.

There was a girl in my class named Barbara Brown who never failed to interest me. One day during a question-and-answer session conducted by our teacher, Miss Sweeny, I noticed blue ink raining down on us. It took a while to ascertain the source of the sudden blue downpour. It came from Barbara's fountain pen, held high above us, which she was shaking desperately. As I recall, she always had her hand up for something and she usually was desperate. Then there was the time she clouted me in the head with a teeter-totter. I have carried the scar from that encounter through the decades. It may look like it resulted from a ferocious struggle, but it was a memento from Barbara Brown.

I had a habit of suddenly, out of the blue, finding myself in what I would call today enigmatic trouble, usually with my teachers. I could never really put my finger on any of a dozen plausible causes, though as I have aged and gained some perspective, I have arrived at one unavoidable conclusion: I usually deserved the trouble I was in.

Sometimes I actually learned from my troubles. On one occasion, I learned a lesson that would shape my adult life and my political leanings. It was my accidental discovery of the Holocaust. My discovery came from another lapse into delinquency. I was in seventh grade and still apparently courting trouble. My teacher, Sister Sarafina, regularly exiled me to the back of the classroom, where she maintained a library of tattered old magazines dating back to World War II, which seemed like ancient history to me, though the guns had fallen silent hardly a decade earlier. There were back issues of *Time* magazine and of the picture magazines *Look*, *Life*, and *Collier's*. There on the pages of these battered magazines I got, at the age of thirteen, my first glimpse of the cadaverous victims of Nazi concentration camps as they were liberated by the astonished soldiers of the US Army. Did it ever dawn on me that if I had been born a few years earlier I might have, with my comrades, stumbled into one of these gruesome concentration camps—or maybe even have been numbered among the American casualties? I doubt it, but still, I was sufficiently shocked by what I saw in those tattered magazines to stand by Israel in practically every scrape that the Israelis were to get into throughout my adult life.

In religion class, we were then studying the Roman persecution of the Christians, but that was long ago. The persecution of the Jews had just taken place, and it was conducted by one of the supposedly most civilized European countries. It was done in the name of *science*, and, I guess, advanced thought. The Nazis were hauling the Jews from all over Europe to concentration camps and gassing them. Some had escaped to the British Isles or North America, but many did not make it. Later I learned that at least six million did not make it. I do not know if it was in the back room of Sister Sarafina's classroom or sometime later, but the idea took root in my mind that the Jews, the Christians, and, later, the victims of the Soviet gulag, ought to stick together. They had a lot in common. That America led the resistance to Nazi barbarism made me proud. In time, it made me equally proud that America led in resisting and defeating Soviet Communism. We liberated Eastern Europe and even the Russians at the end of the Cold War. A milepost in that liberation was a White House dinner for Russia's first elected president, Boris Yeltsin, that I was privileged to be invited to in June 1992.

Toward the end of grammar school or in early high school, I learned another lesson: Some of my neighbors were really famous. One afternoon when I came home from school, my mother beckoned me to the television set. "Mr. F. was just on television," she declared rather proudly. "He said 'I refuse ta answer on the grounds it may incinerate me.'" I presume my mother misinterpreted Mr. F., but I let it go. I shall use the first initial of his last name so as not to disturb his corpse or any surviving relatives. Though by now they would probably be a bit long in the tooth.

I never enquired as to what mother was watching on the television, though I did know Mr. F. His son hung around with us in late grammar school, though by eighth grade his appearances with us had become infrequent. Somewhat mysteriously, he had to help his dad at the family business, which was a liquor store, and therein lies the mystery or one of the mysteries that Mr. F. inspired. The family lived in a mansion in the posh end of River Forest with huge cars in the driveway and domestic staff. It was not how one would expect a liquor-monger to live. And there were other mysteries: bodyguards and much business conducted in the handsomely appointed basement of his mansion from a barber chair equipped with a telephone—a telephone!

As a matter of fact, Mr. F. conducted his affairs much the way Francis Ford Coppola depicted his characters in the famous *Godfather* series, though without a hint of violence. He did live, as I have reported, in a posh neighborhood that abounded with gentlemen who followed his profession. Men with names such as Sam "Teets" Battaglia, Paul "The Waiter" Ricca, and Tony "Big Tuna" Accardo come to mind. You may have heard of them. But as for Mr. F., he was a perfect gentleman, and I never even heard him use the F-word. He even had his "guy" cut my hair when it got too shaggy, and he allowed us to shoot pool in his basement when he was not on the barber chair's telephone. During clement weather, he would spend Sunday mornings seated in a beach chair outside his mansion and wave to us boys when we passed his house en route to Sunday morning Mass.

I lost touch with his son and, of course, with him. Yet years later, one of my pals from River Forest, Tom Lescher, became a proctologist in Florida and he told me that Mr. F. had moved nearby in his sunset years. He became one of Tom's most diligent patients. He was apparently very fastidious about following all the protocols of Tom's artistry. Mr. F. died peacefully of natural causes at a grand old age. All those hours spent in the beach chair on Sunday mornings apparently paid off.

I have one other story from my Mafia trove. At some point during seventh or eighth grade, a classmate, Jackie K. I shall call him, for he had his own Mafia connection—namely, his father—decided that I had offended him. He would pay for me to be beaten up. He was familiar with such modus operandi, for his father had recently been gunned down and left in the trunk of a car in the nearby Lutheran church parking lot. Jackie K.'s plans for me were much more temperate than the plans perpetrated on his poor father. He offered money to the biggest boy in our class, Bill Hanley, to teach me a lesson. Bill was a family friend and would not think of bringing violence down on me, though he did suggest that if I were to feign grievous injury from his blows, we could split his payoff. Owing to a heroic streak in me, I would not consent.

Next, Jackie K. presented his project to Glenn Constantino, another playground heavyweight. Glenn agreed. My goose was cooked. On a sunny day, we presented ourselves for the showdown out on the playground, but I was in luck. Glenn immediately threw a powerful right jab, but it missed, and he stumbled. I responded with an otherwise puny counterpunch, yet it connected. I landed the punch right in Glenn's eye, blinding him. That was it. We were not professional pugilists, and Jackie K. had to forfeit his purse, amounting to as much as a dollar, possibly five dollars. I have always hoped that Glenn got enough of Jackie K.'s loot to buy an ice pack for his eye. He looked terrible.

I proceeded from grammar school to high school equally baffled. In high school, as in grammar school, there was no area of study in which I excelled, though I did swim rather well. This was probably because my summers were spent at my grandfather Tyrrell's vacation house in Long Beach, Indiana, on Lake Michigan, some seventy miles from River Forest. There I met two men who made an impression on me, more of an impression than any teacher I was to encounter until college, Frank Leahy and Gus Stager. Frank was the legendary Notre Dame football coach whose teams had won four National Championships. Gus was the swimming coach at the University of Michigan, and in 1960, he coached our Olympic team. Frank, who lived in Long Beach and had a son my age, was a fervent golfer. With a missionary's zeal, he tried to prepare me for the links. Gus tried to turn me into a champion swimmer. He had more success. In the next two years, I won titles in the Chicago Catholic League swimming championships. I learned about athletic glory amid the trophies and pictures of the National Collegiate Athletic Association (NCAA) championship teams in Frank Leahy's basement, and I *experienced* a modicum of glory after being coached by my first Olympic coach, Gus Stager. My next Olympic coach would be Doc Counsilman.

There was one other thing I picked up in Long Beach, to wit: how babies are made. According to Tony Carey, who has remained my boyhood friend for all these years, babies are made by a mother and father engaging in a preposterous act after hours. Tony was the most energetic fabulist on the beach, but with this story, he had outdone himself, and I told him so. He went on to star at Notre Dame on one of

Ara Parseghian's legendary football teams, and in the 1964 season, he intercepted eight passes. Yet I remember him best for telling me how babies were made even before sex education was introduced in the kindergarten curriculum.

Actually, looking back on my academic career, I find few glints of enlightenment coming from any coursework of mine. I think I am the rare editor and writer who got most of his education in a swimming pool. The one great lesson that set me apart in high school and college was that I never was on a swim team that lost anything, not the Catholic League championships, not the Big Ten championships, not the NCAA championships, not even the Amateur Athletic Union (AAU) championships. When I joined the conservative movement a few years later, there was a romantic aura of defeat enshrouding it thanks to such pessimists as Whittaker Chambers and Russell Kirk, the latter of which was given to rainy-day pronouncements, such as "I am a conservative. Quite possibly I am on the losing side; often I think so. Yet, out of a curious perversity, I had rather lose with Socrates, let us say, than win with Lenin."[1] Well, the hell with that. I always wanted to win and frequently succeeded.

Doc Counsilman was my coach at Indiana University where I was to be a minor figure on his team, but the lessons I learned from him went far beyond swimming. He taught me many things, but most importantly, he taught me to prepare for every event. If you do not do your best in practice, you will not do your best in the championships or when you sit down at your writing desk or when you mount a debating platform or even when you appear on television. Doc taught me something that some unknown mentors taught Winston Churchill and Ronald Reagan: Preparation is never to be neglected. Later on in life when I studied Churchill and when I came to know Reagan, I was struck by how much preparation they put into every speech, every column, every public undertaking. Reagan never gave a major speech without going over it as much as a dozen times—and his critics called him lazy. His good-natured rejoinder was: "It's true hard work never killed anybody, but I figure why take the chance."[2]

Though I was at best a mediocre member of Doc's team that over the years could boast of sixty Olympians and many more world record holders, every now and then Doc would spend time with me working on my stroke mechanics and my conditioning. One day after a long session with me, he exclaimed jubilantly, "By God, you've got it Bobby. You're going to be a world-beater," and so I could swank about the pool for a day or two before collapsing into mediocrity once again.

I think the most productive time I spent with Doc was, for me, not time spent at workouts, but time spent talking to him about life. He had grown up as a liberal. During my undergraduate days, however, he was drifting toward the right. By the time I had founded the magazine, he was a confirmed conservative, in fact, a supporter of President Reagan. I chatted with him long after I had retired from swimming and taken up handball in the handball courts next to the IU pool. Incidentally, Doc was in the 1930s a national champion handball player and a world-class swimmer. As life went on, the magazine made me a larger and larger figure, far surpassing my swimming career, though the magazine's offices remained for a time in Bloomington.

I remember my last conversation with Doc in Bloomington. We were down in the pool and alone. Earlier, when I told him I was moving the magazine to Washington, he warned me to avoid women "who might break up a marriage" and "avoid the limelight"—this from a man who had been in the limelight practically all his adult life. He could not even serve in World War II without attracting the limelight. He crash-landed his bomber in Yugoslavia, and because he got his crew to run to the back of the plane as it touched down, the bomber flattened out and they all survived. His crew would not desert Doc, so Doc had to figure out how to land his plane safely. I believe he attributed the landing to his knowledge of physics. We often called him the Great White PhD.

Now I was stopping by the pool to bid him one last goodbye. I wanted Doc to know that I remembered what he had told me. Yet all I could summon on that sad occasion was: "Doc, I'm leaving for Washington"—long, painful pause—"and, Doc, I'll remember your advice." Slowly the old master of the natatorium, who was in failing health after becoming the oldest man to swim the English Channel, looked up at me and said, "And, Bobby, don't forget what I said about fame." Doc had probably coached more world record holders and Olympians than any swim coach in history. He knew what he was talking about when he warned of the dangers of fame. Fortunately, some ten years down the road, my friends the Clintons effectively limited my fame while I eventually ended their dominance in politics, as you will see, and as Tom Wolfe testified to at *The American Spectator's* fortieth-anniversary gala in 2007.*

Bob Knight, Indiana's legendary basketball coach and a great friend of mine, had a similar admonition for me as I headed off to Washington in 1985. He warned me about the phoniness of fame in such magnets for it as Washington, DC, New York, and Hollywood. The former Pan American Games coach, the former Olympic coach, the winner of three NCAA titles and eleven Big Ten titles warned: "Bob, the wider you become known as a writer, the greater your swimming achievements become in the eyes of the public." Bob Knight knew how easy it is to manufacture additional bogus achievements once one has attracted the public eye, but few get away unscathed.

Think of former New Mexico governor and UN Ambassador Bill Richardson, once a presidential contender. He passed himself off for years as a Major League draft choice of the Kansas City Athletics (and

---

* As reported in our March 2008 issue, Tom addressed the dinner thus: "I submit that *The American Spectator* did a more thorough job with Bill Clinton than Woodward and Bernstein did with Nixon." And our reporter who covered Tom's speech went on to elaborate that our piece, "Living with the Clintons," was "quite literally Exhibit A in the scandal that made Clinton only the second president in US history to be impeached."

helped President Bill Clinton by arranging at taxpayers' expense a UN job for Monica Lewinsky). Or Richard Blumenthal, the senator from Connecticut, who claimed to have served in Vietnam after receiving five deferments during the war and never leaving the United States during it. Perhaps geography was not one of his strengths. Or think of Senator John Kerry's whole career of bogus achievements. It is so easy to just add a little here and a little there, and before you know it, you have won the Congressional Medal of Honor. In fact, in the years ahead, *The American Spectator* gained a well-earned reputation for unmasking frauds. Recall 2017 when *The American Spectator*'s Dan Flynn and I caught the author, William Manchester, claiming a Silver Star, a Navy Cross, a second Purple Heart (atop his legitimately earned Purple Heart), and dozens of other contrived achievements on his résumé and in his bestselling autobiography *Goodbye, Darkness*. I have always been very careful to stress my mediocrity as an Indiana swimmer and as a student, at least until graduate school.

I became a graduate student because of Robert H. Ferrell, one of the few profs that impressed me, and, apparently, I impressed him. Otherwise, how did I get into graduate school? He was a prominent historian, a gifted teacher, and a polished writer who lived to a great age and taught hundreds of serious students at Indiana University when IU was a surprisingly fine place to get an education. Now it is lost in the rabble of politically correct cow colleges. Professor Ferrell had high hopes for me, though I was rather wobbly at first. He insisted that as a graduate student working toward my PhD, I would get As or I would get out. I got As for the first time in my life and ended 1967 with an MA in diplomatic history and a minor in government from two great teachers: Professor Ferrell in history and Charles S. Hyneman, the former head of the American Political Science Association, in government. I continued to take courses toward my PhD, but by then, I had an idea of what I wanted to do in life. Irving Kristol told me I lacked the *sitzfleisch* needed for scholarship, but I could be a journalist. I agreed.

A few years earlier my roommate, Jerry Gerde, after listening to me pop off about politics with the utmost confidence but almost no knowledge, told me to do what he had done—join the conservative Young Americans for Freedom (YAF) and the conservative Intercollegiate Studies Institute (ISI). I did, and my intellectual foundation as a libertarian conservative gained heft. YAF was the conservative activist organization, the equivalent of the left-wing Students for a Democratic Society, though without the SDS's bomb-making facilities. ISI was the scholarly conservative organization that stressed learning. By the late 1960s, there was no scholarly left-wing student organization left. Both YAF and ISI fortified me against the liberal line that was then propounded by the moderately liberal faculty at IU. Professor Ferrell was dubious. Professor Hyneman was more favorably disposed. He had taught such luminaries as presidential candidate Hubert Humphrey and television journalist Sander Vanocur. Charlie had grown skeptical of liberalism. Before he died, I believe Professor Ferrell had, too. Both men would soon be writing for me.

The war in Vietnam, the civil rights movement, and protesting youth had been gaining strength on campuses across America since the early 1960s. By 1968, it was all coming to a boil. That was a seminal year for the 1960s protests. Though my conservative impulses grew with every student protest and every library destroyed (IU's was damaged twice and bombs were going off all over the country), so did my libertarian impulses, propelled by a libertarian's love of liberty and a young man's sense of fun. Along with some of the more literary swimmers, I began hanging around with beatniks and hippies and what were once called bohemians.

Also, in our group, there was Steve Tesich, who went on to become a serious writer, eventually the author of highly acclaimed plays, and an Academy Award–winning movie. The movie, *Breaking Away*, brought him back to Bloomington in the late 1970s to film his vision of a bicycle race that he had participated in when he was a student back in 1963. But in keeping with Hollywood's proclivity to falsify reality,

Tesich had to change the winners of *Breaking Away* from the world-class swimmers and seasoned bicycle riders that they were in 1963 to the impecunious "townies," which they were not and who could not qualify for the race anyway, as they would not be students. Anyway, whatever Hollywood touches it fictionalizes, and when it comes to fiction, Hollywood transmogrifies it.

We also picked up with folk singers from local coffee houses, as IU had a distinguished Folklore Department. I particularly admired Joan Baez and Dave Van Ronk, but I drew the line at Bob Dylan. There was always a hint of contrivance about Dylan, and when I hung about Greenwich Village, there were rumors that he pilfered peoples' music. When in 2016 this rock singer, who in his early days always was in need of a bath and a pair of dry socks, won the Nobel Prize—complete with his theatrics about whether he would accept it—my suspicions were fortified. However, Joan Baez, with her crystalline voice soaring out over an audience, was another matter. Whether she was in need of a bath or not, I never learned. Years after the tumult of 1968, I was invited by NBC to come to Woodstock, New York, to reminisce with some of the original participants, who had somehow survived the ensuing fifteen years: William Kunstler, the radical lawyer, Bobby Seale, the cofounder of the Black Panther Party, and some "pathetico" named Wavy Gravy. I was told Joan would be there too; so how could I resist? For a while, after the fall of Vietnam, she had shunned the North Vietnamese and taken heat because of it.

NBC drove us all out to Woodstock to solemnize the fifteenth anniversary of this idiotic jamboree, and I appeared on stage as the lone dissenter. Andrea Mitchell moderated the show that was called *Summer Sunday U.S.A.* Fifteen years before, I was washing my car or sunning myself as the Woodstockians frolicked in the mud, but I confected a plausible story to satisfy NBC's interest in me. Possibly, I told the producer that, while Woodstock was underway, I was practicing the national anthem on my harpsichord or perhaps I was stamping envelopes down at the local American Legion post—all the activities that the network news expected of a young conservative. At any rate, NBC fell for it. It balanced a panel of several leftists with me, only me. My judgment, which I rendered with Kunstler on my right and Seale on my left, was that all the Woodstock generation could take credit for fifteen years ago was a "growing rate of illegitimacy along with a rise in petty lawlessness, drug addiction, welfare, venereal disease, and mental illness."[3] Kunstler was not amused, nor was his colleague Wavy Gravy.

The other thing that I remember about the fifteenth anniversary of Woodstock was how melancholy the leftists were. They drank beer throughout the show, and by the time the taping was over all were downright lugubrious. Wavy Gravy blubbered that: "It is strange to see lines on faces that 15 years ago looked so young."[4] Bobby Seale confided to me that a corporate deal for him as cofounder of the Black Panthers to write a cookbook had fallen through because Bobby failed to turn in the contract's obligatory number of "low-salt recipes." Well, Bobby, what did you expect with Ronald Reagan in the White House? Even I felt a little blue. Joan Baez never showed up. She taped her interview from a studio in Manhattan. Possibly she had even reneged on her repudiation of the North Vietnamese. Yet one thing never changes: the leftists' addiction to politics and lying. A couple of weeks later, Kunstler complained in *The Washington Post* that I left Woodstock in "a limousine."[5] Actually, *everyone* on the show left Woodstock in a limousine—Bill, even Wavy Gravy, who was by then sobbing uncontrollably. We were all guests of a giant corporation.

Always, during my brief period of being fetched by folk singers and hippies, I dissented when they began to move from a libertarian's free-spiritedness to their left-wing obsessions, which constantly menaced freedom. I never saw what the folk singers and Hollywoodians admired in Che Guevara, Fidel Castro, or Mao Zedong. All I had to do was read Armando Valladares's *Against All Hope*—his Cuban prison memoirs—to comprehend the immutable evil of Communism, and there were hundreds of other books chronicling Communism's métier, preeminently those of Aleksandr Solzhenitsyn. Even when American national interests called for support of Chile's General Pinochet or of the Argentine military, their usefulness and appeal did not last very long. Compare the longevity of General Pinochet and the Argentine regime with that of the Communist regimes in China, Cuba, and Vietnam.

There was a lot of youthful madcap in the 1960s and early 1970s, and naturally, *The American Spectator* was part of it. After all, we were barely twenty years old in the run-up to the magazine's founding, and I was but twenty-three when I put our first issue to bed. I know of no other intellectual magazine started by college students that went on to become a national magazine and lasted for more than fifty years. So, it should not surprise anyone that the formative years of the magazine were not marked by sobriety, much less sophistication. That changed pretty quickly.

There was the time I disposed of my 1952 Packard sedan from a fifty-foot cliff overlooking the placid depths of a quarry made famous by an elegant diver in Tesich's movie *Breaking Away*. Possibly, inspired by a scene starring James Dean in *Rebel Without a Cause*, I remember getting into my car—nicknamed Midnight, which I paid sixty-five dollars for the previous year—while some teammates pushed it toward the precipice. The idea was that I and a compadre riding shotgun would leap from the vehicle just as it was about to go over the cliff. We hardly made it out of the car, but what a spectacle the Packard made when it landed in some twenty feet of water, its roof smacking on the surface of the quarry as it descended slowly amidst a profusion of bubbles and foam. It settled quietly on the quarry's bottom.

Of course, the police got wind of the car's watery demise and sent down divers to reconnoiter. Then they went to my residence, in a trailer camp, just off campus. Fortunately, I was not home, and they never came again. Today I would be jailed, if not for attempted murder, then almost certainly for an environmental violation.

I had one final brush with death that ended my fascination with wild rides for good. One night Eddie Kin, a promising swimmer from Indianapolis, appeared at my bedside in a dormitory at IU and wakened me to go for a ride with him. He wanted to show off his restored hot rod. Like an idiot, I agreed, or maybe I should say like a *college student* I agreed. It was about 11:00 p.m., and all I had to do the next morning was to attend class. The car was a sleek coupe from the early 1950s. I piled in and off we went to a quarter-mile running track off campus. The night was dark, but Eddie figured out how to get his car onto the track and accelerate it around the first turn and head up the back straightaway. We were going about thirty miles an hour when suddenly the white lines on the track proved to be more substantial than white lines. They were the ends of a set of bleachers that a crew had apparently pulled forward onto the track for the next day's events. Eddie slammed on the brakes, but too late. The boards of the bleachers had penetrated the hot rod's roofline and protruded neatly around my head. If they had come any closer, they would surely have penetrated my skull.

Suddenly, an eerie quiet descended on the track. I brushed aside the remnants of Eddie's windshield. Eddie restarted his hot rod, for on the driver's side the boards caused little damage. We limped back to campus, and Eddie got the bright idea to park his wrecked car in front of a construction site and claim his hot rod had been stolen. I returned to my dormitory and tried to go to sleep. I never saw Eddie again, though I did see the campus cops. During their uneventful interview with me, they told me the owner of the car had left it parked in front of what would soon be their new headquarters. Well, at least my pre-magazine adventures involved only fast cars, never unwilling women, as apparently was the case with Bill Clinton.

Though there were *willing* women whom I resisted. For instance there, was my trip to the whorehouses of Terre Haute, Indiana. It is a good story and ends with my virtue intact, though it has been told before. During Christmas break toward the end of my graduate work,

I was finishing a research paper before returning home for the holidays. One evening, two left-wing friends stopped by to announce the good news that one was going to elope the next day with his preternaturally ugly girlfriend. They wanted me to solemnize this important event by my taking in the whorehouses of Terre Haute with them. They had even brought some cheap wine to make the fifty-mile drive even more pleasurable. Brothels, as a site for coitus, did not appeal to me on several counts: I am careful about how I spend my money; I am shy and do not make new friends easily; finally, I am a hypochondriac. And there were also questions of morality—I believe it is immoral to exchange bodily fluids (to use the *New York Times'* coinage from the early days of AIDS) without the requisite affection and tax breaks. Yet my friends were in need, and I was bored.

Terre Haute was at the time the Pigalle of southern Indiana, and so we had no trouble finding the red-light district; it covered most of the town. (I believe the authorities have now replaced it with a university.) Once in the right neighborhood, we only had to walk the dark streets for a block or so before sin found us. Ghostly old frame houses stood but a foot or two from the sidewalk. Soon, from behind a dimly lit screen in a window at shoulder height, painted lips whispered lewd enticements. Instantly, my comrades clambered onto the porch and through the front door. In the vestibule, where pale pink wallpaper peeled from dirty crumbling plaster, a naked light bulb dangled above our heads, casting grotesque illuminations on us and three ebony working girls in black ballet outfits and wigs.

They immediately began their bargaining. My friends were eager and paid a high price. Soon they were gone, and I was left with my scruples and a very temperamental lady of delights who also happened to be about the age of my grandmother—though not as nice. Coitus was now completely out of the question. I tried to be polite. But I am afraid that I couched the reasons for my purity in terms that were somewhat unfamiliar at a whorehouse. The highbrow in me came out. While this elderly black lady spoke in an earthy dialect of her special talents, I am afraid my protests sounded didactic, perhaps even haughty. Of a sudden, she either adjudged me a homosexual or a nut and briskly departed to her quarters. I like to think she went off to read a good book. I know grandmother would have.

Now I was free to browse. The old house was beginning to creak in lascivious rhythms. Groans and sighs sounded as I meandered down a narrow hall toward the back of the house. At the end of which, I found a kitchen where an ancient black cook stood staring pensively into a pan of greasy chicken parts. We were then living through the great days of the civil rights struggle, and I was properly gung ho for black emancipation. Thus, I attempted to strike up a hearty conversation.

Unfortunately, the chef was not much given to hearty conversation, or, for that matter, any talk at all beyond an occasional wary grunt. He did tell me that he had cooked in whorehouses since the 1920s, but that was all. Possibly the lady to whose unemployment I had just contributed was a friend. I tried another line of conversation and another. Like so many young white men of the time, I was earnest to show my goodwill to blacks, and when simple conversation failed, I decided to compliment the chef on his chicken. Alas, I went too far. Though I only meant to point to a particularly inviting wing, the old man abruptly determined that I was about to grasp the morsel, and he bellowed fiercely: "Git yo filthy hand away from dat," he warned, pretty much putting the kibosh to our friendship. I nervously withdrew into the street, feeling like a dog. That night I may have protected my health and virtue, but I had failed miserably in advancing racial understanding—perhaps another time and under more wholesome circumstances.

For a short period of time in 1966, I was employed by YAF to spread the message of libertarian conservatism throughout all the campuses in the state of Indiana. At the time, YAF was much larger than SDS, though we never got the publicity that SDS got. As I was to demonstrate within a couple of years, YAF's reliance on learning was never quite as newsworthy as SDS's reliance on violence. Nonetheless, though the 1960s are even today known for left-wing violence and sexual liberation and drugs, YAF and related conservative groups had larger memberships than SDS (and the Young Socialist Alliance), and there were few druggies on our side. In fact, the youth vote went for Richard Nixon in 1972—in 1968, 15 percent of the youth vote went for the segregationist Democrat George Wallace! Actually, the conservative movement in those days seemed to be gaining ground, and by 1980, with Ronald Reagan's presidential election, we had in fact won. Still, there was a madcap atmosphere surrounding our endeavors even when they were au fond serious.

I need, however, to relate one more madcap moment from the world of sports before moving on to the world of politics in the late 1960s. It has to do with my friendship with Kenny Sitzberger, who was destined to be an Olympic champion in the 1964 Olympics and dead by the time he was thirty-eight. His life in the 1960s and tragic death might open our eyes to how fame and drugs do not mix.

Helping Doc win national titles in the pool was his jolly, albeit shrewd, sidekick diving coach, Hobie Billingsley. Hobie lived to an ancient old age and was almost as successful with his divers as Doc was with his swimmers. One afternoon, Hobie asked me during a poolside chat if I would help him recruit a Fenwick High School diver who was four years behind me at Fenwick and in his last year there, Kenny Sitzberger. Hobie had been as kind to me at IU as had Doc, so of course I began seeing Kenny as often as I could on trips home to River Forest. He was a neighbor of ours and already a city champion. Under a great coach like Hobie, he would someday be an Olympian.

One evening, Kenny and I were having a beer or two in the back of Jimmy Guilfoyle's tavern on a busy Chicago thoroughfare, North Avenue. We had about had our fill and so we proceeded to make our exit by walking the length of the bar to the front door. As we did so, I noticed that the Irish guys were gathered at the bar and the Italian guys were across from them in the banquets. Once again, "diversity" was being practiced in the 1960s, and it had its usual effect. As I recall, I distributed a few, choice, ethnic slurs as I passed between the two mildly hostile groups, and by the time we got to the front door, what looked like an archway of bodies—from the Irish on my left and the Italians on my right—had locked in fisticuffs to the ruin of Jimmy Guilfoyle's tavern. The place was, in no time, a mess. Unfortunately, Jimmy Guilfoyle was standing at the front door and fingered me as the provocateur. I still remember his Solomonic decree pronounced as though he uttered it just yesterday: "Bobby Tyrrell, you'll never have another drink in here." I was back in a few weeks.

Rather pleased with ourselves, Kenny and I proceeded up North Avenue a few paces, whereupon two rather massive Italians emerged from Jimmy's catastrophe and confronted us. The larger of the two stripped off his coat, heaved it out into North Avenue and prepared to do me violence after yelling at his Sancho Panza to retrieve his coat from the street where it was now being pummeled by every passing car. Apparently, his Sancho took offense at the big fellow's tone and refused. This proved to be the break we needed. The big fellow took reciprocal offense at Sancho's reluctance to retrieve his coat and the two squared off, thus allowing our hasty getaway under the cover of darkness. My last sight of the two bully boys was of them walloping each other fiercely while the big guy's coat was still flapping in the street every time a vehicle went over it. I attributed their impromptu fisticuffs to strong drink.

Kenny and I laughed about our adventure at Guilfoyle's for years. He went on to IU and to the 1964 Olympics in Tokyo where he won a gold medal on the three-meter springboard. He then began a sixteen-year career as a sports commentator for ABC Sports that ended on New Year's Eve in 1984 when he got in a fight at his home, hit his head on a coffee table, was put to bed, and never woke up. He was thirty-eight years old, and whether his death was an accident or a homicide remains a mystery. At the time of his death, he was under a subpoena as a federal witness in a cocaine-trafficking case, which only adds to the mystery.

Kenny probably should have slowed down by the end of the 1960s. For a certitude, I had slowed down. For one thing, I was now an officer of YAF, and run-ins with the authorities would be unseemly. What is more, by 1967, I had embarked on a very pleasant full-time job. I was the founder and editor in chief of a conservative magazine. As things turned out, it would be the only job I ever held. Who says a dead-end job needs to be disappointing?

Chapter III

"YOU'VE GOT YOURS. THERE IS NOTHING PEOPLE IN WASHINGTON CAN DO FOR YOU."

*O*ne evening in the 1990s in Washington, I was talking with Lally Weymouth, the daughter of Kay Graham, then the owner of *The Washington Post*, and expressing my disdain for one aspect or another of the increasingly feverish Washington rat race. Lally was a unique Washington figure. She was a talented journalist and did not need to be in the good graces of anyone. She had talent. She had money. And she had a place to publish practically anything that fetched her muse. As I grumbled on, she remarked, "You've got yours. There is nothing people in Washington can do for you."[1]

The Washington rat race for personal advancement has continued around me for more than fifty years with increasing intensity, but, contrary to what some of my critics have said, it has never consumed me. I arrived in town with my own magazine. That was all I wanted or needed. As Lally said, "You've got yours. There is nothing people in Washington can do for you." What is more, I had my principles, as Margaret Thatcher reminded me during a particularly tricky episode with the Clintons. No one could take them from me. I guess that made me a unique Washington figure, too. In Washington, as in other places, I was my own man. I had not thought about that before.

At one point during the Clinton years, a group of conservatives suggested I run for governor of Virginia. The year was 1993, and that would put me up against George Allen, who eventually won the governorship. I did not then know George, and I considered a run. I even sought the advice of Art Finkelstein, a successful conservative political strategist from New York. Art came down and listened over lunch at the Cosmos Club in Washington to my rendition of all the things I would be giving up as editor in chief of *The American Spectator*. Then I toted up what I would be gaining as governor of the great state of Virginia. The only thing I could think of was a chauffeur-driven car with a police escort. Art said, "You'd be crazy to give up *The American Spectator*." I agreed. The governorship was not for me. Art did not charge me a consultant's fee, not even airfare.

By the time Lally imparted her wisdom to me, I had been editing *The American Spectator* for more than two decades. That, too, was something that I had not fully taken into account. I had my own magazine and the friends and associates to pay for it and to fill it with vitality. When I founded the magazine, I was unaware of how having a magazine under one's name is like having a beautiful woman on one's arm. It drives some bystanders wild. They think they can edit a magazine. They think they can write a magazine article. They think they can found a magazine. If they fail in the first three endeavors, they think they can take over an established magazine. I have survived at least six takeover attempts: one was friendly, another was ostensibly friendly, three were hostile, and the sixth was *really* hostile. In fact, it threatened my pleasant life with a stretch in the hoosegow.

That sounds farfetched, but it took place in the Clintons' 1990s, under the Clintons' Justice Department, when so many things seemed farfetched. Remember Paula Corbin Jones? Remember Monica Lewinsky? What about Vince Foster or "Filegate"? At *The American Spectator*, we dubbed the Clintons' attempt at a hostile takeover of the magazine "the Bait Shop Junta." The Clintons and their FBI investigators actually traced our subversive activities all the way back to a remote bait shop in rural Arkansas belonging to Parker Dozhier who also doubled as a trapper and a fly fisherman—but more on that in Chapter X.

The White House even produced what it called a "media food chain," explaining how we at the *Spectator* manipulated the entire media—even the British media. The information was contained in a 332-page report written up by a young White House aide working in an obscure corner of the Old Executive Office Building. Defending the magazine against the charges set me back over a million dollars. Nonetheless, given the fact that Bill and his lovely wife, Bruno, were involved, I had a lot of fun at their expense. Though my lawyers were horrified when I spoke so cavalierly in public. Well, I say live dangerously or you are not going to live at all.

If you read *The American Spectator*'s stories from the 1990s, I think you, too, will be amused. Thanks to the Clintons' harassment of *The American Spectator*, I am—as Seth Lipsky has said in *The New York Sun*—the most thoroughly investigated editor in America, possibly in American history. That is a title challenged by only a few relatively obscure Communist publications, and Communists have never been known for having a good time. Yet, with enemies such as the Clintons yapping at my heels, life has been amusing, even if it cost me over one million big ones. As the song goes, "Don't Cry for Me Argentina," though my friend Madonna was singing, I suspect, about something loftier than the Clintons, and for more on Madonna, you will have to wait for Chapter VII.

It all began back in the spring of 1967 when my leadership of the Young Americans for Freedom (YAF) in Indiana got off to an admittedly inauspicious start. The radical Students for a Democratic Society (SDS) won the student body elections at Indiana University, making IU the first major university to fall to the barbarians. The chief barbarian was Guy Loftman, a slight scarecrow of a man who led SDS on campus. He was elected student body president on April 13, 1967. Incidentally, though he came from out of state, he never left Bloomington, Indiana, not even to attend law school, and forty-seven years later when I was invited to speak at a symposium on campus, he showed up dressed like a janitor and attempted in his narcissistic way to monopolize the evening with a long-winded spiel about the rich and the poor, the white and the black, the Giant Corporations and something about Ebola in Africa. He jabbered on as though 1967 had never ended, and for him, I assume it never had. My guess is that for five decades his rant has remained essentially the same, perhaps deleting a line about the whooping crane some years back, perhaps adding a line more recently about transgendered household pets.

This state of arrested adolescence from which Loftman has obviously suffered since the spring of 1967 is a general affliction suffered by most 1960s radicals to this day, assuming they have not died from a drug overdose or beriberi or some ghastly sexually transmitted disease. I am told that in the 1960s many of Loftman's cohorts suffered from head lice. Perhaps later in life, they suffered from worms. Suffice it to say, you would not want to be their bunkmate.

At some point in the late 1970s, the Left went into hibernation mostly on college campuses, in government bureaucracies, and in the public school system where they had sought easy employment. Though the Left's most decrepit hangers-on to this day are still staggering into rehab facilities or the street shelters of our great cities. Of course, most of the Left snapped out of it during Bill Clinton's presidency, and they really came alive during the presidencies of Barack

Obama and Joe Biden. One of the SDS leaders, Obama's friend Bill Ayers, will be remembered for his timing. It was colossally flawed.

In an interview published on September 11, 2001, to introduce his long-awaited memoirs to the nation, Ayers told the *New York Times* that "I don't regret setting bombs" during the 1960s and "I feel we didn't do enough" bombing.[2] As I said, bad timing. You might recall September 11, 2001, as being the day on which the al-Qaeda terrorists flew hijacked airliners into Manhattan's Twin Towers, the Pentagon, and a vacant field in the Pennsylvania countryside, killing 2,977 people and injuring countless more innocents. Ayers and the SDS will be remembered for numerous acts of violence and bad timing. They were a public relations firm's nightmare.

But back to the spring of 1967—Loftman's election represented for me, the executive director in Indiana for YAF, a setback, almost a personal humiliation. There I was with an office in Bloomington from which I was to evangelize for liberty and limited government, and the SDS takes over the student government right under my nose. On the other hand, SDS's victory presented me with promising prospects. Eventually, I was going to need a real job. One could not be a student leader forever, as Loftman would find out in a decade or so. I needed gainful employment, and slowly out in the misty future, a plan was taking shape. If my friends and I were going to take the campus back in the spring elections of 1968, we would need a magazine, and once we had a magazine, it could become a national magazine, the voice of the young Right. I could move from being the executive director of YAF to being an editor, a journalist, an intellectual. Surely that would be a full-time job!

As the months passed and our magazine took shape, I was discovering that YAF and the students around it constituted an exceptionally gifted group of young people. They, of their own initiative, organized a political party. Called the Impact! Party, it numbered hundreds of students from fraternities, sororities, and dormitories. They raised funds for the party. They decided on who would be its candidates. When the spring elections arrived, we would be back in charge of the student government without the help of Karl Marx, Friedrich Engels, or the Communist Party of the USA.

Though, now it can be told. These students were always a bit short of funds. I turned to the university's president, Joseph Sutton, a former officer in Army intelligence and rumored to have been associated with the CIA. He covered the students' shortfall and saw to it that my right-hand man did not flunk out of school that spring. We continued working on two fronts: the journalistic front where things looked promising and the political front where John Von Kannon helped manage our political operation. He would remain my friend and colleague until his death almost fifty years later. September 5, 2015, was a sad day for me.

When I say that the students around me constituted an exceptionally gifted group of young people, I am not exaggerating. No fewer than half a dozen of them went on to make a name for themselves in the national conservative movement, its foreign policy organizations, its public policy organizations, and the pro-life movement. One even found employment on Capitol Hill. Robert F. Turner led the national Victory in Vietnam movement and went on to distinction at the University of Virginia School of Law. James Bopp would become a leader in the national antiabortion movement. Von Kannon eventually became the leading fundraiser at the Heritage Foundation. Steven McKinley Davis would join the staff of Representative Phil Crane from Illinois. All were around me in those days. Yet, for now, we had a magazine to get out in the fall, and I had just the fellow to assist me, Steve Davis, nicknamed Jefferson back in the days when Jefferson Davis was remembered (if he was remembered at all) as the saturnine Southern statesman who lost a war for Southern independence that cost this country 620,000 deaths. Though today it is dismissed by perpetually angry and ignorant Americans as a delaying action against freeing the slaves and nothing more.

Steve was a hunter, an angler, and a quick study in learning Linotype and other mysteries now lost in the haze of more than fifty years of technological advances in the world of computers. It is a world that none of us back then could even imagine. He could also write (and still does) but for the most part, Steve provided the technical know-how, and I provided the prose. In the fall of 1967, *The American Spectator* came out under the name of *The Alternative*. It was the work of young rowdies, but we had a lot of help from adults, one being an eventual Nobel Prize–winning economist at the University of Chicago, Milton Friedman.

I journeyed to his cramped office at the university to ask him for an appraisal of our product and, as I recall, an article. Milton said we would fail unless we charged money for *The Alternative*. I responded that the money we were laying out with our free campus-wide distribution should be considered a promotional expense. Though I rarely disagreed with Milton, when I did, I never won an argument with him, save this one. On the other hand, by our February 1972 issue, we had gone through our "promotional expenses" and were charging money. I think our customers liked our irreverence and pugnacity. The off-campus magazines of the Left offered sex and drugs. We offered irreverence, combativeness, and literacy. Irreverence and literacy won out. After all, it proved difficult to get up in the morning after a night of sex and drugs.

In fact, sex and drugs were instrumental in wrecking the whole New Left movement. As an intellectual movement, it did not have many years left. On the right, what would eventually be known as the Federalist Society, the Heritage Foundation, the Cato Institute, and our publishing endeavors were just getting started. More than fifty years later, we were all still going and the hippies, the yippies, and the Communists were being packed off to the geriatric wards.

The early issues of the magazine were somewhat stilted from a typographical point of view. They looked like the kind of magazines that are produced by the airline industry for bored travelers, though they had their charm, and looking back on them, they reveal the several currents of thought that Davis and I were then susceptible to. The first current of thought was the madcap. In early issues, there was poetry written by an inmate at the Indiana Girls' School, a penal institution, if memory serves. There was a notice from the "Student Committee to Tar and Feather Guy R. Loftman," and "The First Annual Mark Hanna Natural Gas Award," which went to a professor who, incidentally, smoked like a chimney *in* class. In the October/November 1968 issue, George Washington Plunkitt made his first regular monthly appearance in essay form, though he became a regular in our November 1970 issue in an epistolary form. His monthly department was known as "The Bootblack Stand," and you will hear more on him anon. There, Plunkitt proffered advice to solicitous politicians who wrote him earnest letters, for instance, Richard Nixon, Massachusetts senator Teddy Kennedy, and Jane Fonda, the callipygian cutie who even when well into her seventies prided herself on her well-rounded rump.

We also relied on a department called "Brayings from the Left" to collect the fatuous pronunciamentos of left-wing cranks and liberal sages. Reading back on their utterances, you will doubtless detect early traces of what we at *The American Spectator* now call virtue flaunting. In the April 1972 issue, we changed the title of the "Brayings from the Left" department, at the request of Professor Sidney Hook, to a more serious-sounding title, "The Current Wisdom." We still use it. Sidney, from his post in the philosophy department at New York University, would remain a mentor to me for years. I, along with *Spectator* stalwart Bill McGurn, was even asked to blurb Sidney's autobiography years later.

The department would continue through the decades collecting nonsense from liberals who steadily became more nonsensical until, by the twenty-first century, they were calling themselves not liberals but Progressives or even radicals. Today, after some fifty years in print, "The Current Wisdom" can be read from beginning to end as a reliable guide to the decline and fall of a once well-intentioned, if wrongheaded, point of view. It has run from the early days, from Charles Reich, the author of *The Greening of America* and a virgin until at some point in middle age he became aware that his penis was a dual-use technology, to modern times and the less literary Congressgirl Alexandria Ocasio-Cortez, who has yet to write a book or even a letter to the editor.

November 1970 witnessed the inauguration of the monthly wrap-up of the news called "The Continuing Crisis." The Crisis's inaugural column began thus:

> Smitten by campus violence Mr. Nixon convoked the Presidential Commission on the Causes of Campus Unrest under the intrepid Mr. Scranton. Mr. Rhodes, the only student on the Commission, blamed Governor Reagan for "murder" and President Nixon for making speeches which were "killing people."

Does anyone wonder where Mr. Rhodes is today? It is astounding how year in and year out for the past fifty or so years the successors to Mr. Rhodes have been essentially repeating themselves without much adjustment for changing times. Implicating President Reagan and President Nixon in murder is a preposterosity. Will Mr. Rhodes's successors be making the same charges in 2024, by which time America will probably have its first LGBTQ president?

The second current of thought in the magazine was supplied by the scholars. In Volume One, Number One, we ran Milton Friedman's piece in which he made "The Case for a Volunteer Army." In the next issue, we published yet another article critical of the draft, this time written not by a libertarian but by a traditionalist, which shows the breadth of support the voluntary army had among both libertarians and conservatives in those days. The author was Russell Kirk, a stalwart of the conservative movement and a frequent writer for *National Review*. Later, we published another University of Chicago economist, Yale Brozen, and we began a series of articles by the British writer

Anthony Lejeune. We also ran articles by lesser-known writers and by writers who would never be heard from again.

One writer I was particularly pleased to publish was our music critic, whose name was Frank Octave (really!) Brunell. He published a series of pieces on classical music and had been, incidentally, the world record holder for the four-hundred-meter individual medley. No other intellectual review in the history of our country could boast of a music critic who was also a world record holder, but then no other intellectual review was begun by one of Doc Counsilman's swimmers.

About this time, the name Sandy Weeder began appearing as a sketch artist for *The Alternative*. He was really Elliott Banfield, and once he decided we were going to make a go of it, he would be with us for years to come. His father was Edward Banfield, the distinguished author of *The Unheavenly City*, a book about urban problems that could profitably be read right up to the present moment. Ed was also on the Harvard faculty and the Banfields represented a growing trend at *The Alternative*, to wit: publishing two generations from the same family. There were the Banfields, the Kristols, the Moynihans (Pat's son Tim was a sculptor who produced a striking statue of H. L. Mencken for our office), and the Steins, Herb and his son, Ben, who is with us still. The magazine was becoming a family affair.

A third current contributing to the early magazine came from the senior writers at *National Review*, who were essential for keeping us on a path that was a little less madcap. They provided essays and reviews, but mostly they provided interviews. In the early years, we ran interviews with *National Review*'s publisher, Bill Rusher, book editor, Frank Meyer, and a senior editor, Ernest van den Haag, who became a member of our stable of writers as well as at *National Review*. Finally, there was the advice, encouragement, and even the presence of *National Review*'s founder and editor in chief, William F. Buckley, Jr. In 1966, I had sent him a check for $264,000 in answer to his yearly appeal to loyal readers of *National Review*. At the time I had just $27 in the bank, but if Buckley said he needed $264,000 to cover his annual deficit, I was willing to write the check. Luckily, he was not willing to cash the check. For a certitude, it would have bounced, possibly into outer space.

Bill was the conservative movement's guiding light. Certainly, he was our guiding light. He visited us in Bloomington on October 17, 1968, debated a flamboyant university professor, and appeared in a photo spread in our December 1968–January 1969 issue. The photographs were taken by Kevin Berry, another world record holder and the 1964 Olympic champion for the two-hundred-meter butterfly. Bill even delivered original copy to *The Alternative*. He invited me to dine in his Manhattan town house and asked me to attend *National Review*'s editorial meetings. For years he was a human dynamo, criss-crossing the country with a message of freedom and occasionally stopping in Bloomington.

There was in the early years another steady, if discreet, source of writers that helped us along, the writers of the very competent Nixon speech-writing team. Its link to us was John Coyne, a superb literary stylist and master craftsman of books, essays, and reviews. He lined up writers from the president's staff, such as John Avey (really Bill Gavin), Aram Bakshian, Ben Stein, and eventually in one capacity or another Pat Buchanan and Bill Safire, who soon moved on to the *New York Times*. Coyne and Bakshian have been with us for years, and Stein's "Diary" even appears in the digital version of *The American Spectator*.

John fed my appetite for articles on Jack Kerouac, the Beatniks, and McSorley's Old Ale House, the latter being Manhattan's last male-only pub. Such contrarian pieces set us apart from what was by the early 1970s a growing crop of off-campus conservative magazines. Today, John says there was nothing like our magazine being published by young people in America in the late 1960s and early 1970s. Needless to say, that holds true right up to the present time. He, in part, made it so.

The final source of articles appearing in the early years of the magazine was Irving Kristol and *The Public Interest* writers. They introduced an elegance to public policy writing that has completely disappeared from the American scene, but while they were alive, there was hope that public policy need not be incomprehensible to the civilized mind. Irving, along with Daniel Bell of Harvard, coedited *The Public Interest*, and he came to be called the godfather of the school of thought that dominated *The Public Interest*, neoconservatism. We, though an organ of the New Right or modern conservatism, cultivated the neoconservatives assiduously because I had recognized early on that they were a vibrant source of new ideas for conservatism. Moreover, I recognized that they had no place else to go for allies. Liberalism by the 1970s was already on its way to the goose-stepping conformity and infantile rants of the Trump era.

The Alternative, soon to be renamed *The American Spectator*, gained its first historic distinction by serving as a bridge on which the neoconservatives could cohabit peacefully with the conservatives. Bill Buckley and Irving Kristol became genuine friends in part because of their shared relationship as mentors to *The Alternative*. In the 1990s, the sons of the genuine neoconservatives, namely Bill Kristol and John Podhoretz, the son of the neoconservative editor of *Commentary*, Norman Podhoretz, were perfectly happy to be called neoconservatives. It helped them to make their way in the world of ideas. Yet, truth be known, they were not neoconservatives but *conservatives*.

To be a neoconservative, one had to be a liberal at one time, ideally a Trotskyite as Irving had been. Bill Kristol and John Podhoretz were never Trotskyites or, for that matter, even liberals. As will become apparent in this memoir, I have known them both. They worked for me. Bill appeared on our masthead starting at age sixteen. He was a conservative. In the 1990s, it would be accurate to call Bill and John "hawks" in foreign policy but conservative hawks rather than neoconservative hawks. Such slovenliness in describing one's political leanings came to typify the journalism and even the scholarship of the 1990s.

The original neoconservatives around *The Public Interest* were alarmed by the overreach of their original liberalism. They wrote

about such topics as "the rule of unintended consequences" and liberalism's tendency to "define deviancy down," and other manifestations
of liberalism's overreach in the 1970s. Admittedly, neoconservatives
favored a strong foreign policy, but having a liberal past and concerning oneself with liberalism's contemporary excesses was essential for
one's neoconservative credentials. Irving and Norman were joined
by Daniel Patrick Moynihan and Nathan Glazer and dozens of other
writers from *The Public Interest*. Eventually, Jeane Kirkpatrick joined
the original neoconservatives and in time she became an indispens-
able board member at *The American Spectator*, where turbulent times
lay ahead; she was always there for me. I considered her true blue.

Irving and Pat had died by the time we arrived at the next seismic
disturbance in conservative politics, the 2016 election of President
Donald Trump. In the 1990s, Bill Kristol and John Podhoretz were
comfortable wearing their fathers' colors of neoconservatism. In 2016,
they were even more comfortable wearing the colors of the Never
Trumpers. In Bill's case, once he had driven his brainchild, *The Weekly
Standard*, off the road, he picked up with a publication called *Bulwark*.
Its partial owner was a left-wing billionaire named Pierre Omidyar.
My friend of fifty years had now taken up with his lifelong enemies.
His father would not be pleased. John's father certainly was not pleased
with his own son. Norman told me so.

It might surprise readers of this memoir to discover that the first
neoconservative to appear with any frequency in the early *Alternative*
was Daniel Patrick Moynihan, who went on to become a mildly liberal
Democratic senator before becoming a pretty much standard-issue
liberal—such is the typical evolutionary process for members of the
Democratic Party since the late 1960s.

Yet before he entered the Senate, he was close to us. In early issues
of the magazine, he supplied us with revised speeches, one delivered at
Fordham University for our November 1970 issue, another, a revised
speech he gave at the White House at the end of his term there. It was
titled "Reflections on Mr. Nixon" and it appeared in our February 1971

issue. He was a supporter and a warmhearted friend to me. He visited our communal home where I lived with the Baron Von Kannon. It was a decrepit farmhouse in which we maintained both our residence and our offices. We called it "The Establishment." Pat's son, Tim, did art-work for us. When Pat served President Nixon as a presidential coun-selor, he hired a summer intern, Bill Kristol, who was soon to be raised to the position of senior editor on our masthead. Later, when Pat was made American ambassador to India, he greeted my son's birth with a silver cup engraved:

Patrick Daniel Tyrrell
From
Daniel Patrick Moynihan

After Moynihan defeated Bill Buckley's brother, Jim Buckley, for Jim's seat in the Senate, we drifted apart as I have said, but we remained friendly. Once, while returning to Washington, we found ourselves on the shuttle together and enlivened an almost empty flight by enunciat-ing lines from Yeats back and forth across the nearly empty plane. As I recall, I intoned fragments of, "An Irish Airman Foresees His Death" and Pat replied, "Parnell came down the road, he said to the cheer-ing man: 'Ireland shall get her freedom and you still break stone.'" Then I remember telling Pat during Bill Clinton's travail with Monica Lewinsky that I admired his statement made on a Sunday morning television program that if Bill lied under oath about his involvement with Monica, Pat would vote to impeach. His response was succinct. Looking pained, he replied that I should tell it to his wife, Liz. She was always the ritualistic liberal in the family. When it came time for the Senate to vote on Clinton's impeachment, Pat contradicted his state-ment made on that television show weeks before. He voted no.

One night in Washington in the summer of 1970, I wanted to take my new Washington correspondent, George Will, out to dine with Irving's young son Bill, while Bill was serving as an intern for Pat in the Nixon White House. Autumn was approaching, and George's first piece would be coming to us shortly. Eventually, George would be doing one or even two articles a month until he left us around the summer of 1972. His regular column was titled "Letter from a Whig," revealing in those days his uncertain grasp of American history. A more appropriate title for George's column would have been "Letter from a Tory," but he stuck with Whig for some reason. His PhD was, after all, in political science, not history.

The evening proved to be painful for me. To begin with, George insisted on Chinese cuisine, which has no acknowledged dessert. Moreover, the night was sweltering. Sweat dripped from George's nose, which he did not seem to notice. Worse still, I recognized early that George did not feel particularly comfortable with me as his employer and he spent the whole evening ingratiating himself to a very bright fellow who was, of course, only seventeen years old. On the other hand, Bill was the son of Irving Kristol whom George, then an aide to an obscure Colorado senator, did not really know. As we made our way through the mounds of chop suey and General Tso's chicken, I marveled at how George could be so obsequious to a teenager. If Bill wanted to talk about The Beatles, George would have eagerly welcomed this démarche and might even have begun banging the table.

By 1972, George was off and running—or climbing—at *National Review*, *The Washington Post*, and ABC, but he left a curious stench as he heaved himself up the ladder. Readers of our magazine kept coming up to me, asking why George spoke so ill of his time at *The Alternative*. I could not explain it. Did he not know that his snide remarks would inevitably get back to me? What is more, cross words never passed between us. No great issue divided us. Though, in fact, about the only time we were together was with Bill over Chinese cuisine and, somehow, I remember his nose dripping. Why did he not just get up and get a Kleenex?

Yet reflecting back on that evening, I have to wonder: Why did the Fates put me in a Chinese restaurant with George Will and Bill Kristol so many years ago, and why did the memory of that evening stick in my mind through all these years? Some fifty years down the road, both Bill and George were to commit political suicide in the election of 2016, George, by calling upon his readers to vote Democratic rather than Republican. That is to say, to vote for Hillary, his sworn enemy, against Donald Trump in the presidential election; and Bill, by doing much the same thing and killing off *The Weekly Standard*, thus putting forty or so people out of work two weeks before Christmas.

What is more, Bill, out of his self-absorbed treachery, put in peril the cachet that a handful of small intellectual reviews had struggled for years to build up. Until Bill overreached, we all could claim some authority over the realm of political ideas. Now Bill and George and others like them had demonstrated that they and their magazines had very little influence to crow about. Was it that the Fates wanted to reward me for keeping a cool head in 2016? Or was it that the Fates did not really like these two prigs very much? Certainly, it could not be the cuisine, could it?

Among my mementos of self-absorbed writers, there is a letter from George protesting that *The American Spectator* claimed in its advertisements that he was a contributor. He charged the magazine with making a false claim. I thought it might interest you:

> Dear Bob,
> Considering that it has been something like a decade since I have written for *The American Spectator*, and it may be that long before I do so again, I think it would be in the interest of honest advertising for you not to include my name in your advertisements as someone your subscribers are apt to read.
>
> Sincerely,
> George

I, of course, hastened to respond with my customary goodwill, reminding him of a splendid piece of his that we had published not *ten* years ago but *two* years ago. I never heard from him again.

At any rate, my plans for the magazine seemed to be coming to fruition by the late summer of 1970. *The Alternative* had indeed become the national voice of the young Right. We had secured funding from the generosity of Hoosiers: one being the electronics genius Sarkes Tarzian whose son, Tom, is on our board still, another being Harold Ransburg, a prosperous Hoosier businessman, and finally Mrs. Eli Lilly, from the Indianapolis pharmaceutical family. A timeless myth of American political life is that conservative pockets are bottomless. The truth is the opposite. The Left outspends us by roughly six to one, but we have managed to spend our largess more prudently.[3]

Mrs. Lilly was helping us with an annual grant of $10,000 a year, but more importantly, she told us that if we had the corporate structure of a charitable foundation known to the IRS as a 501(c)(3) she could increase her contribution considerably and she could perhaps prevail on the Lilly Foundation to contribute. Her advice amounted to grants of more than $100,000 a year. Of greater moment—and actually of historic significance—this kindly old lady's advice put us on the road to solvency for more than fifty years and laid out the blueprint for many magazines five decades later when her blueprint was followed by such titles as *Harper's*, *The Atlantic*, and even the Associated Press allowing them to stay on the newsstands when the market for intellectual magazines and publications had declined. Once our magazine was seen as the struggling waif of American journalism. Now it can be seen as a magazine that was fifty years ahead of the competition.

Soon, thanks to Mrs. Lilly's prescience and the generosity of other Hoosier contributors, we could move from our first headquarters in a mobile home within the shadow of the IU football stadium to our old farmhouse standing on forty acres some ten miles outside of Bloomington, which we called "The Establishment." It was to be the first substantial home for our magazine, and on its barstools—which were sawed-off-tree-trunks—we drank heartily with such eminences as Bill Buckley, Pat Moynihan, and Frank Meyer from glasses that in truth were discarded jelly jars. Von Kannon, who by now claimed the nickname Baron Von Kannon, kept The Establishment reasonably tidy and full of fun. Late at night, our distinguished guests, say Bill or Pat, might avail themselves of our front porch to answer nature's call. In fact, I once playfully chided Bill that his motto might be "Void Where Prohibited."

The old farmhouse was isolated and quiet, though every autumn local hunters would, without warning, turn our Hoosier hillside into a shooting range for deer, grouse, a stray dog, whatever caught their eye. The clatter of gunfire inspired one of my colleagues, at the time our circulation manager, Ron Burr, to carry a .22 pistol in a shoulder holster, making him look far more menacing than any camo-clad hunter.

The bucolic campus of Indiana University gave birth to more than an SDS-dominated student government. It nurtured a couple of *indignados* who surpassed all the student government Marxists. They were Bill and Emily Harris who left IU sometime in the early 1970s to join the idealists of the Symbionese Liberation Army (SLA) in sunny California where they joined in robbing banks, killing bystanders, and kidnapping Patty Hearst, the newspaper heiress. They were eventually locked up, but before the cell doors clanked shut on her, Emily explained to a local journalist that she had taken up arms to protect herself from my circulation manager with the .22 pistol. How she found out about him remains to this day a mystery.

At some point in the early 1970s, we received an unsolicited letter from the very wealthy Pittsburgh philanthropist, Richard Mellon Scaife, telling us that he would like to give us a grant. All he needed was our 501(c)(3) letter from the IRS allowing us to accept his foundation's grants. The Baron Von Kannon, who as publisher was in charge of such matters, and I began ransacking The Establishment looking for the IRS letter. You might think it would be kept in a file cabinet, but I am not certain that, at that point, we even had a file cabinet. I was in my early twenties, the Baron was in his late teens, and Davis was hunting or fishing as the seasons warranted. We had no luck looking throughout the house.

In desperation, I walked out on the lawn and peered across the refuse dump that we used to dispose of our garbage and to prevent further erosion of our driveway. There, sticking out of a smoldering pile of garbage, was our slightly smudged IRS letter. I can still see it in my mind's eye. I have always considered this discovery one of several miracles that got us to the twenty-first century.

Now we had money from Dick Scaife, from the Lillys, from Sarkes Tarzian, from Harold Ransburg, and lesser funders. We were on our way. We linked up with students at the University of California at Berkeley, the University of Chicago, and—most important—Harvard University, which today is referred to in our offices as "Harvard State University," owing to its crass venality and cow college direction. We had, indeed, become the national voice of the young Right.

Back in the 1970s, Harvard was, of course, overflowing with left-liberals, but there were conservatives there, too. They and their left-wing colleagues gave Harvard the rightful claim to being a great university, which it is no more. In the 1970s, faculty members from Harvard, such as Ed Banfield, Nathan Glazer, Harvey Mansfield, Pat Moynihan, and James Q. Wilson, often contributed ideas and pieces, as well as lesser-known members of *The Public Interest* journal. Now all those minds are gone from Harvard and have been replaced by something called "diversity," which does not, in practice, mean diversity at all. Rather, it means regimentation, the regimentation one might find at any cow college.

The late 1960s and early 1970s were for us, the editors of a conservative journal, a time full of excitement but touched by tragedy. I have already mentioned my encounter with Bob Kennedy on stage in Bloomington and my much happier meeting with Governor Ronald Reagan in Indianapolis back in 1968. Moreover, there were such stars as Bill Buckley, Milton Friedman, Irving Kristol, and Pat Moynihan to put a spring in my step. What is more, the ability to say anything I wanted to say about anyone at all was immensely invigorating, even if I was probably not reaching as large an audience as I imagined. Yet, reflecting back on those years, I am struck by the violence that kept manifesting itself amid the unfolding sense of intellectual possibilities.

In 1968, the deaths of Martin Luther King Jr. and Bob Kennedy cast a gloom over the country, and that was not all. There was the rioting that accompanied the King assassination and the raucousness at the Democratic Convention in Chicago led by the usual cast of radicals, namely Tom Hayden, Abbie Hoffman, and Jerry Rubin. Reflecting on it with the hindsight of several decades, the violence that erupted in the late 1960s seemed to prefigure the Episodic Chaos that was to come.

I went to the Chicago demonstration with my brother, Roger, and walked along the police line established in front of Chicago's Conrad Hilton. Rog knew some of the Irish and Italian cops. They were his contemporaries. We stood between the cops and the protestors, watching the protestors provoke the cops, giving them the finger, sneering at them, ensuring, with every passing minute, that the attack would come. We prepared for our escape.

Years later, on the Bob Grant radio show in New York, I appeared with Hayden who was curiously subdued. Did he know that I was standing between the cops and the "kids," as the media affectionately called them, shortly before the cops attacked? Had he read my recollections of the onslaught? I do not know. All I do know is that when I asked him to tell Grant's audience what he had coached the relatively innocent "kids" to shout, he completely shut down. I offered my help, saying: "Go ahead, Tom, tell us what you coached the demonstrators to say." As I recalled to him it was: "Hey Mick, Hey Dago, who's home fucking your old lady?"

Very recently, my friend, the anti-euthanasia writer Wesley J. Smith, told me an intriguing tale bearing on these events. After the Vietnam War ended, Jerry Rubin experienced an unexpected transition from Communist to entrepreneurial capitalist, first making money in the early 1980s, New York City, "social networking" scene, and eventually moving to California, where he hoped to become a multi-level marketing (MLM) magnate. As part of achieving that goal, Rubin retained Smith to ghostwrite a book that Rubin hoped would gain him national recognition as an industry leader. (The book would never be written because of Rubin's untimely death.) Smith told me that the two planned for the first chapter to explain Rubin's evolution from committed subversive to proud capitalist. In their preparation for writing that story, Rubin told Smith that the 1964 "Free Speech Movement" in Berkeley was definitely Communist-led—no surprise there. As for the infamous events of Chicago, Rubin admitted that pro-test leaders intentionally fooled the police into believing they had tens of thousands of like-minded cohorts in the city eager to tear the town apart—when in actuality, there were only some five thousand trouble-makers. The ruse worked. The cops overreacted to the radicals' jeers in a "police riot"—just as Rubin and his coconspirators had hoped. And there I was, in the middle of the action.

Back at Chicago's Grant Park some fifteen years earlier as "the kids'" taunts were reaching a crescendo, I thought it was time for my brother and me to take our leave. We made an orderly retreat. A few minutes later, all hell broke loose. We rushed into the lobby of the Hilton and watched the cops pummel the poor ignorant demonstra-tors. Whose side were the inhabitants in the lobby of the hotel on? Well, they were mostly mainstream media, so you will understand that they were very indignant with the cops. But that does not mean that they were opening the hotel doors to the kids. If memory serves, the media kept the doors of the hotel tightly blockaded. The cops cracked a few more skulls and trundled the survivors off to the calaboose. Hayden, Hoffman, and Rubin were nowhere in sight. Possibly they were consulting their lawyers.

I attended other anti-war rallies in the late 1960s and early 1970s, always as a journalist, never as a participant, much less a counter-demonstrator, though that was where my sentiments lay. The memory of one anti-war rally, in particular, has never left me.

The demonstration took place in Washington on July 4, 1970, and I was with Bill Kristol and Arnie Steinberg, a journalist who was to become a shrewd political consultant over the decades. The rally featured the usual chants and oratory: "All We Are Saying Is Give Peace A Chance" or "Make Love, Not War" or this: "I Don't Give a Damn for Uncle Sam." Journalists and cameramen were all around us, but there was one scene that never made it into the newspapers or the evening news. It was when a small band of World War II vets appeared on a hillside carrying a "Victory in Vietnam" banner above their American Legion caps. They were spat upon and abused. Yet, stoically, they continued their march. They had fought bravely three decades earlier against Nazis and Japanese militarists, and they were just as brave on July 4, 1970. If they had the bodies that they had in World War II, my guess is that the so-called peace demonstrators would have been more irenic, perhaps even respectful. The vets never dropped their "Victory in Vietnam" banner.

The rioting and the anti-war demonstrations continued. One of the grimmest days was May 4, 1970, the day the Ohio National Guard clashed with students demonstrating against the war at Kent State University. Four students were killed. For some reason, I was called to Chicago from Bloomington to appear on the nationally televised Irv Kupcinet Show that evening. Appearing with me in what turned out to be a grab bag of a show was Pete Rozelle, the commissioner of the National Football League, Aileen Hernandez, the head of the National Organization for Women (NOW), and John Filo, a Kent State student photographer who had taken what became the iconic photograph of a fourteen-year-old runaway girl kneeling over the body of the dead Kent State student, Jeffrey Miller. You might think that, given the day's events, Filo would be the center of attention that evening. The photograph he snapped earlier in the day was all over the media that night and it won him a Pulitzer Prize that year. But you would be wrong.

The center of attention was Hernandez for her ludicrous claim that, within a generation, women would be about as numerous as men in the National Football League. All that was holding them back was something called "institutional sexism." I assumed institutional sexism was something that had been dreamed up at a women's studies department at one of America's great universities, perhaps even at Harvard State University. According to Ms. Hernandez, institutional sexism had been stunting American womanhood's growth for generations. Pete Rozelle was speechless. Even Irv was agape. I thought it might be appropriate to take advantage of Ms. Hernandez's authoritative presence and ask her where the big, beefy ladies might dress and whether they would be even beefier than the already elephantine Ms. Hernandez? Irv did not invite me to comment.

Looking back on the violence of the late 1960s, the melodramatic oratory, the bovine demonstrations, the mindless street theater, I am not so much taken by the gaudiness of it all as by the monotony of it all. What Vice President Spiro Agnew said of slums in those days can be said of the Left's mass demonstrations: "If you've seen one city slum, (read, mass demonstration) you've seen them all." In the early days of the magazine, we made our own contribution to the era's street theater, but it had none of the sameness of the Left's songs, chants, and pious oratory. Indeed, our street theater caused IU's dean of students, Robert Shaffer, acute acidosis, painful embarrassment locally, and undue notoriety beyond Indiana. I am pretty sure it made Shaffer a comic figure at Columbia University and even at IU.

We proved by our effort at street theater that violence was the way the Left got attention, not by humanitarian acts or by intellectual endeavors, but simply by violence. Throwing a pie at a prof would be one way. Bombing the Pentagon would be another. The yippies, inspired by Abbie Hoffman and Jerry Rubin, began with pie-throwing and eventually advocated petty larceny. The SDS led by the likes of President Barack Obama's pal Bill Ayers inclined toward bombing and robbing banks. The liberal profs did not approve of the weaponizing of either bombs or pies, though they did very little to punish the pie-throwers, and they generally left the bombers to the FBI. However, when we on the right even pretended to throw a pie, we were ostracized by the bien-pensants as storm troopers. The violence of the Left, at least the violence of the non-murderous Left on campuses and in the streets, had a way of transforming born blanks into Gandhi-like figures, at least temporarily. I first met the yippie Jerry Rubin of Chicago Seven fame in an Indiana field, where he told the assembled that their recent pie-thrower, a born blank named Jim Retherford, was a martyr, though there were no signs of violence or even of discomfort on Retherford's person.

He did, of course, soon return to oblivion, which was preferable to Rubin's final posting. Rubin died of injuries sustained on November 28, 1994, while jaywalking across Wilshire Boulevard in Los Angeles, that being a slightly more dignified culmination than his fellow Chicago Seven defendant, Abbie Hoffman. Abbie preceded Rubin in death by eight months, reportedly dying in a chicken coop, though others have reported that he died a suicide after imbibing alcohol and approximately 150 phenobarbital pills. Both revolutionaries failed to reach the average life expectancy for a white male from their age group, Rubin by six years, Hoffman by ten years. My research staff has not been able to locate Retherford's whereabouts.

His ephemeral celebrity came at that point in the late 1960s when left-wing students were attracting easy notoriety by ambushing university dignitaries with a pie to the face, particularly at public lectures when the dignitaries might least expect it. On October 14, 1969, Clark Kerr, the former president of the University of California and one of the postwar founders of what was then called the "multiversity" or "megaversity," was addressing some four hundred students and faculty when his assault took place. Retherford, a former student and short-lived editor of the short-lived Bloomington underground newspaper *The Spectator* (no relation to *The American Spectator*), hit the bespectacled Kerr in the face with a meringue pie before being taken away

67

in handcuffs. That was about the end of Retherford's notoriety, and it should have ended street theater on campus except that a light bulb went off in my cerebrum.

In November, we had planned an event called "Alternative Week" featuring conservative speakers and even a debate between Frank Meyer, an ex-Communist and at the time *National Review*'s book review editor, and a local radical faculty member who had nothing so colorful as Communism in his past, though he was hard left. Why not add another debate to our "Alternative Week" lineup featuring me and a bogus prof? It could even be *educational* proving my thesis that violence begets fame or at least good public relations. True, we did not have a celebrity leftist like Jerry Rubin to attract the media, but why not try?

We actually had among our circle of friends a fellow who could be a perfect ringer for a radical professor. He was a twenty-six-year-old part-time student whose penchant for booze and cigarettes had aged him sufficiently to allow him to pass for a middle-aged prof. What is more, he was bewhiskered, given to tweedy coats and baggy pants, spoke with a gravelly voice, had the hauteur of a full professor, and—one thing more—he was an absolute idiot. Yet his one incontestable talent was that he could exude the cant of a run-of-the-mill radical prof with aplomb while prattling on about poverty, racism, and American imperialism as though he had just discovered them.

He would be perfect! But just for the sake of authenticity, we gave him the vaguely familiar name of Professor Rudolph Montag. With a name like that, no one at Indiana University would think to question his bona fides. What is more, we added a sonorous title, something about urban studies at Columbia University. The learned Professor Montag was bound to draw a crowd, but taking no chances, we added the title to his November 11, 1969, appearance: "The Urban Crisis," calling it "A Debate between R. Emmett Tyrrell, Jr. and Professor Rudolph Montag of Columbia University." Two hundred and fifty attendees turned out, many of them young faculty eager to see me get clobbered by the Ivy League.

I began the debate with quite possibly the most boring public address I have ever made. I was, after all, dealing with a full professor. To which Professor Montag, seated behind me, theatrically rolled his eyes, and knowingly tsk-tsked my asseverations, much to the approval of the left-wingers in the audience. Then the magnificent Montag rose to rebut me. He stood about 5'6" and strutted over to the podium. Launching into his rebuttal, he began with something like: "Oh poor, poor Mr. Tyrrell. I knew you would say something like this." Then Montag put together a speech incorporating sentence fragments, paralogisms, absurd statistics, and asinine platitudes, which were completely incomprehensible to the ordinary human ear. It was a colossal performance, and oddly enough, the audience sat in rapt attention to the idiot. As I recall, he was answering an admirer's fawning question just as a two-hundred-pound IU wrestler from our group came lumbering down the aisle at the appointed time shouting, "Montag, you goddamned Communist." *Kersplash*, his pie landed in Montag's mustachioed face, spilling down onto his tweeds and making a dreadful mess.

It was beautiful, and the prof did not miss a beat. With cream dripping off him, he lamented, "Ah, I deserved that"—par excellence, liberal guilt! According to our transcript, which has lain in my attic for more than fifty years, Montag's left-wing admirer then volunteered, "I do hope you don't think *I* was responsible for that." Not at all. The becreamed prof was hurried out of the auditorium with the Baron Von Kannon furiously mopping him off with a towel—curious that the Baron brought a towel with him to a university lecture, no? The next day Montag was quoted as telling a local newspaper reporter that "I do hope we can lessen the tension that made this boorish young man do this thing with the pie." Maybe we should have allowed him to hold a press conference, after all.

In the meantime, the presses were rolling across the Midwest. The *Chicago Tribune* carried the news to the entire area. *The Indianapolis Star* carried it to the four corners of Indiana, and lesser newspapers did, too. Never had "Alternative Week" gotten such ink. My thesis was validated.

Alas, not everyone was happy. The next day, Dean Shaffer called me and delivered the news. There was no Professor Montag at Columbia University. "Are you sure?" I asked. How shocking. Columbia's own dean of students had notified the shaken educator. Now he was lecturing me on the essence of true conservatism (how many times would I be subjected to this lecture in the years ahead). He went further. He notified me that our conservative group had committed an act of "violence." That was no way for true conservatives to act. I tried to tell him that our skit was "street theater." It should be seen in contrast to what the left-wingers had done to Clark Kerr. Kerr was an unwilling victim. Whereas Professor Montag was an eager volunteer. The distinction was lost on the learned dean. Reasoning with him was hopeless.

As I have said, for more than fifty years, I have been immured in what is called a dead-end job. I have been editor in chief, apparently for life. Frankly, I cannot understand what economists and sociologists are grumbling about. This job has suited me just fine. Yet, there have been times in which it has been imperiled. One such time came in August 1972. I had been editor in chief for just over five years when I was faced with a grave threat to my way of life. A powerful man was about to offer me a real job at the very seat of power in our nation's capital, the White House. Would I take it? Certainly, today a young man living in a cornfield would, indeed, grab it. Here is what took place.

On that August afternoon at The Establishment, while I was comatose with a pollen-induced hay fever attack and my secretary, Miss Mulholland, was nursing another of her hangovers, the telephone rang. The call was for me, and so she tiptoed up the stairs to my second-story office, where she knocked on my door to announce that there was a very commanding figure on the telephone. "He says he is calling from Washington, DC," the impressionable girl said. I told her to tell him I would call him back once the pollen had relented. I returned to my siesta. An hour or so later, she again was at my door and she was uncharacteristically emphatic. The man was on the telephone again and he told her he was the vice president. "The vice president of what?" I snapped. "He says he is the vice president of the United States," she replied. Well, I had my doubts.

I picked up the telephone and Spiro T. Agnew rattled on for a few minutes with various pleasantries to which I blurted out: "This really is the vice president." To which the vice president answered: "Of course it is; who else would it be?" He went on to say that he had been reading me and liked my "fighting spirit." Would I join his staff in Washington? I looked out at the pollen-laced fields and was fetched by a sudden offer of liberation. No more hay fever. And yet, I hesitated. The Lilly Endowment had recently processed a three-year grant to the magazine. Things were looking up. I made my case for staying in Indiana. Vice President Agnew seemed to understand. He said something about "this crazy city" referring to Washington and asked me to serve as a consultant. I could fly around the country with him, watching him give speeches, occasionally writing speeches, and learning the ways of Washington. I agreed to serve part-time.

Rather amusingly, Miss Mulholland mistook my new position as "consultant" for a "counselor" when she revised my vita sheet. For years, thereafter, I was misrepresenting myself as a counselor to the vice president every time I sent my vita sheet out to a television studio, a publisher, or whomever. No one in official Washington ever caught on. If they had, I would have been doomed, written off as a poseur. It happens in Washington—which abounds with poseurs—all the time.

My trips with the vice president were memorable. He is now not thought of as a very important political figure, but in his day, he had an arresting presence. When he walked into a room, heads turned. He gave some stirring speeches. He was the first national figure to raise the issue of political bias in the media with an unforgettable speech in

Iowa on November 13, 1969. There, he questioned the media's "concentration of power" in the public forum. He said,

> Is it not fair and relevant to question its [the media's] concentration in the hands of a tiny, enclosed fraternity of privileged men elected by no one and enjoying a monopoly sanctioned and licensed by government? The views of a majority of this fraternity do not, and I repeat, do not represent the views of America.[4]

That speech ignited the conservatives' complaint about an elitist handful controlling the news. The fire has burned for more than fifty years, picking up a few additional complaints along the way, and ending with Donald Trump's famous complaint about "Fake News." Democracy is the best form of government devised by mankind, but obviously it is not the most efficient.

One day, I saw the vice president toss something that I thought looked valuable into his wastepaper basket. Later in the afternoon, I retrieved it. It was the key to the city of Cincinnati. I have kept it through the decades, always in my living room, always in an exalted spot. Few people have ever asked how I got it. Actually, I am not sure that *anyone* has asked how I got the engraved key in my living room, and now that I have mentioned it here, there is always the possibility that Cincinnatians will want it back.

On another day, having landed in Air Force Two at Andrews Air Force Base and while helicoptering back to the White House, the veep launched into how he relished signing autographs. He asked if anyone else had had any experience with autographs, collecting them, exchanging them? Well, I told him that I had actually *signed* autographs as an Indiana swimmer, neglecting to mention that when the autograph seekers saw that they had neither the autograph of an Indiana Olympian nor the autograph of a world record holder, my transient fans moved on. The vice president was impressed, though my story did not win me many admirers on his staff.

I kept supplying him with speeches calling for clean government, thinking that the boss would inherit the presidency when Nixon was driven from the White House. None of my speeches were ever used. I found out why when, in early 1973, the story broke that an investigation of him was underway. In October, he was gone. So were my hopes for being a presidential speechwriter. I now settled into my dead-end job with renewed enthusiasm, reporting on rowdy student riots, civil rights protests, the winding down of the Vietnam War, and the approaching ordeals of Richard Nixon.

Years later, when I became acquainted with the Clintons, I would discover that during the late 1960s and early 1970s they, too, were engaged in what they might have called public service, Bill at Oxford where among other things he ducked the draft and heaved marbles under the hooves of struggling police horses in London's Grosvenor Square, and Hillary slaving away at the *Yale Review of Law and Social Action* in which police were depicted as pigs. The *Review* was defending the Black Panthers and Hillary shortly thereafter would be off to California to work for the former Communist Robert Treuhaft. In the 1990s, the Clintons would lie about their youthful far-left activities by simply denying them. I have never had to lie about my youthful activities, though I would rather keep that story about the vice president's key to the city of Cincinnati entre nous.

The Clintons, John Kerry, Al Gore, and many of their peers on the left began lying about their lives early on and kept lying to the very end. As for my mendacious confrères on the political right, they lie, too, but not as frequently or as egregiously. The left-wing media keeps the right-wing pols relatively honest while allowing the left-wingers to run hog wild. The *Wall Street Journal's* James Taranto has gained fame and rightly so by naming the phenomenon an example of the Taranto Principle, that is to say: The media, by indulging the Left but not the Right, actually encourages the Left's flights into fantasy. Thus, we have seen Hillary Clinton, for instance, tell whoppers that Newt Gingrich would never attempt.

I tried to help my former boss when he was driven from office. At first, I tried to help him move out of his office. He had always treated his Secret Service detail well, and they volunteered to help him move on weekends. Also, I attended an elegant dinner at the Agnew residence on May 22, 1975. Along with his erstwhile political assistant Dave Keene, who would be a friend of mine for years, and Tom Charles Huston, an ex-Nixon aide and fellow Hoosier, we laid out a plan for how Agnew might use a foundation that I gave him to further conservative interests. The foundation was broke.

Agnew talked that night of his friendship with the Saudis, saying: "Once you earned their friendship, they would always honor it." Our plans never came to much, though when word of a foundation hit the newspapers, I was temporarily tainted. The magazine lost a couple of writers owing to the controversy, one being David Brudnoy, whom time has forgotten. He compared my involvement with the fallen Agnew to Pearl Harbor or some such shocking historical event. Looking back on Brudnoy's tergiversation, it seems to serve as a preview of what was to come years later during the Clinton scandals, when Bill Buckley and Pat Buchanan deserted me over Troopergate and later when Bill Kristol overacted to the candidacy of Donald Trump. After the Brudnoy furor quieted down, I tapped Elliott Abrams, a fine writer and objective reviewer, to review Agnew's memoirs, *Go Quietly...or Else*. Abrams found that the ingenuous Agnew had indeed admitted to taking money from contractors. He admitted to it in his book.

That night, along with the foundation business, Agnew expressed his frustration. He talked of earlier plans for a run at the presidency, presumably after Nixon's second term. Agnew said ruefully that Nixon had promised him a pardon, which he obviously had reneged on. Now, Nixon, Agnew said, "detested" him. Agnew seemed lonely and apprehensive. Is it possible that he wrote his memoir thinking it was all right for the governor to take money from construction companies? His successor as governor was Democrat Marvin Mandel, who was convicted in 1977 for the same sort of behavior. Welcome to Politics As Usual in the Maryland Free State.

I do know this: If I had taken the job that Spiro T. Agnew offered me, you would not have this book in your hands.

Moreover, I would not have been editor in chief for life!

Chapter IV

RICHARD NIXON AND THE MOST ELEGANT MARTINI OF THEM ALL

*I*t has been said that the 1970s actually prolonged the havoc of the 1960s. That was the view of those who adjudged the 1960s catastrophic. Others, the celebrants of the 1960s, were no happier, as they glumly watched their dreams—bred of the 1960s havoc— go aglimmer. As the celebrants of the 1960s aged, they forsook their jeans for business attire but did so with remorse. They feared that they had sold out to "The Establishment" (not to be confused with our farmhouse in Bloomington). There was even a movie about their transformation called *The Big Chill*, which its Hollywood producers with cavalier insensitivity promoted as a "drama/comedy." Well, truth be known, both sides were wrong. The 1970s have proven to be more ominous than their critics from either end of the spectrum thought.

The decade, it seems to me, was actually the next stage in what was to be, for America, fifty years of Episodic Chaos. Possibly the Chaos will continue. The America of the 1950s and before was almost a different country from the America of the late 1960s and beyond. The 1950s were years of normalcy, as were the years of the 1940s, the 1930s, and the 1920s—despite a World War, Depression, Prohibition, and "the flappers." Up until the late 1960s, things on the home front were settled and little was challenged. There were relatively few demonstrations, relatively few riots, no mass shootings, no impeachments, and when you entered a public toilet, there was no controversy unless you were what was then recognized as a deviant.

In fact, the America of the 1950s and what preceded it was amazingly prudish or, to use the word then in use, puritanical. In the pre-1960s, one rarely encountered the word sex in the news, certainly not in the headlines. By the 1990s, sex was everywhere. It had seeped into more and more news stories, as had racism and violence. Sex even made it into the Oval Office in the 1990s.

The 1920s up through the 1950s and early 1960s were years of domestic tranquility compared to what was to come. What was to come afterward was, as I have said, fifty years of Episodic Chaos. Possibly the Chaos was the consequence of the mass media's ability to excite its nationwide audience and to keep its agog clientele on the edge of their seats from one wild moment to the next, from feminism to Watergate to Iran-Contra, and on and on to the presidency of Donald Trump with its attendant helter-skelter. On the other hand, possibly these fifty chaotic years were the consequence of an ongoing breakdown of authority from the late 1960s through to the 2020s with every moral certitude being challenged, many moral certitudes discarded, and no end in sight. Whatever the cause, during my life, I have seen a near-total collapse of the moral authority of institutions—and still America whirls on.

For fifty years, no area of American life was safe from the intrusions of the post-1960s revolutionaries. Moreover, the revolutionaries promised no end to the Chaos. They fiddled with boys' roles. They fiddled with girls' roles. They fiddled with what we smoked, now banning tobacco, now legalizing marijuana. There would be no dictatorship of the proletariat, certainly no dictatorship of the billionaires, only the unpredictable dictatorship of anarchy. The weight of the Founders' Constitution became evermore oppressive to the maestros of *change*, but what would replace the Constitution? The smug answer was *change*.

The only value that the maestros of change steadfastly adhered to, through high seas and calm waters, was *disturbing the peace*, as will become apparent in the course of this memoir. The one value that the so-called liberals have never discarded in more than fifty years has been to disturb their neighbors, which in most criminal codes worldwide is at least a misdemeanor and in some Islamic polities a felony punishable by stoning. The soi-disant liberals turned their backs on cigarette smoking and reversed their prohibition on marijuana smoking, but they never lost their itch to molest their neighbors. We conservatives favor the tried and the true, sustained by constitutional liberty. Those on the left—whether they call themselves liberals, Progressives, or radicals—favor perpetual disruption. Most polities promise peace and quiet at some point. The American Left promises only disruption, sempiternal disruption. One has to wonder, is their project even rational?

Whatever the cause for the Episodic Chaos over the past fifty years, it has almost perfectly enshrined the life of our magazine and much of my life, too. Every few years, the call goes out for *change*—not normalcy—and usually the call for *change* is answered. Yes, there have been peaceful interludes, but then comes the Chaos. For instance, in the early 1970s, Watergate intruded, and President Richard Nixon, having just won one of the greatest landslides in American history, was given the boot in no time at all. Watergate overtook the headlines, with more than two dozen White House aides eventually being jailed. It would take some forty years to uncover the evidence that neither

President Nixon, nor his lawyers, nor even his prosecutors understood the meaning of a tape that cooked his goose. Had Nixon understood, as researchers now have, that the so-called "smoking gun" tape had nothing to do with the Watergate break-in, he might never have resigned, a matter I shall turn to in due course. How many more unnecessary Watergates have we, the citizenry, been put through?

Perhaps the first stirrings of the 1970s came during the 1968 Democratic Convention, while the Democratic Party was experiencing another of its periodic civil wars. All of these civil wars have been begun by disgruntled adepts of the Left going all the way back to the time of President Grover Cleveland. Some historians have traced this fractiousness back even further. The Democrats have disgruntled people on their right, for instance, in modern times such racists as Governor George Wallace of Alabama and Governor Lester Maddox of Georgia, both Democrats. Yet for some reason these bigots can never get out of their hayseed environs. It is hard to imagine a George Wallace planting himself in the Republican Party. Contrary to the received opinion—what *The American Spectator*'s readers recognize as *Kultursmog*—compared to the querulous Democrats, the Republicans reside in a pool of serenity.

At any rate, the Democrats' most recent series of civil wars began in 1948 when the insurgent radicals and Communists supporting former vice president Henry Wallace were beaten back by the Democratic establishment. The radicals of 1948 spent the next two decades sharpening their anti-American rants, developing their utopian giveaways, and distancing themselves from the Communists. Then they returned to the political fray in force in 1968.

They were the adepts of a New Politics. Some ran wild in street demonstrations that overran Grant Park and along Chicago's Michigan Avenue. I gave them their due in Chapter III, and doubtless, we shall hear from them again when they transiently attract our attention for bumping off a bank or blowing themselves up while fashioning bombs in their affluent families' basements. Few of these hotheads ever made lasting headlines and those that did usually ended badly. Recall if you will the late Jerry Rubin, hit by a car while jaywalking on Wilshire Boulevard in Los Angeles not far from President Ronald Reagan's retirement office, or the late Abbie Hoffman who may have expired in a chicken coop.

Others bathed, brushed their teeth, and filed into the conference rooms of Chicago's cavernous International Amphitheatre. They would cause less property damage indoors but more lasting disorder for the Democratic Party and the nation. They developed a plan. It would be fully implemented for the 1972 convention. It insured that the struggle between the establishment Democrats and the radicals would last for decades until sometime in the second decade of the twenty-first century when the masters of the New Politics renamed themselves the Progressives and finally won out. There were no liberals left in the establishment to beat.

In the 1968 Democratic Convention, the establishment Democrats were still strong enough to win the nomination under the banner of Vice President Hubert Humphrey, beating the more radical—but utterly charming—Senator Eugene McCarthy,* also from Minnesota, who could claim to have tested his popularity with voters in the primaries. Humphrey never ran in a single primary. Some of his people, acknowledging Senator George McGovern's "decency" and idealism in launching a brief stand-in campaign for the assassinated Bob Kennedy, gave McGovern and his New Politics acolytes a consolation prize. They would set up the Commission on Party Structure and Delegate Selection for the 1972 convention, hoping to avoid the open warfare of 1968.

Called the Reform Commission, McGovern was named its chairman by the head of the Democratic National Committee, Senator Fred

---

* I became friendly with the senator in the 1990s when we did a series of television programs out of Montreal. By then, he was bored by ideological politics, and after taping our show, we would head off to the bar to have a couple of drinks and catch up on the latest Washington gossip.

Harris, who himself was sympathetic to the New Politics. The Reform Commission was crawling with McGovernites, though the establishment seemed oblivious. The Commission's youthful staff was led by Gary Hart (baptized Gary Hartpence). He was a deeply committed McGovernite who would move on to the McGovern campaign in 1970. Before leaving, he began drafting the rules for selecting delegates in 1972, and there were few establishment figures to stop him and his allies. Their reforms were extensive, but one reform was to have colossal consequences for the Democratic Party in 1972, for the nation in the years to come, and for black Americans for generations. The reform was affirmative action.** The Reform Commission's work was to reverberate across the land for years to come, especially for blacks, and for the adepts of "identity politics."

Once affirmative action became the law of the land, anytime a black person wanted to make a legal case about his or her employment, he or she could. On the other hand, anytime a black person attained a position, especially a position involving some expertise, there would be doubts about the merits of his or her employment. Affirmative action seemed to last forever. Had it never been implemented, by the late 1980s—certainly by the 1990s—blacks would have been making their way into the professions free of legal hassles and doubts about their capacities much as the Irish, the Italians, and other immigrants had years before. Of course, blacks were not strictly speaking immigrants. It took longer for their ancestors to arrive in any appreciable number in the middle class. Yet, by the 1960s, they were making great strides—a point almost never made. By 1978, the

---

**   Interestingly, affirmative action in its first iteration by President John F. Kennedy was perfectly sensible. In 1961, his Executive Order 10925 ordered federal agencies for the first time to take "affirmative action to ensure that applicants are treated equally without regard to race, color, religion, sex, or national origin." Bravo! Then, in 1965, President Lyndon B. Johnson reversed things. He signed Executive Order 11246 changing the point of Kennedy's Executive Order from *nondiscrimination*—"without regard to"—race, and so forth, to one that sought "results" based on race, and so on. Alas!

eminent black sociologist William Julius Wilson was right when he concluded in *The Declining Significance of Race: Blacks and Changing American Institutions* that class had become more significant than race in American society.

At the 1972 Democratic Convention where the misbegotten policy of affirmative action began, blacks, women, and youths (persons under thirty and over eighteen) were to be represented in state delegations as they were physically represented in their state. With that reform, the 1972 convention was handed to the New Politics, and the New Politics nominated as their presidential candidate South Dakota's George McGovern, the "decent" candidate, the public-spirited candidate, the candidate who stepped out of a modern smoke-filled room, one that allowed no smoke—but plenty of wheeling and dealing.

Yet the "decent" candidate's cunning began to desert him. He had already staked out some of the most extreme positions ever presented at a national convention. For instance: He favored amnesty for draft dodgers, a 37 percent across-the-board reduction in defense spending, and a "demogrant" of $1,000 annually to all American families whether they needed it or not. As a result, President Richard Nixon's position in the polls grew ever more formidable.

Then, as McGovern and his people rolled toward the convention, in an April 27 column syndicated columnist Robert Novak quoted an unnamed liberal senator "whose voting record differs little from McGovern's." According to Novak's source, "The people don't know McGovern is for amnesty, abortion and legalization of pot." When they find out, "he's dead."[1] McGovern's adversaries, both Humphrey, who remained in the race, and the Nixon people, referred to the Democratic front-runner as the "Triple-A" candidate who supported "Amnesty, Abortion, and Acid." Soon, McGovern's search for a running mate became a trial. Teddy Kennedy turned him down, so did Humphrey, Senator Walter Mondale of Minnesota, Senator Edmund Muskie of Maine, and others. Finally, Senator Thomas Eagleton of Missouri, after undergoing only a cursory background check, accepted

McGovern's offer. Almost immediately rumors began to spread about Eagleton's mental health.

Two weeks after being chosen as McGovern's running mate, Eagleton admitted to having been repeatedly hospitalized in the 1960s for depression and that his regimen included electroshock treatment. Initially, McGovern declared that he stood by Eagleton "1,000 percent." However, pressure on Eagleton increased. On August 1, eighteen days after being chosen, he withdrew at McGovern's request. Pandemonium followed. There were questions raised about McGovern's judgment, about his process of selecting a running mate, and about the wobbly progress of the campaign. Thirty-five years later, Novak identified the 1972 source of his "Triple-A" quote. The source was Eagleton, who by then had passed away. Yet back in 1972, his loquacity with Novak might be forgiven. How was Eagleton to know that in two and one-half months he would be McGovern's choice for veep?

McGovern went on to suffer one of the worst defeats in American history. He won only the People's Republic of Massachusetts and the District of Columbia. It was the largest margin of defeat in any postwar election. At the magazine, we were relieved to see McGovern and his radicals go down, though we noted that Nixon gained but twelve seats in the House while losing two seats in the Senate. He could have used a much stronger showing in the House and the Senate, for back in June, there had been a break-in at the Democratic National Committee headquarters in the Watergate Hotel. The break-in was taking on a growing importance.

Of course, in the years before the 1972 convention, the peace movement had steadily spread throughout the country and certainly within the Democratic Party, where it was about to preempt the estab-lishment. A preview of how strong the peace movement was becoming and what lay ahead in the 1972 presidential election came in the spring of 1971. On April 24, 1971, a huge anti-war demonstration barged into Washington. I attended the demonstration with my fellow conserva-tive writer and infiltrator of left-wing extravaganzas, Arnie Steinberg, then the editor of the Young Americans for Freedom's (YAF's) national magazine, the *New Guard*. The April 24 demonstration was sponsored by something called the National Peace Action Coalition. (Apparently there was no conflict between "Peace" and "Action" in the comrades' minds.)

I use the term "comrades" advisedly. The National Peace Action Coalition was dominated by the Socialist Workers Party and the Party's youth cadre, the Young Socialist Alliance (YSA), both of which groups comprised the Trotskyist Communist movement in America. Incidentally, the YSA was then the left-wing equivalent of the YAF and was always, when I was young, much smaller than YAF but much more likely to get into the headlines. You will recall my efforts at street theater in Bloomington with the estimable Professor Rudolph Montag. In my last chapter, I scrupulously recorded those efforts, and, of course, noted that ultimately, they were destined for failure. Yet I think you will agree, they were a lot of fun.

So, the National Peace Action Coalition was far to the left, but that did not prevent at least two Democratic congressmen from attending its glorious demonstration. Nor did it prevent the apparent front-runner for the Democrats' 1972 nomination from endorsing the Coalition. That would be the man who, but three years before, had campaigned as Hubert Humphrey's hawkish running mate, Senator Muskie. The winds of change were gusting in the early 1970s, and Muskie would go with the wind.

In 1970, on the eve of the midterm elections, Muskie had given an unusually good speech—unusually good for him—on national television. Whereupon, he suddenly found himself in the unlikely role of Democratic front-runner. I say unlikely because he was about to endorse bald-faced Communists. The demonstration orchestrated by Trotskyists and endorsed on April 24, 1971, by Muskie was not like any gathering of Democrats I had ever seen anywhere. As Arnie and I walked through the crowd, the aroma of marijuana was strong. The pro-Vietcong propaganda was in abundance, as were leaflets and bulls for other subversive causes. There were militant blacks and angry whites and total crackpots. This was not a Vietnam Victory crowd. This was a Vietcong Victory crowd, and Muskie, the Democratic front-runner, was seeking their support as though they were just another union belonging to the American Federation of Labor.

Muskie's endorsement of the National Peace Action Coalition startled the establishment, though by 1971 any candidate with a hope of nomination had to join the herd. Muskie fell in with the other front-runners in ratings posted by the liberal Americans for Democratic Action (ADA). There was Muskie with an ADA rating of eighty-five, Humphrey, the establishment's favorite, with a rating of eighty-nine, and not to be outdone in reaching for the slightly outré Democratic voter, McGovern, with a robust rating of ninety-six. Interestingly, all this changed a year later. In 1972, as the election approached, Muskie detumesced and lowered his ADA rating to a more mainstream rating of seventy. Humphrey's rating plummeted to an even more mainstream rating of sixty, and McGovern, the Robespierre of 1972, came in at a very conservative forty-five. Why the Democrats' radical ratings declined as the election approached is a mystery to me, but there you have it.

Yet, as I have noted, change was in the air. Muskie's candidacy would wilt, but in the early 1970s, he had become very different from the hawk he was in 1968. As Robert Novak wrote in his memoir, "Muskie and his team felt a genuine kinship to the war protesters and other radicals," by the spring of 1971. Doubtless, McGovern and Humphrey did, too.[2]

The feeling of kinship with the radicals was spreading throughout the Democratic ranks. By the convention, Humphrey even agreed with McGovern on the war. He was now ready to cut off support for the South Vietnamese. His reasoning? He told Novak that he would "because I believe that it is no longer in our interest to be there."[3] Such fluidity of thought among the Democrats provoked Margaret Thatcher years later to quip: "Lose a country, gain a restaurant."[4]

However, Muskie was a prosaic speaker, which is why his initial 1970 speech was such a surprise. He was also highly emotional and, as he was soon to demonstrate, he possessed a mercurial temper. His rapid decline began with the Democrats' first primary in New Hampshire. There he had one of the most famous temper tantrums in American political history. Provoked by William Loeb's right-wing *Manchester Union Leader*, he appeared in front of the newspapers' offices and delivered an overwrought presentation. His voice cracked, and he appeared to be crying. Some thought he had been drinking.

In the New Hampshire primary of March 7, he did badly, winning only 46.4 percent of the vote to McGovern's 37.1 percent. From there it was all downhill with one more amusing display of temper a week later in the Florida primary against the racist governor of Alabama, George Wallace. Wallace won with an antibusing campaign, beating Hubert Humphrey and Senator Scoop Jackson from Washington. Incidentally, Scoop was about the last Democrat we at the magazine could admire. Muskie finished a dismal fourth, but that was not all. He went on national television from Miami to assail Wallace and the 42 percent of Florida Democrats who supported him. He said they were possessed of "some of the worst instincts of which human beings are capable."[5] Now he was finished, and it would be forty-four years before another presidential candidate would direct a similar attack on her opponent's base. Hillary Clinton called Donald Trump's base the "deplorables," and she met a fate similar to that of Muskie. She lost to Donald Trump in 2016.

Novak recalls another amusing story about the stupendously self-absorbed Senator Muskie. In 1971, when Muskie was still the Democrats' front-runner with polls even showing him ahead of President Richard Nixon, Novak was invited to lunch in Muskie's Capitol Hill hideaway. After a heavy meal, including preprandial drinks, wine with the main course, and a hefty dessert, Muskie offered Novak his views of the world and his ideas on how to fix the world. Then he asked Novak for *his* "views on the world." About one minute into Novak's recitation, the prospective presidential candidate fell fast asleep. It was not a light drowse. It was a deep slumber with snoring, gurgling, and various gastric noises. Novak abruptly shut down, hoping to awaken the somnolent senator, but the senator continued his restless siesta. Next, Novak cleared his throat. He even coughed. That did it. Muskie awakened with a start, and Novak hurriedly said, "And those are my views, Senator." To which the great man replied, "Very interesting, Bob."

Years later, after I moved the magazine to Washington, Bob and I became close friends. He became a reliable contributor to the magazine, a member of our monthly dinner club, known as The Saturday Evening Club (which never met on Saturday evening), and a member of the magazine's board of directors. During the Clintons' assault on us, he became an occasional, but well-intentioned, critic. He is the only person whom I have ever known in public life who, when it became apparent that I was right about the direction of the magazine and he was wrong, called me on the telephone and apologized. No one else has ever done that. I miss him terribly.***

During the 1968 and 1972 Democratic and Republican Conventions, we were still in our larval stage at the magazine. We did not have the funds to send reporters to the conventions, much less the inclination to attend them. We were too busy editing and writing. Sometimes I would write two or three articles, an issue often under assumed names. My favorite was George Jean Nathan, the name of Mencken's old partner. Even George Will, then our Washington correspondent, would often contribute more than one piece. Other rising young members of Washington's conservative community wrote for us, too, though most were careful to write under a pseudonym, the

---

*** There was one person in private life who had second thoughts about ending his friendship with me over Bill Clinton. That would be the New York developer and art collector Sheldon Solow. During our Troopergate imbroglio he called and said our friendship was over. But during the Lewinsky affair he called back and said "Bob, I apologize. Clinton's a bum." Our friendship revived.

favorite being C. Bascom Slemp, who early in the twentieth century was Calvin Coolidge's secretary.

Then, too, in our first years, we were living pretty much from hand to mouth. Though the Baron Von Kannon did lead a few of our fellow students down to Miami Beach as volunteers for the 1972 Republican Convention. They went as members of our local chapter of the Young Americans for Freedom, though they went as conservatives first and Republicans second. Their hearts were still with Barry Goldwater. They were young and idealistic. I wondered how their Goldwater bumper stickers went down with Richard Nixon's Brooks Brothers–clad lieutenants. Within a few months, of course, we would all be for Richard Nixon. We agreed with M. Stanton Evans, the conservative wit, who always got a laugh from a conservative audience when he would declare, "I never liked Richard Nixon—until Watergate."

I cannot recall what the Baron did down in Miami Beach, aside from drinking beer and handing out Goldwater material. I suppose he had pamphlets booming the magazine and YAF literature arguing for the volunteer military, elimination of the minimum wage, and victory in Vietnam, all typical conservative issues of the time. Looking back on those days, I am reminded that the ideas propounded by the Goldwater candidacy, which was so soundly defeated in 1964, were the ideas of the future for conservatives, not the ideas of the past. In the years ahead, we developed still more ideas, such as antimissile defense and supply-side economics.

Eventually, we conservatives took over the Republican Party under the leadership of Governor Ronald Reagan, the man whose short-lived presidential campaign I was supporting back in June 1968, shortly after my eerie encounter with Bob Kennedy. Under Reagan's leadership, we would take over the government of the United States in the election of 1980 and implement many of our conservative policies. But for now, I had to get married. I married Judy Mathews in 1972, and we vacated The Establishment in 1973, moving into a vast house in Bloomington built around an elegant goldfish pond with a stately fountain that I insisted was an original Bernini. The house had a large office across from the pond, which I shared with my editorial staff. Judy was a bit startled by the move. Eventually, we had three children there and an astonishing dog.

It had a bloodline similar to that of the Prince of Wales, which made him a little high strung. He was an English bulldog, and I eschewed the accepted names, such as Strathtay Prince Albert or Lord Winston, and I named him Irving, *Irving Kristol*. The kennel was not pleased when I registered Irving's name. Irving consumed much of my wife's furniture before I sold him for a pittance. It was either Irving or the furniture, and some pieces were elegant antiques. On the first day in my new house, after my wife went off to work, I fell into the goldfish pond.

As for the magazine, we were steadily developing a following nationwide, and by 1975, our circulation stood at thirty thousand. The June–September 1974 issue was our last under the name of *The Alternative* and it was also the last issue of the magazine published from The Establishment. It featured a cover article on the liberal economist John Kenneth Galbraith, who was to serve as a favored punching bag for us for years. Our pugilist this time was Harold Demsetz, the distinguished professor of economics at UCLA. Also featured on the cover was Irving Kristol (the man, not the dog), writing on "Utopianism, Ancient and Modern." The cover also featured two other well-known writers, Arnold Beichman and Ben Wattenberg, two liberals in transit to the right.

Our next issue featured a refinement in our name from *The Alternative* to *The Alternative: An American Spectator*, and we had moved into our first real office, 102 West 6th Street, looking out on the Bloomington square. It overlooked the Monroe County Courthouse with its Civil War–era artillery and other monuments to faded glory that always arouse the suspicions of modern-day leftists who want to extirpate the past and sometimes do. One such monument was the infamous water fountain of the Woman's Christian Temperance Union

(WCTU) which the abstemious gals raised in 1913. I never saw it as much of a threat, though when the ladies first sponsored it, they were obviously anti-Catholic and adamantly opposed to alcohol even for medicinal purposes, even when used for such salubrious preparations as cough medicine or perhaps a seasonal fruitcake.

By the time we inhabited our spot above the Courthouse, the tee-totalers were as rare as the original Potawatomi Indians, and I would laugh at the ladies' memory. Occasionally, at the end of a long day, I would grab a staff member and head down to the WCTU water fountain to filch some of its blessed juices for a scotch and water to be enjoyed upstairs. I am told that the WCTU fountain is now gone, a victim of the left-wingers' hysteria about Confederate memorials and the American past in general. Someone apparently convinced them that the WCTU was a tool of the Ku Klux Klan, possibly the ladies were even in league with the slave trade. At any rate, if you want a mild libation, there is a bar down the street where, supposedly, the 1927 hit "Stardust" was composed by Hoagy Carmichael, a Hoosier. If you are in luck, the bartender might even serve medical marijuana.

The Baron and I spent the early days in our new offices sharpening up the magazine and developing its departments to serve as platforms for highlighting the noxious ideas and absurd behavior of those who roused our ire, mostly soi-disant liberals, ideological leftists, and, in general, opponents of American democracy, which included left-wingers and right-wingers, too. One might think that we were also engaged in devising elaborate schemes for avoiding the draft, much as Bill Clinton and like-minded patriots did at the time, but there was no reason for us to be obsessed with the draft. I was about the only person in our crowd old enough to be drafted and when I went home to Cook County, Illinois, to take my physical, the nurse asked me how long I had suffered from high blood pressure. I told her I had never tested for high blood pressure. "Ah," she said, "you just did." Well, possibly it was because I had had to use the facilities since the early morn when a burly sergeant announced that the next recruit to claim that he had to relieve himself would suffer some horrible fate. I took note, and the sergeant remained calm, but for me, it was the beginning of a day of extreme anxiety.

Actually, by the early 1990s, after decades of listening to erstwhile war protesters braying that Americans who failed to serve in Vietnam despite supporting a strong foreign policy were "chicken hawks," I became interested in the question of how many draft-age men served in Vietnam. It became obvious that a large number of young men failed their physicals in the 1960s and early 1970s. Just as a large number of young men back in the late 1930s failed their physicals—something like 50 percent. There was, after all, no need for their services until December 7, 1941. Thankfully, we never suffered a December 7 attack in the 1960s.

I called the Vietnam Veterans of America Foundation and talked to Ken Burez, then the associate director. He told me that 30 million to 35 million men came of age from 1964 to 1975, the Vietnam War years. Approximately 2.9 million, he said, actually went to serve in Southeast Asia. That figure sounded a little high to me. More recently, we consulted with the Selective Service System. According to the Selective Service, 2.15 million men served in Vietnam during the war, which comes to about 8 percent of the generation, which the Selective Service now estimates at 26.8 million men. Forty percent served in the military in places other than Vietnam. Fifty-seven percent, or 15.41 million men, were considered deferred, exempted, or disqualified. Even if I went to the bathroom the morning of my physical, I probably would not have served in Vietnam. Few of us qualified as chicken hawks, even in the 1970s. The term is a canard.

So, in the early 1970s, I was, I guess the contemporary term would be "weaponizing" the departments of the magazine, and they would remain our weapons of ridicule for fifty years. I take it as evidence of the encroaching weakness and ultimate death of liberalism that no liberal magazine or pundit ever attempted to compete with us in the department of humor, much less wit, in the more than fifty years of our existence.

As mentioned briefly in Chapter III, there was the "Bootblack Stand." From it, George Washington Plunkitt counseled, for instance, Senator Edward Kennedy on safe driving. In my mind's eye, I can see Plunkitt counseling, "Always wear a seat belt, Senator, and if you can still find someone to ride with you be sure that your passenger does too." And he might advise George H. W. Bush on how to deal with Jane Fonda. Jane might have just returned from visiting North Vietnam where she found our POWs unsympathetic. "History will judge them severely," she averred in a schoolmarm tone.[6] There were others, too, who sought his advice.

Another department was the "Current Wisdom," an omnium-gatherum of ignorance and fatuity where, for instance, columnist Pete Hamill in the *New York Post* justified the condition of American POWs as "prisoners because they committed unlawful acts"[7] and where the Reverend Philip Berrigan called the POWs "war criminals."[8] The most famous of our departments was perhaps "The Continuing Crisis" that for decades served as what Bill Buckley at one of our annual dinners called a collection of "ironic amalgamations" juxtaposing serious happenings with the utterly goofball.

A famous specimen from the "Bootblack Stand" appeared in our June–September 1973 issue:

Dear Mr. Plunkitt:

The recent outbursts of Jane Fonda against our POWs are inexplicable to me. I do not know what she is up to, but I am sure she is up to something. After all, who isn't?

Sincerely,
George Bush
Republican National Chairman

Dear George:

The intentions of Madame Fonda are really quite simple, but then what does one expect from a creature whose complexity is on a par, say, with the amoeba? What Madame Fonda is really up to when she calls our POWs war criminals and the like is nothing less than the 1976 Democratic presidential nomination. She obviously thinks that if she continues uttering these audacious political pronouncements, the Democrats will crown her—a development dearly to be desired by all high-ranking Republicans. For if she wins the nomination, there will be no need ever to bug her headquarters. All Americans will be instantly aware of the most fleeting thought to gambol and lurch through her mind.

—GWP

A specimen of the "Current Wisdom" from the same period (October 1974) might remind contemporary readers of our longtime absorption with radical enemies, in this case, the youthful and idealistic bank robbers and bomb throwers of the Symbionese Liberation Army (SLA) as they were perceived by the left-wing *Nation* magazine:

REPORT FROM L.A.: Definitive report on the SLA's last stand from one of *The Nation*'s resident imbeciles:

There is not as much difference as law-abiding citizens would like to believe between the psychology of the SLA and that of FBI agents and most police in battle. In this instance, both sides were imbued with the politics of desperation and unlimited force. Locked in combat, the actors, lawful and lawless alike, behaved as if their roles had been written for them in a movie script, stripped of everything human except violence without limit.

—*The Nation*
June 1, 1974

Another weaponized department was our "Worst Book of the Year Award" at first called "The Harold Robbins Award," and then "The J. Gordon Coogler Award," a slightly tonier-sounding name for a writer who was even more insipid than Harold Robbins. Coogler was a real dolt. He advertised from his office, "Poems written while you wait," and he earned a living wage doing just that.

The department lasted from 1974 until 2008, after which I had tired of reading bad books. Though, if anything, they became even worse as we entered the digital age with semiliterates volunteering their tomes to publishers everywhere and editors being a thing of the past. The first winner of The Worst Book of the Year award was Peter Schrag, whose *Test of Loyalty: Daniel Ellsberg and the Rituals of Secret Government* was about the trials of the sainted Daniel Ellsberg, who, without authorization, released the Pentagon Papers to the public. Another memorably bad book was produced by the writer who became our Coogler laureate for 1980, Bertram Gross. His contribution was *Friendly Fascism: The New Face of Power in America*. It was, as was Schrag's effort, a dreary and ill-informed book about the fate that America faced from its government in the years ahead. Obviously, Gross's prediction was off by at least forty years. Then the danger of fascism came from the Left, and few of the citizens thought it friendly.

One happy anomaly in this otherwise dismal parade of literary efforts was our 1979 awardee, William Shawcross. We gave him the award for his book, *Sideshow: Kissinger, Nixon and the Destruction of Cambodia*. Our reviewer, Peter Rodman, now sadly deceased, noted errors in the book and other problems, but Peter formed a friendship with William, who turned out to be an admirable man, and both men went on to contribute mightily to the strength of, for instance, the

NATO alliance and to their respective countries. It fell to me to tell William in 2011 that we had rescinded his award and, truth be told, our board of directors wanted it back. Some thirty years after the fact, the board wanted it returned! I even visited William's home in London, expecting to find the handsome trophy on his mantelpiece or in some other exalted place. But, no, I could not ascertain where he had placed the objet d'art, and before I could inquire further, he offered me a beer and after that a second beer and we forgot the fracas completely.

Finally, there was the aforementioned "Continuing Crisis." I wrote it for the sheer fun of it, and the idea was to mix in the oddball with the portentous and, when the occasion warranted, to throw in the solemn. It was supposed to be a wrap-up of the previous month with offbeat things that caught my eye. For instance, in the June–September issue of 1974, I noted that:

> In New York City, Mrs. Milton Kravenstall has brought a class action suit against the President for 'consistently and maliciously interfering with my sleep,' and Mr. Claude Hammer, also of that fair metropolis, has promised to sign a reciprocal suicide agreement with the President so long as the President acts first.

That was pretty much all in fun, though Mrs. Kravenstall and Mr. Hammer were real-life people.

Yet by the time I wrote "The Continuing Crisis" in our October 1974 issue, the Crisis had turned grim, then solemn. In July,

> Mr. Nixon had to deliver sixty-four tapes to Judge John J. Sirica for use in the criminal trial of Mr. Nixon's former Assistant Presidents. Just as this black cat had crossed Mr. Nixon's path the House Judiciary Committee voted out three articles of impeachment against him, setting the stage for an August 19th impeachment debate, a performance that was never to be, for by August 5th those sixty-four tapes revealed

that Mr. Nixon had lied about his knowledge of and his role in the Watergate coverup.

From June 17, 1972, onward the Watergate Hotel/office complex was mentioned with increasing frequency in the news, for it was there that five men were caught in the offices of the Democratic National Committee after hours, in offices that were not their own. One of them had worked for the CIA and now was employed by the Committee to Re-Elect the President (soon dubbed, ironically, CREEP). Two others arrested shortly thereafter had similar spooky backgrounds and also now worked for CREEP. It did not look good for the Republicans, and by January 30, 1973, when the seven men were found guilty, the speculation was that they did not act alone. At the magazine, we were intrigued by the early Watergate stories, though at first, they did not loom large for us. There were so many other stories, and besides, some of our best writers were on the White House staff: Aram Bakshian, John Coyne, and Ben Stein. Eventually, of course, Watergate became a huge story for us. In fact, along with the fall of Vietnam, Watergate became an early instance of the Episodic Chaos that was to engulf America in the years to come.

The traps were by now set for catching President Richard Nixon. The seven break-in defendants were scheduled to be sentenced on March 23. Earlier that week, one of them, James McCord, wrote the presiding Judge John Sirica telling him that the defendants were lying and that there had been a cover-up. Also, that same week, on March 21, John Dean, Nixon's lawyer who had been running the cover-up, finally got around to telling the president some specifics. He was dispatched to Camp David to prepare a report that the president would use to call for a renewed investigation—but it was too late. Sirica released the McCord letter at the sentencing hearing, the people running the cover-up panicked, and the cover-up quickly collapsed. Dean broke with the White House and hired a Kennedy-clan lawyer. Dean quickly changed sides and Watergate stories dominated the news.

A year later, the seven cover-up defendants were indicted, including Nixon's attorney general, John Mitchell, his chief of staff, Bob Haldeman, and his assistant for domestic affairs, John Ehrlichman. Then on July 24, 1974, the Supreme Court unanimously upheld Special Prosecutor Leon Jaworski's subpoena for sixty-four additional White House tapes, and the president's lawyers announced that he would comply. The House Judiciary Committee on July 27 adopted the first of three articles of impeachment, for obstruction of justice, abuse of power, and refusal to comply with House subpoenas. On August 5, the White House released the transcript of the smoking gun tape, where Nixon was heard to agree with his staff's suggestion that they stop FBI interviews of two individuals by getting the CIA to claim that the individuals were part of a CIA operation. Nixon's remaining support collapsed entirely and on August 8 he threw in the towel and agreed to resign.

Yet here we are decades after the Supreme Court's order triggered the release of the tapes, and recent revelations have cast doubt on the judgment that the smoking gun tape revealed that Mr. Nixon had, as I mistakenly wrote in the October 1974 "Continuing Crisis," "lied about his knowledge of and his role in the Watergate coverup." In the fall of 2019, *The American Spectator* published an article by Geoff Shepard titled "Nixon's Resignation Reconsidered." Geoff was a former member of Nixon's Watergate defense team, and in his article, he proved categorically that President Nixon's lead defense lawyer, Fred Buzhardt, had misunderstood the import of the smoking gun tape. Nixon did not recall the specifics; only John Dean did, and he kept its import secret.

It was a tape of a conversation between the president and Haldeman that was recorded on June 23, 1972. Looking back on the conversation from August 1974, Buzhardt had mistakenly thought that Nixon and Haldeman were referring to the Watergate break-in when Haldeman said that an FBI investigation "goes in some directions we don't want it to go." But Geoff's research revealed—and he made a very convincing case—that history has made a stunning mistake about the depth of Nixon's involvement in the cover-up that cost him the presidency. Haldeman was not talking decades ago about getting the CIA to restrain the FBI from investigating a Watergate-related operation. Haldeman was talking about something entirely different. Haldeman was talking about the idea of getting the CIA to restrain the FBI from pursuing interviews with two witnesses whose only knowledge concerned Democratic donors who had made perfectly legal donations to the Nixon campaign. Geoff wrote in his *Spectator* piece that the sole purpose of the June 23, 1972, conversation between Nixon and Haldeman was to prevent disclosure of the names of the two prominent Democrats who had contributed to Nixon's campaign under the assurance that their donations would remain confidential. Geoff also learned that the idea was John Dean's. By August 5, 1974, more than two years after his conversation with Haldeman, Nixon had apparently completely forgotten the import of his June 23, 1972, conversation, and Haldeman was long gone. Nixon could not convince his own staff that he and Haldeman had not been talking about Watergate. Thus, he resigned.

Does anyone else agree with Geoff's thesis? Actually, John Dean, the orchestrator of the cover-up all those years ago, the one who forwarded the phony idea of CIA involvement, which Haldeman shared with Nixon on June 23, and the betrayer of his sole client, the president, appears to have kept the truth from the world since 1974. But in his 2014 book, *The Nixon Defense*, all of that was pretty much ignored, even by the book's reviewers. Still, Dean revealed his secret. Here it is:

> When revealed by order of the U.S. Supreme Court in late July 1974, this became known as the "smoking gun" conversation, because it was viewed as hard evidence, demonstrating beyond question, that Nixon's final defense about the Watergate break-in…was bogus, which doomed the Nixon presidency. Ironically, this

conversation has been mistakenly understood as an effort by Nixon and Haldeman to shut down the FBI's entire Watergate investigation. This appears to be the case only when viewed out of context. In August 1974, when the conversation was revealed, and Nixon and his lawyers had to focus on this conversation, he [Nixon] had long forgotten what was actually involved; they [Nixon and his lawyers] assumed it had the same meaning as everyone else did. In reality, it was only an effort by Haldeman to stop the FBI from investigating an anonymous campaign contribution from Mexico that the Justice Department prosecutors had already agreed was outside the scope of the Watergate investigation. In approving this action, however, Nixon slightly expanded the request, saying that the FBI should also stay out of Howard Hunt's CIA-related activities. In fact, this conversation did not put the lie to Nixon's April 30 and May 22, 1973, statements, and had Nixon known that he might have survived its disclosure to fight another day. This is not to say, however, that Nixon's April 30 and May 22, 1973, statements were not a lie, as countless other conversations later revealed. In short, the smoking gun was only firing blanks.[9]

Perhaps it is time for historians of a revisionist inclination to turn their attention to Watergate as Geoff Shepard did in his piece.

Though Nixon's speechwriters and his vice president had been friends of mine during his presidency, I never met RN until August 21, 1978, and then it was under conspiratorial circumstances. It was during my first book tour, and the book was titled *Public Nuisances*. Nixon accounted for Chapters 16 and 17 of that book. As mentioned earlier, I was no fan of Richard Nixon, though I certainly preferred him to George McGovern. En route to a television interview in Los

Angeles, I stopped off in Corpus Christi (geography has never been my strong suit) to visit with my friend Anne Armstrong, the former US ambassador to Great Britain. She arrived at the airport with her attractive daughter, Katharine, who would drive me to the Armstrong Ranch after dropping her mother off in the city. After lunching at the King Ranch, it was on to the Armstrong Ranch. Between the Armstrong Ranch and Corpus Christi, there is only one ranch, the King Ranch. Texas is spacious. The Armstrong Ranch was enormous but not as big as the King Ranch, then claimed as the largest ranch in the world, and also the setting for the movie classic, appropriately named *Giant*.

After a very long drive through uninhabited prairie and brush-lands, we arrived at the King spread just in time for lunch with two of the Kleberg daughters whose family owned the ranch. Then it was back into the car for another trudge to the Armstrong Ranch. Texas is a big place, and by the time we arrived at our destination, animals had begun to emerge from the brush. I cannot recall what kind of animals, but I was not about to leave the car to find out. It was now late in the afternoon, and Katharine told me we would be joined at dinner by the Kleberg girls and their brother, who turned out to be a big, rangy guy, dressed like a cowboy though without the six-shooters. The girls had spent the afternoon surfing in the Gulf of Mexico, after which they would gather up their brother back at the King Ranch and join us. According to my calculations, they drove more than two hundred miles that afternoon. As I was discovering, Texas is a big place for any-one who is not from Texas.

That night we had a Texas-sized feast and enough wine and scotch to assure a Karamazovian hangover the next morning. Anne and her husband, Tobin, withdrew after coffee, and we young people continued to party. At one point the Kleberg brother, who was sprawled across a lounge chair, asked, "Well Bob, what do you think of Texas?" Looking out across the expanse as far as the eye could see and watching those creatures leaping and gamboling in the moonlight, all I could say was: "It's big." What else was there to say?

The next morning, nursing a clangorous hangover, I departed while everyone in the house was asleep. But first, I penned a very polite note to Katharine. She had been very sweet. I never saw her again until one morning in 2006 when on the television broadcasting from the Armstrong Ranch came a spokesperson for the ranch to explain Vice President Dick Cheney's shooting accident during a quail hunt there the day before. The spokesperson was Katharine Armstrong. She had weathered the decades well.

I arrived at Los Angeles International Airport, signed for my rental car, and took off on the sixty-mile drive down the coast to San Clemente, once the seat of the "Western White House." Ken Khachigian still loyally working for "the boss" would be my host for dinner, and despite my enduring hangover, we had a lively chat at the end of which came the conspiratorial part. Ken said, "the boss" is looking forward to seeing you at 10:30 tomorrow. I objected, though I had been sufficiently anesthetized by an evening of Ken's Nixon stories to stifle my admittedly weakening reluctance.

The next morning, I headed down the hill to Casa Pacifica, encountering a crowd of colorful surfers headed to the beach (the Western White House was situated on the precise point where massive waves roll in from Hawaii). I passed the former president's numerous aides in the hallway, including Diane Sawyer, soon to be a talking head on one of the morning news shows, and his distinguished speechwriter, Frank Gannon, who was reading from a stack of London newspapers. Nixon always maintained a particularly urbane and literate team of speechwriters, some of whom have worked with me right up to the moment that this book was finished.

I was ushered into the ex-president's library for coffee: There the scoundrel sat, slouched in a reading chair that appeared to be floating on a surface of discarded books, magazines, and newspapers. Nixon, with a pipe at his side, wearing reading glasses, looked like a fellow editor. Had Khachigian set me up? If so, Nixon's makeup artist should have been shot. I shall never forget my first close-up glimpse of that famous face. Cartoonists had been too charitable. The face shocked. It did not have creases; it had ravines, gullies, dried creek beds. The jowls hung. Eyebrows sprouted wildly. The skin was raw, peeling, and discolored. The voice was strong, but there was fluid in his throat, the consequence, perhaps, of a recent cold. We talked for two hours about history, politics, and related books. He asked me to come by again in the afternoon. Reluctantly, I agreed. Thus, began a friendship that was to last the rest of his life.

The character of a sphinxlike man such as Nixon is often like a crystal, sometimes like a diamond, occasionally like a lump of coal. Different facets of his character are drawn out by different conditions around him: different persona, different demands, different goals. Occasionally, no goals whatsoever. So it was with the former president. The Richard Nixon that conferred with Mao Zedong revealed a different side of himself than the Richard Nixon who campaigned against Hubert Humphrey or visited with Margaret Thatcher or smoked a pipe with me.

That afternoon we talked about history, sports, politics, and, fleetingly, religion—he was interested in the subject and in Malcolm Muggeridge, the deeply religious Christian journalist who had recently converted to Catholicism and who was a friend of Mother Teresa. Of course, Nixon often talked of Winston Churchill, Charles de Gaulle, and other world figures, and so we did that afternoon. Yet something had been nagging at me since the summer of 1974. I waited for a pause and asked him about the Watergate break-in and the cover-up. What did he know? I remember his response as though it were yesterday. He slumped, hesitated, and replied, "That's *the* question." He said he neither knew of the planned break-in ahead of time nor any specifics of the cover-up prior to his meeting with John Dean on March 21, 1973. I was not convinced that he was telling the truth. Now, all these decades later, I believe him. I have seen Geoff Shepard's evidence, and I have read John Dean's confession. Nixon was not lying.

Ed Cox, the former president's son-in-law, has for years said that I reintroduced the thirty-seventh president to the world of conservative intellectuals. My managing editor from our early days, the very perceptive Adam Meyerson, agreed. In a piece on me for *Vanity Fair*, he volunteered to the *VF* writer that I had met the former president "in the mid-seventies, when nobody was talking to Richard Nixon. And afterwards when Nixon wanted to come back and again talk to journalists and intellectuals, the person who organized his re-emergence was Bob Tyrrell." Well, why not? RN liked many of the same things I liked, such as America, such as the give-and-take of ideas, such as writers. I was pleased to bring the writers together with him. In the course of doing so, I learned how to make a splendid martini.

I recall a dinner we had at Nixon's Manhattan townhouse with a leading French journalist at the time, Patrick Wajsman. Also invited were several American journalists and my close friend, the futurologist, George Gilder. Years later, George was to step in and assist me in protecting *The American Spectator* from the vengeful Clintons. RN had an excellent Chinese cook that night and some bottles of superb bordeaux. Inspired doubtless by Wajsman's presence, he compared each bottle's vintage with the year's political events both in America and France. When he arrived at 1968, the year of his election, he was surprisingly vague about the grape, whose quality was not high. When asked to account for it, he hesitated and then dolefully observed that 1968 was the year of de Gaulle's fall. He obviously admired de Gaulle, perhaps he even identified with him.

On another occasion, late in 1979, following his book tour in Europe, I rounded up twenty young journalists and historians to join him in his suite at the Waldorf Towers. It was the first time I saw him undertake a performance for which he was to become renowned in his years as an elder statesman. He gave us a guided tour of the world's trouble spots, commenting on them as they related to Western interests. When he got to Iran, one of our historians asked him about the Shah's treatment of the riotous crowds at Teheran's Jaleh Square. The former president pronounced coldly that the Shah was "insufficiently brutal." Perhaps, as John Dean implied in his 2014 book, it was to America's good fortune that Nixon did not survive the smoking gun tape and live, as Dean said, "to fight another day." It might have been a bloody confrontation. He had given way on a disputed presidential contest in 1960. He might not have been so docile the second time around.

For years, RN actually got stronger as he grew older. From the time I first met him in August 1978, on into the 1980s, the appalling face steadily returned to the health of the face that once filled our TV screens from the Oval Office. Slowly, I came to realize that the face, which I had first seen up close in San Clemente, was the face of unconcealable suffering. As Watergate receded into the past, the therapy of writing books proved to be cosmetic surgery for RN. Through the years we talked regularly, occasionally face-to-face, but more often on the telephone. One day, he called me at my McLean, Virginia, home and asked me what "we" knew about this guy, Oliver North. Iran-Contra had just made him infamous.

I said that North was a war hero, but the rumor going around was that he had threatened some guy who hassled his wife when he was in Vietnam. RN fired back in his inimitable style, "Well, what's wrong with that, Bob? We don't have anything against that, do we?" It is a good thing there were no reporters from *The Washington Post* in the room. Then he had a word with my son, Patrick. It was January 9—their birthday. P. D. was sixteen. RN was seventy-seven. One of my fondest memories of RN came months later when I brought my playboy friend Taki Theodoracopulos out to RN's New Jersey home for dinner.

Taki was much more cultured than a mere playboy, and he and the former president hit it off that night. So, months later, when the New York press reported Taki's arrest for trying to enter the UK through

Heathrow Airport with an envelope of cocaine protruding from his vest pocket, I should not have been surprised by RN's morning telephone call. He wanted to know how he might console Taki. I said I thought he could send Taki a hacksaw in a package with RN's name on the return address. That would probably get by his guards. Instead, he sent a simple letter of encouragement, and later Taki told me the guards were impressed.

I remember Richard Nixon for many good times and many heuristic moments and for one thing more. I took a group of writers out to his home in Saddle River, New Jersey, for dinner. There he mixed me the best dry martini I have ever had. I have counseled five presidents, and visited with a sixth one, Bill Clinton, as you will see in Chapter X and Chapter XI; but only RN mixed me a martini. It was a specialty of his. He called it an Eisenhower martini.

Back in 1974, after Nixon had departed on Air Force One for the last time, I called one of his speechwriters, John Coyne, who was to write for us for decades. I offered my condolences. Being from Chicago and the equally barefisted political environment of Indiana, I had pretty much worked out my explanation for the politics of Watergate. As history has unfurled Watergate's mysteries, my explanation has been vindicated. Geoff Shepard's revelations only add to my vindication.

Here is how I explained it to Coyne. In politics, there are formal rules and there are informal rules. The formal rules have to do with ethics, the law, those virtues a politician claims to be admired for. The informal rules have to do with what, in the Watergate days, were called "dirty tricks" or political dark acts. They are what a politician can go to jail for. After Nixon resigned, people began poking around the behavior of the FBI, the CIA, and eventually Nixon's predecessors in office. Investigators deposited their findings in six books, known as the Church Committee report, or more formally, the final report of the United States Senate Select Committee to Study Governmental Operations with Respect to Intelligence Activities. The report came out on April 29, 1976, and it made my case for the informal politics of presidents. That is to say, the shady practices occasionally resorted to by all presidents since Franklin D. Roosevelt, even by the avuncular Ike. The report renders this judgment on page VIII of Book II:

> Fundamental issues concerning the conduct and character of the nation deserve nonpartisan treatment. It has become clear from our inquiry, moreover, that intelligence excesses, at home and abroad, have been found in every administration. They are not the product of any single party, administration, or man.[10]

The report goes on to chronicle the widespread practices of surveillance of American citizens by government agencies, including the CIA, the FBI, and military intelligence units, undertaken in the name of national security and without court-issued search warrants. These practices occurred under President Nixon, but they also occurred under his predecessors, stretching back to Franklin D. Roosevelt. We now know that they continued right up through the presidency of Donald J. Trump.

The Church report revealed such routine practices as surreptitious wiretapping, surreptitious mail opening, surveilling "subversives," both Americans and the foreign born, and, of course, surveilling political opponents. No president thought he would be impeached or prosecuted for such activity. For instance, Barry Goldwater knew that LBJ had tapes on him, but impeaching LBJ would be almost un-American. That was what Richard Nixon thought, too. People who knew Nixon well, for instance Ed Cox, report that Nixon never thought the behavior practiced by his administration would be grounds for impeachment. In the summer of 1974, he learned otherwise. The informal ways of politics were not going to be extended by the Democrats to him. Once again, we see the Democrats break with precedent, and the consequence has been Episodic Chaos for America. The cause of their break with precedent is, of course, their unscotchable political libido. Republicans have nothing to match it but principle, as I shall be chronicling.

Back at the magazine, we were having a grand old time. I had purchased a Cadillac limousine, much like the one Bill Buckley owned to convey him to and fro on his busy schedule in Manhattan. The only differences were that there was no place to go toing and froing in Bloomington, and besides, my limousine was quite dilapidated. I had purchased it third-hand, possibly fourth-hand, from a funeral parlor. Nonetheless, it was in demand on several occasions, at least one of which was provided by my friend Tom Tarzian, the son of our supporter Sarkes Tarzian. Tom had heard that I was cutting a dashing figure about town in my limousine, and he asked if I would convey him and a distinguished guest to Indianapolis in my limousine, which Tom had never actually seen. I agreed to meet them at the Tarzian newspaper, the *Courier-Tribune*. When I learned our guest was to be the previous year's short-lived Democratic candidate for vice president, Senator Tom Eagleton, I could smell a news story. At the appointed hour, I rolled up to the *Courier-Tribune* building in my spacious rattletrap and welcomed the senator aboard. In he came, obviously startled by my ancient conveyance. But the senator was taking his meds and presented no danger to anyone. The chauffeur I had engaged for this occasion was completely sober, and we had a very pleasant ride to Indianapolis, though I noted that Senator Eagleton was wearing his seat belt all the way.

In the spring of 1975, I picked up Pat Moynihan yet again at the Indianapolis airport—this time in a Porsche—and transported him to the campus where he was scheduled to speak before dining at one more banquet in The Establishment, now the home of the Baron Von Kannon, still our publisher, and Ron Burr, who had become our circulation manager now that we had a circulation department and some money to promote the magazine. Money, contrary to our critics, would always be an issue for us. In fact, money was a problem for the conservative movement from the start. Research shows that over the years the Left has outspent the right by roughly six to one as reported earlier, even as the conservatives continued their half century of growth.[11]

Pat was impressed by how fast I drove him down to Bloomington in my new Porsche. He asked me if I had, as had his Harvard colleague James Q. Wilson, taken Bob Bondurant's course in high-speed driving. To Pat, there was a course available for almost everything. I had not, and as I recall, Pat tapped the clasp on his seat belt to be sure it was secure. Pat spoke in a heavily accented argot whose exact origin was, as with Bill Buckley's, difficult to discern. Yet it lent his presence when he spoke in public with a forbiddingly imposing air, especially at the United Nations. He was our ambassador there from 1975 to 1976 and a commanding presence he was. As did Winston Churchill, Pat had a mild speech impediment, which hindered both men on the podium not at all.

At The Establishment that night, he was his usual congenial self, which is to say a mixture of the serious and the urbane, but this evening there was something else. As the crickets chirped outside and Beethoven played sotto voce in the background, Pat said he thought "the world will drift for two or three years." He said the "Nixonians" had been "empty men who would set conservatives back." Then he added that he saw *The Alternative* as a "source of information" and he was "surprised by the large circulation" (for a small intellectual magazine) and the "esprit de corps" of our staff.[12] Much of what he said that night he had recently written in *Commentary*. As for his high praise of our magazine, I was pleased but surprised. There was none of Irving Kristol's superciliousness coming from Pat Moynihan. It was a good night.

However, he had me off balance all evening with his combination of outspokenness against the "Nixonians" and his friendliness toward the magazine. I would be a close friend of his for the next few years, visiting with him at the Democratic National Convention and sharing drinks with him and his aide, my handball buddy, Penn Kemble. After he defeated Senator Jim Buckley, he drifted—as I have said—into the increasingly regimented thought of the Democratic Party. We were still friends, but no longer close friends. There was that trip on the shuttle where we shouted lines from Yeats back and forth. There was an appearance at the Saturday Evening Club in Washington. I have always wondered if, at his last evening at The Establishment, he glimpsed the future: the rising strength of our young gang of some-what daring thinkers; his coming years of growing isolation, cowed by his party and cowed by a woman he seemed to hate, Hillary Clinton, the successor to his seat in the Senate. Pat was a great figure. Of all the neocons, he was the best, with the eventual exception of Jeane Kirkpatrick, about whom more later.

We did share one more memory together. That would be May 20, 1998, at St. Patrick's Catholic Church in downtown Washington and afterward at Bob Novak's home, where a small group of us got together to celebrate Bob's conversion to Roman Catholicism. Pat was a Catholic through and through. I was, too, and now the Prince of Darkness, as his colleagues on television called Bob, had joined us. Bob's conversion came about because of a feeling of emptiness he had borne within him for years. There was also his family's shared longing for the Holy Eucharist and because of something more. He had a mys-terious exchange with a woman student whom he had met at Syracuse University. They spoke briefly of their religious commitments: hers apparently fervent, Bob's apparently lax. She ended the exchange with words that he said "shook" him. Upon being told by Bob that he did not "at the present time" plan to join the Church, she said, "Mr. Novak, life is short, but eternity is forever."[13] Bob concluded that the Holy Spirit was speaking to him through the Syracuse student. I do too.

As I have gone through my notes of that faraway evening in Bloomington with Pat Moynihan, a sobering thought occurs. That evening there was no mention of the fall of Saigon by anyone pres-ent, though it took place shortly before, on April 30. Twenty years of war, more than fifty-five thousand Americans dead, billions of dollars expended, and now it was over. As my friend, Seth Lipsky, the editor and founder of *The New York Sun* who had served in the war, was to write years later, "On the ground in Vietnam, our GIs did just that [won]. In the most famous battle, Tet in 1968, our soldiers trounced the Communists. The cause of free Vietnam was betrayed in the US Congress, which had been turned by the anti-war movement."[14] Yes, the same idlers who smoked marijuana, handed out pro-Vietcong pamphlets, and assaulted old veterans waving a "Victory in Vietnam" banner, had won the hearts of senators such as Muskie and McGovern. In the end, who were the true defenders of freedom, the men in their sweaty fatigues thousands of miles from home or the overgrown children in their tie-dyed T-shirts basking in the shadow of the Lincoln Memorial?

The Vietnam War has endured as another of the 1970s' moments of Episodic Chaos. When it reached its denouement in Congress in 1974 and 1975, it was the Democrats who ignored the pleas of President Gerald Ford and Secretary of State Henry Kissinger and voted to end support for Free Vietnam. Incidentally, one of the most vehement senators who met with President Ford and insisted on leaving our Vietnamese allies to their fate was a young senator from Delaware. He was Joe Biden, the same Joe Biden who forty-six years later hastily pulled our troops out of Afghanistan. Joe has mastered the strategy of defeat. President Ford wrote about it in his memoirs.

Chapter V

A GREAT
GENERATION PASSES

*B*y the mid-1970s, the conservative movement was growing
steadily, though we still only composed a small group of individuals in comparison with the liberals who surrounded us.
The joke still was that the conservative movement could fit comfort-
ably into the corner telephone booth, assuming you can still envision
a telephone booth. We were composed of academics, editors, writers,
a handful of hangers-on, and an audience of avid readers. The avid
readers were as important to our movement as they are to any intellectual movement, but looking back over a distance now of more than
fifty years, it appears to me that we never acquired enough avid readers. At one point in the 1990s, *The American Spectator*'s audience was
approaching three hundred fifty thousand, making us the largest intellectual review in the country and probably the largest in the world. But
this did not last. The Clinton administration came down on us with
their investigations. Also, there was talk of congressional inquiries.

I recall one day waiting in the greenroom while Representative John Conyers, the Democrat from Michigan, was being interviewed by Brian Lamb on C-SPAN. It was April 2, 1998, one day after April Fools' Day, if memory serves. Brian asked the congressman what would become of *The American Spectator*, which was then the focus of ongoing Democratic wrath. Conyers said, "Well, we're looking into them." Brian told the congressman that I was his next guest. I hastened to the entranceway of the studio, expecting to meet the great man as he exited. Yet, somehow, the great man never came out. Possibly, he jumped out a window. At any rate, he went on to suffer a long period of investigations himself and he retired in 2017 amid charges of sexually harassing female members of his staff and secretly paying them hush money with taxpayers' funds. Prior to that, his wife spent time in a federal prison on bribery charges. Incidentally, we shall encounter similar culminations as we read on. At the magazine, we consider such sad endings to be examples of the "Tyrrell Curse." Aside from government investigations, of course, there were also instances of the media harassing us. Yes, the media was harassing *us*. I recall Geraldo Rivera leading either an NBC or a CNBC crew (they all look alike with their baseball caps on backward) outside our office windows about this time. What had provoked him were our "scandalous" stories about Bill Clinton's harassment of women and his shady fundraising schemes, all stories, by the way, that have been vindicated. Yet soon we were fighting for our lives, and our circulation suffered.

Also joining us in the telephone booth in the early days was a small group of foundations—the Earhart Foundation, the John M. Olin Foundation, the Lilly Endowment, the Smith Richardson Foundation, the Bradley Foundation, and the foundations belonging to Dick Scaife, the Pittsburgh philanthropist without whom modern American conservatism would be much reduced. There were not a lot of conservative foundations in those early days, but those that were with us were extremely generous and well managed, and their officers thought strategically about their philanthropy. I have come to the conclusion that it was not a lack of talented writers or a lack of money that prevented conservative magazines from acquiring an avid readership capable of competing with the Left's audience. It was the lack of a stable, reliable pool of readers from which to draw an audience. The Left had the universities. We did not. We had nothing equal to the network of universities that would allow a stable community of readers to gestate and spread.

For years I had assumed that, encouraged by an atmosphere of freedom, the curiosity of adventurous minds would choose cool reason over infantile emotion and reach out for truth at our great universities. That is how a place for conservatives would be insured in academe. Yet, the arrival on campus of identity politics, tribal behavior, and other anti-intellectual preoccupations made my hopes appear fanciful. By 1985, I, at last, gave up on the universities. The decision has made my life ever more pleasant. Today, I rarely raise my voice in public. I can read widely without fear of someone peeping over my shoulder. And when I talk about ideas, it is usually in the company of adults.

At his foundations, Dick Scaife had Dan McMichael and Dick Larry organizing strategy and overseeing funding. His largesse was sent to every corner of the conservative movement, a movement that in a dozen or so years would command the White House—from Goldwater in 1964 to Reagan in 1980! Not bad, Dick! Dan and Dick Larry, with the help of Dick Scaife's foundations, funded academics, think tanks, magazines, and single-interest shops. Naturally, they helped to finance books and studies. In the early 1970s, apparently satisfied that the Scaife investment in our magazine had borne fruit, Dick Larry enlisted me in two ventures that allowed the magazine to broaden its interests and its reach.

The Scaife foundations funded a study of television coverage of the 1972 Democratic primaries that allowed me to work with Irving Kristol and Paul Weaver, an assistant professor at Harvard, whose thesis on television coverage of elections first appeared in the winter

Public Interest. Now our organization, The Alternative Media Analysis Center, would put Paul's study to the test by analyzing the 1972 Democratic primaries. A couple of years later, Scaife funded my book *The Future That Doesn't Work: Social Democracy's Failures in Britain,* broadening our interests and increasing our reach.

As I have said, the first study was my inaugural opportunity to work with Irving and *The Public Interest* writers. The second, *The Future That Doesn't Work,* introduced me to the intellectuals of Europe. Friendships that began with that book have endured and multiplied through the years. Irving also helped me with *The Future That Doesn't Work,* lining up British writers with whom he had worked while he was coediting *Encounter* magazine in London after World War II. Now we would rely on them and some Americans to chronicle socialism's fall and to adumbrate Thatcherism's rise. His own contribution to *The Future That Doesn't Work* was appropriately titled "Socialism: Obituary for an Idea."

The youngest person on our staff when we assembled it in Bloomington in 1972 had a year yet to go in high school, the very bright Joe Duggan. Joe now remembers the "parade" of writers who came out to Bloomington to visit, consult, and, finally, write our report. The parade, he recalls, "Was really quite something." There was Paul Weaver from *The Public Interest* and the Harvard Government Department. His thesis, that television covers primaries as though it were covering a horse race, held up very well and attracted national attention to the magazine.

Along with Paul was another Harvard figure, Roger Rosenblatt, a gifted writer who would leave Harvard eventually to make his mark briefly at our magazine and later on in television and by writing engaging books. There was Terry Krieger, also from Harvard, who served as a consultant on our project, and Marc Plattner, the assistant editor of *The Public Interest,* who served the project as an analyst and writer. Finally, there was Robert Asahina who served as a consultant for us on the project and went on to edit numerous conservative books, among them my 1992 book *The Conservative Crack-Up*. Joe also remembers Bill Kristol, who apparently turned up in Bloomington that summer and was Joe's age, though he had no role in the project.

Then there was this curiosity: Alan Keyes. He began college at Cornell and left there for Harvard under some pressure. Black militants were threatening him with machine guns, which even among the academics in the wilds of Ithaca, New York, was considered controversial. It was the first of many memorable marks that Alan made in his life. His next mark was with me on our 1972 project. It was not as heroic as his Cornell exit, though it was memorable. Alan did research for me. He was very bright, had a first-class analytical mind, and, as I recall, was extremely eloquent.

He was also, as they now say, a gentleman of color, though to listen to him hold forth you would think he was a citizen of ancient Athens, living just down the street from Pericles. He had studied under the classics professor Alan Bloom at Cornell and was now studying under Ed Banfield at Harvard. He was at this stage of his education either an Aristotelian or a Platonist. Frankly, I have forgotten. Alan was eventually to leave a mark on several other different, if far-flung locales, not the least of which was as the Republican chosen to oppose Barack Obama in Barack's run for the Senate from Illinois, though Alan's residence was in Maryland. The race was Barack's only run for national office before he glided into the White House. It is a shame that Alan lost. He would have been a colossus in the Senate, where he would have been a mellifluous successor to Illinois' Senator Everett Dirksen. But he lost, garnering only 1,390,690 votes to 3,597,456 votes for Barack.

Alan also lost with me. He had a way of telling others on the staff to get him groceries. A frequent candidate was young Joe. One day, I overheard him send Joe out for a quart of milk. This had to stop, and so I called him aside and told him we were parting company. Utterly unperturbed, he looked out at some distant object he spied apparently over my left shoulder and intoned, "Tyrrell, you are my moral and intellectual inferior." Well, I could not argue with that, but I did reply: "Alan, on that we can agree, but you are still fired…and you have twenty-four hours to clear out."

After the departure of Alan Keyes, things quieted down and we executed the tasks required to put together our *Report on Network News' Treatment of the 1972 Democratic Presidential Candidates*. We got it out in time for the autumn election, and the *Report* attracted our first national publicity, the flavor of which is conveyed by one of our early champions, Bill Buckley. In his hugely popular syndicated column—at the time the most widely read column in the country—he wrote under the headline "The Casting of the Presidency" that

> [t]here is continuing interest in the reporting of Presidential races, and now we have a most interesting analysis, published by a group put together by *The Alternative* magazine, entitled *Report on Network News' Treatment of the 1972 Democratic Presidential Candidate*…. Everyone will be interested in it, demonstrating as it does a) that McGovern was made by the television media; and (inferentially) b) that he was destroyed by the television media.

Well, I am not so sure about point (b), Bill. McGoo did a pretty thorough job of destroying himself.

At any rate, it did not take very long for Dick Larry to ring me up and suggest yet another Scaife-endowed book project. Dick Scaife was interested in a scholarly account of how socialism was faring in Britain, and with the assistance of Irving and his wife, the Victorian scholar Gertrude Himmelfarb—both of whom had lived in London after the war—we gathered up a group of British writers, including Colin Welch and Peregrine Worsthorne, editors at the *Telegraph* papers, Samuel Brittan from the *Financial Times*, and Patrick Cosgrave from the London *Spectator*. Thus began a relationship with the *Spectator* that would last for decades. From this side of the Atlantic, we enlisted such writers as Irving, Harry Schwartz from the *New York Times*,

Leslie Lenkowsky from the Smith Richardson Foundation, and from Harvard once again, James Q. Wilson. The Baron and I were soon flying off to London to oversee our project and to stop off on the way back in Dublin to oversee the flow of Guinness. As the essays began coming in from our writers over the months, the prospects for socialism in Britain did not look very promising. So funereal were they that I could confidently title the book *The Future That Doesn't Work: Social Democracy's Failures in Britain.*

By the book's publication, things looked bad for Britain and were getting worse. I noted in my introduction to the book that Britain had now inherited from Turkey the title of the "Sick Man of Europe." The problem, I wrote, was that

> [s]ocial democratic ideas almost all spin off from the fundamental tenet that government must attend to every need of the citizenry, and England's social democrats have constantly enlarged the number of these needs. The cost of English government has so expanded that it now devours some 60 percent of the nation's Gross National Product.[1]

The consequences were exorbitant taxation, high inflation, and social unrest.

In brief: Social democracy, or socialism, is very inefficient because it lacks incentives, discourages individual initiative, and hobbles innovation. It spends too much time looking for good causes to spend money on as it limits productivity. Capitalism provides jobs, whereas socialism provides welfare. Capitalism provides products that people want based on consumer sovereignty. Capitalism puts money in workers' pockets so they can buy what they want. Socialism practically bankrupted Britain until Margaret Thatcher came along proclaiming: "There is no such thing as society. There are individual men and women and there are families."[2] Capitalism encourages entrepreneurship and innovation, allowing men and women to be free and prosper.

Yet social democracy, or socialism, never goes away no matter how much capitalism outperforms it. It lurks in the shadows as Communism. It struts its false promises from the sidelines as socialism. Socialism's secret reward is not economic; it is *aspirational*. Its aspiration is moral superiority. Today its adherents engage in what is called "virtue signaling." It would be more accurate to call it "virtue flaunting."

Of the top-tier writers I enlisted to contribute to *The Future That Doesn't Work*, the most interesting by far, and the most tragically flawed, was the Irishman Patrick Cosgrave. He lived in London with his dog, an English bulldog, whose name told you a vast amount about its owner's tastes. The dog was named Winston, Winston Churchill, which perhaps made more sense than the name I gave to my bulldog, Irving. Patrick, though born in Ireland, was a total Churchillian. He had written for us before and would write for us briefly again.

His essay in *The Future That Doesn't Work* was an engaging tour de force about the Conservative Party's failure in Britain from World War II to 1975 and the rise of Patrick's heroine, Mrs. Thatcher. From the mid-1970s until his fall in 1979, he wrote brilliantly, became increasingly close to Mrs. Thatcher, and roamed widely as the political editor of the London *Spectator*. I saw a bit of him in London and thought he, a man about my age, was made for our gang at the magazine. I considered making him our British correspondent. There was only one problem: alcohol. He was a hopeless drunk and as he aged, which was rapidly, his problem intensified. One night in 1979, after he had become special advisor to Mrs. Thatcher, he climbed into a taxi with her and threw up on her shoes—she was wearing them.

Now at *The American Spectator*, we have always found booze as a launching pad for jokes and witticisms, just as we have found sex as a laughing matter. Yet booze and the carnal arts have also been the occasion for tragedy. Think of Representative Wilbur Mills from Arkansas and his late-night Tidal Basin follies with the "Argentine Firecracker" of years gone by, or of a more recent Arkansas politician and his amorous adventures in the Oval Office. The Baron and I, or for that matter most of those attached to the magazine, even when we were young, usually drank with an invisible governor on our person. A few drinks of an evening, even when watered down by the Woman's Christian Temperance Union fountain, and the buzzer would gently go off. In all our years at the magazine, I can only recall one or two writers who shared Patrick's problem. Heavy drinking has always struck me as an awful waste of fine wine and ardent spirits. Margaret Thatcher, though known for her loyalty to her staff, dropped Cosgrave like a stone. I am afraid I did, too.

He could have been one of the great political writers of his generation. He died penniless and in obscurity at the turn of the century. His problem was not only booze but also political power. It swept him away. Like a lot of political writers, he assumed that because he wrote about politics and rubbed shoulders with politicians that he had political gifts, too, such as timing, courage, judgment, prudence. That night in the taxi, he had no reason to doubt that he had them until *yawp*. After all, he was the special advisor to the head of Britain's Conservative Party, soon to be prime minister. People who write about the exercise of political power often make the mistake of thinking they *have* political power or the capacity for using political power. I have observed this delusion more often than I care to admit.

Sports writers are susceptible to this delusional thinking, too. But just because they write about a great athlete does not mean that they think they can match his feats. To the contrary, they usually know they cannot. There is a reality check governing a sportswriter. There is no such reality check on a political writer. The sportswriter writes about athletes, but most know that they cannot suit up for an event and expect victory. They have those reality checks on them: a tired body, a sagging stomach, aching knees. With politics, there is no reality check. When Patrick talked about his heroes, Churchill or Thatcher, one could see a peculiar light come into his eyes; in his mind, he was talking about his equals. Bill Kristol, too, in recent years might have that light come into his eyes.

Today, in America, political writers are frequently given to the same delusional thinking as poor Patrick. They think of the political world as their peculiar domain. When conservative activists in Virginia suggested that I run for governor, I am sure that, at least fleetingly, I shared their delusion. Other poor fish have acted on similar delusions. I think this is what drove so many Never Trumpers toward Trump derangement syndrome. They came to hate Trump beyond all rational limits. He had wandered from the realms where he had amassed billions and starred on reality TV into *their* realms, *their* secret realms, *their* realms of fantasy in which they are not mere hacks but statesmen and jugglers of realpolitik. Like Churchill, they conversed with Stalin and Franklin Roosevelt—or imagined that they did. Then, in winning the 2016 presidential election, Trump punctured their fantasies and encroached upon their vast self-importance. He showed that they were not necessary. It drove them mad.

As luck would have it, we were arriving in London just as a great generation of intellectuals was about to call it quits in London and other European capitals, for instance, Paris and Rome. We arrived in time to latch on to them. I had been reading their work for years, and now I could avail myself of their knowledge. Writers such as Malcolm Muggeridge and Paul Johnson in Britain, Luigi Barzini in Italy, Jean-François Revel and Raymond Aron in France, and a dozen more writers of heft. All are gone now, but when we sought them out, they were alive and would be active for at least a decade more, some even longer.

In the case of Muggeridge, he gave me the benefit of his imagination, which was comic, religious, literary, and political, but his political views were usually helpful only when he was assessing Communists and the Communist sympathizers. His political commentary too often entailed calling someone an idiot, which was vastly amusing but not very informative, especially when that someone was Margaret Thatcher or Ronald Reagan. When he spoke of Winston Churchill as

"a ridiculous figure," which he often did in the postwar period pursuant to an easy laugh, I would draw the line. Certainly, the late Adolf
Hitler, toward the end of his days, did not dismiss Churchill as a ridiculous figure, nor did the late Benito Mussolini.

Malcolm, back in the 1930s, had been among the first Western
intellectuals to arrive in Moscow hoping to find the New Jerusalem.
He arrived with his wife Kitty in 1932, but by the spring of 1933, he
recognized that he had placed his hopes in a Slavic version of Hitler's
polity. The only difference was that the German version was more efficient than the Slavic version, just as nowadays it appears that the contemporary Chinese version of Hitlerism is more efficient than the old
Slavic model. Malcolm and Kitty returned to London in 1933 to the
antipathy of the journalistic herd, who always thought that men such
as Muggeridge and George Orwell had been too eager in jumping to
dark conclusions about their comrades.

Paul Johnson was not as amusing as Malcolm, but he was a more
serious writer and probably had a greater range. He was as deeply
religious as Malcolm, though not as theatrical. As a journalist and a
historian, Paul wrote from the perspective of what he called a radical empiricist. That is my perspective, too, I would like to think. His
judgments were always sound and occasionally audacious. In the late
1990s, he appeared on C-SPAN and when asked about his loyalty to
The American Spectator answered that he wrote for us and was loyal to
us because "I take a fatherly interest in it [*The American Spectator*]....
And I'm very interested in the way that paper has put itself on the map
in recent years."[3] He was alluding to our exposés of the Clintons.

Paul was as astute as Malcolm about Communism, though on economics and politics in general he was Malcolm's superior. The same
can be said for Raymond Aron and Jean-François Revel, though these
Frenchmen followed the same crooked path that the neoconservatives
were following in America. Norman Podhoretz and Irving Kristol
took their time coming around to free market economics, and Milton
Friedman would probably have judged them as shirkers, though Irving

did become a leading supply-sider. As for Jean-François, he could be surprising. In 1978, we dined together, and he surprised me with his favorable assessment of Milton's free market economics. I reminded him of his past skepticism of Milton. "Ah," he replied, Milton's "old ideas are now being applied to new conditions." In the 1970s and 1980s, there was a discernible movement from leftist ideas to conservative ideas among certain intellectuals. This explains the evolution of the neoconservatives. A similar evolution was taking place in Europe. Certainly, among the Europeans that I courted. I thought it would continue for years, given Ronald Reagan's victory in the Cold War and his revival of the economy from the drear of President Jimmy Carter. It proved not to be that simple.

The last of the intellectuals that I was interested in was Luigi Barzini, though about him I was not so sure at first. For years I had read him, but he seemed too fashionable for me. On that, I could not have been more wrong. He turned out to be utterly civilized and shared all the values of the others, which is to say pro-American values. There had been for years a virulent anti-Americanism in Europe. One might call it, as the German Josef Joffe has, the anti-Semitism of the world-weary European Left. But there was also a pro-American element in Europe, and all my targeted intellectuals shared in it. If anything, Luigi was more pro-American than the others. An Italian who had lived in America throughout the 1920s and attended Columbia University, Luigi, once I got to know him, struck me as just another Italian American right out of Manhattan's Little Italy.

That reminds me of a discovery I made on my early trips to Rome and Dublin at about this time. Walking the streets of those ancient cities revived in me memories of the Irish neighborhoods I had known in Chicago and of the Italian neighborhoods I had known in Chicago and New York. There was something in the air, the smells, the sounds, and the rhythms of life. Did the immigrants bring those qualities from the Old World with them? That had to be the case, but it is hard to believe. The bulk of the Irish and Italians had come a century before.

Luigi was handsome, urbane, very soigné. He had been a polo player and was a fine horseman. He sailed and eventually reviewed one of Bill Buckley's books on sailing for me. He knew Hollywood figures who would visit him in Rome where he lived with his charming lady friend, the Contessa Vivi Crespi, an American by birth. One visitor from Hollywood was Clint Eastwood during his spaghetti western days. Luigi also knew television figures such as Johnny Carson of NBC's *The Tonight Show*, and, of course, Gore Vidal, a prominent nuisance in my book *Public Nuisances*. Gore, who lived in Rome, was always unavailable for drinks when I was visiting Luigi. That was too bad, for I had enjoyed many laughs at his expense in the magazine and my books. I owed him my thanks or at least a proper apology. But it appeared he took himself quite seriously, despite all the silliness in his books. He remembered every jab I had taken at him, Vivi Crespi told me.

Luigi wrote superbly in both Italian and English, in magazines such as *The American Spectator* and books such as *The Italians*, a book he originally wrote in English. Ever on the lookout for rising talent, I asked him one day who would be the next Barzini. He pulled on his Marlboro and smiled sheepishly: "There won't be another Barzini." He was, of course, right. A similar response might have come from any of my other targeted intellectuals. They were the culmination of an era, combining learning, manners, culture, and, of course, public service—Luigi had served in the Italian Chamber of Deputies for fourteen years. They were prominent in the public life of their countries, and now they are gone.

After publishing *The Future That Doesn't Work*, I got the idea that by publishing such Europeans we could add a distinctive quality to the magazine. Thus, our annual budget included trips to Europe and a hefty set-aside for wining and dining. It was all part of my scheme to lure the European intelligentsia into our pages. People such as Jean-François, Luigi, and, by 1978, a newcomer, Kenneth Minogue of the London School of Economics, took even their gastronomy very seriously, especially Jean-François. Once, while visiting with me in Bloomington, he snatched a fellow guest's unfinished dessert. It was only half consumed! Why waste a dessert?

According to my scheme, their work would receive a favorable review in the magazine, though the work might have come out years before. Then I would send the reviews on to them. I would arrange to meet with them when I got to Europe—that being two or three times a year. I would invite them to dinner at some posh restaurant, and, *hesto presto*, they would be writing for us. My strategy never failed. My table manners are legendary.

I have mentioned Minogue because he was very bright, very amusing, and because his prescient 1963 book, *The Liberal Mind*, served as a guidebook at the magazine. It apprehended practically every goofball project of the liberal mind, often years before anyone was even aware of what was afoot: modern art, sexual hygiene, and rejiggering the anatomy to conform with ideological desiderata. Then there was arms control, global cooling, global warming, on and on it would go. Minogue apprehended most of them. We readers of *The Liberal Mind* saw it all coming thanks to him, and we even knew *why* it was coming. The book was among the earliest and certainly it was the most far-sighted of all the studies of that disease, which has afflicted the West throughout the postwar period, right up to the present. The disease is not Communism, not fascism, but liberalism. That affliction has metamorphosed with time into stages, such as progressivism and socialism. Minogue's seminal discovery was what he called "the suffering situation" known today as victimization, and if you can claim victimization, you can claim the world. Minorities claim victimization, bicycle riders claim it, tree huggers claim it, and so forth. The various victims have claimed victimhood ever since 1945. Ken became a great friend. His book is a classic.

One of the rejuvenators of the pro-American Europeans of the late 1970s and early 1980s was the emergence of Eurocommunism. It became a hot topic amongst the intelligentsia and seeped into politics, particularly in Italy and France. I remember Antonio Martino, then a recent student of Milton Friedman's at the University of Chicago and teaching economics in Rome, telling me in the late 1970s that rich Italians had their private planes gassed up and ready for an urgent flight from Italy if the Eurocommunists ever took power. The thugs never did, and Antonio went on in later years to attain two seats in the government of Silvio Berlusconi, minister of foreign affairs and minister of defense.

I visited my targeted intellectuals in their homes and their clubs and at least three of them—Malcolm, Luigi, and Jean-François—visited me in Bloomington. Early on in this memoir, I mentioned visiting the Muggeridges and the Longfords in Malcolm's country home near the village of Robertsbridge, a verdant old community of ancient cottages and country estates deep in literary and Cold War lore. I made my contribution to the literary lore of Robertsbridge when I brought one of America's great writers, Tom Wolfe, to visit Malcolm and Kitty with his incomparable wife, acting at the time as *The American Spectator*'s art director, Sheila Wolfe.

I first met Tom through the good offices of Lewis Lapham, the editor of *Harper's* magazine. We had drinks at the St. Regis Hotel in the King Cole room in late 1976. Lewis would distinguish himself, at least with me, by doing a hilarious review of Jimmy Carter's insipid autobiography in our magazine. He was a ritualistic liberal and friendship with him was unfortunately hopeless, but on Jimmy, he was sublime. Tom's politics in 1976 were opaque, though I had my suspicions that he was one of us or at least on his way to becoming one of us. Friendship with him was easy. He was a great gent, and we remained friends until his death. Editing him, however, was nerve-racking. He *had* to make sure that everything was perfect. We had a magazine to close. He never missed a deadline, though he sure came close.

At any rate, Malcolm wanted to meet Tom, or Tom wanted to meet Malcolm, and so with the Wolfes, I clambered aboard the train at Charing Cross Station for the hour-long ride to Robertsbridge. What followed was a few hilarious hours at the Muggeridges' place capped by a joyous jaunt walking single file up the spine of a very steep hill: Malcolm in the lead, laughing uproariously, next Tom in his white linen suit, a white felt homburg on top, next me, and finally, Kitty bringing up the rear with Sheila and the daughter of one of Malcolm's old friends, "Sister Fifi," she was called. She wore a wild religious habit with an immense conical headdress. In her youth, she had been a showgirl. For once, Tom's attire was not the most conspicuous as we made our promenade over the ancient hills and fields once crossed by Roman legions and Celtic Kings, Norman knights and Cistercian monks, and now us. Visitors from afar, who flew in from thirty-five thousand feet. On the train back to London, Tom captured Malcolm's aerie perfectly when he called it "A little bit of heaven." Soon Tom would be writing for us, too.

The magazine was maturing. By the late 1970s, I had succeeded in luring my European targets into our pages, publishing such articles as "Solzhenitsyn Reconsidered" by Malcolm, "Return to Respectability" by Luigi, "A Note on Eurocommunism" by Jean-François, and Paul Johnson began with book reviews. For instance, he began with such books as *Caveat: Realism, Reagan, and Foreign Policy* by Alexander Haig. Yet later, Paul contributed all sorts of pieces that went on for decades. Of my targeted intellectuals, Paul lived the longest, surviving on into the 2020s. We offered our readers the work of the neocons, the cons, the libertarians. It was the full menu of writers on the right, so long as they were civilized. We even offered the work of wayward liberals and socialists (remember we are talking about the civilized 1970s, not to be confused with the barbaric 2020s). Moreover, our layout was taking on the airs of the stately thanks to Elliott Banfield's elegant sketches and Sheila Wolfe's sharp eye for design.

Also, we were undergoing a name change. In our June–September number of 1974, we published the last issue bearing the name *The Alternative*. Frankly, I had tired of receiving over-the-transom articles about alternative lifestyles and first-person pieces by florists and vegetarians. Our October 1974 issue bore the name *The Alternative: An American Spectator*, which was purely transitional. By November 1977, we came out fully dressed as *The American Spectator*. Irving Kristol counseled a less drastic change, but I had my reasons, and they had nothing to do with aping the British *Spectator*, which I suspect was Irving's worry. Rather, my reasons had to do with an American literary tradition that in the 1970s was defunct, though still admired by some civilized readers. We saw ourselves as heirs to the 1920s tradition created by H. L. Mencken and George Jean Nathan. That being a tradition of sophistication, skepticism, iconoclasm, and risibility. It had disappeared by the 1930s, though the skeleton of Mencken and Nathan's old *American Mercury* was still rattling around. I wrote Alfred Knopf, who had been the publisher of *The American Mercury* in Mencken and Nathan's day, inquiring if I should buy it now. Knopf was emphatic. The old *Mercury* was too enmucked in anti-Semitism and other poisonous tendencies. I should take my millions elsewhere.

As luck would have it, the name of *The American Spectator* was available. The original magazine had been founded in November 1932, with Nathan being among the founding editors who also included Eugene O'Neill, Theodore Dreiser, and several others. That gave the original *American Spectator* the literary bloodline we aspired to, and the name *Spectator* conveyed a sense of distance from any subject we might take up. As the years have lengthened, the appetite for literary pursuits has withered with the drying up of the literary afflatus. Yet politics was all around us, and it was in politics that we were to make our mark.

When Nathan and his fellow editors gave up their *Spectator* in 1935, an obituarist writing with Nathanesque whimsicality in the *New York Times* averred: "Following their pledge of thirty months ago that when they tired of editing *The American Spectator* they would 'retire to their estates' the editors announced yesterday the discontinuance of the periodical."[4] Thus, the price of retrieving *The American Spectator* from obscurity seemed reasonable. We picked it up for $0.00

and even coaxed one of the original *American Spectator* writers into our first issue, James T. Farrell, whose name appeared on our cover. And so, with our November 1977 issue, the new *American Spectator* was born with a cover featuring Buckley, Farrell, Kristol, Muggeridge, and me, along with a banner proclaiming "Our Tenth Anniversary." The original *Spectator* lasted thirty months with eminent writers such as Nathan, O'Neill, and Dreiser. Ours passed the half century mark some years ago. Technology changes, business models change, but *The American Spectator* you always have with you.

Our tenth-anniversary dinner was held in New York at the St. Regis Hotel on December 6, 1977. The Baron Von Kannon had been working on it since the summer. It was to be our first big dinner, with fine wines, plenty of booze, and, according to the report subsequently published in our February 1978 issue, "180 satisfied diners [who] had devastated the nation's last flock of whooping cranes." That was a joke. Not one whooping crane perished that evening. For years, we had scrupulously reported on the migratory birds' arrival in—I believe it was in Texas. The birds were on the endangered species list, and the worrywarts in the nascent environmental movement fretted over their shrinking numbers. It has now been decades since their last incoming flight was reported on, either because the last whooping crane has croaked or because the birds have become so plentiful as to have become a public nuisance, much like the wild turkey—which stands, by the way, as our logo.

THE AMERICAN
SPECTATOR

The dinner was typical of the conservative movement at the time. People came from all over. I flew in early in the afternoon to get situated, and as I arrived, so did truckloads of firefighters with hoses at the ready. The room where we were to dine was reportedly ablaze—a false alarm, possibly a political opponent's dirty trick. At any rate, the firefighters withdrew, and the evening went off without a hitch.

In those days, the conservative movement was not as fractious as it became sometime later, certainly by the 1990s. We all celebrated together. Bill Buckley toasted everyone in the room, saying, "I believe that there is a greater concentration of beauty, brains, and culture here tonight than ever assembled anywhere in the history of the world." Bob Nisbet, the erudite sociologist saluted me—I had just been named one of Jaycees' Ten Outstanding Young Men of America, adding my name to a list that included over the years the likes of Henry Kissinger, the three Kennedy brothers, Richard Nixon, and other notables. Norman Podhoretz, then editor of *Commentary*, gave a toast to how we had all aged. Irving Kristol toasted the Baron, and the *New York Times'* Bill Safire served as master of ceremonies.

The Baron could not be with us that night. He had come down, days before, with myeloblastic leukemia. I had come into the office early in the week of our party and found my friend exhausted and wearing a ghastly pallor. I knew it could not be good. He had been suffering from a flu-like illness for weeks. I sent him immediately to see my old college roommate, Dr. Chet Jastremski, once the fastest breaststroker in the world, now the man who would diagnose my dear friend Baron Von Kannon. By 8:00 p.m. that evening, the Baron was diagnosed with cancer. He was given ten days to live.

Not knowing what else to do, I called Father Jim Higgins, the Baron's priest and mine. The Baron was a recent convert to Catholicism. Father Higgins was blunt: "Bob, get over to the hospital. I will be waiting." Sure enough, he was there, standing with his little black bag containing the oils and the prayers for the last rites of the Catholic church. Led by Father Higgins, we breezed past the astonished doctors and nurses and proceeded directly to the antiseptic room where the Baron was lying. Smiling from ear to ear, he received the last rites of the Catholic church. As we withdrew once again, passing the startled members of the medical corps, I felt we had just executed a flawless military mission and left Satan broken in our wake. Precisely forty years later, the Baron was told he again had cancer. He called me and said he would fight it again. He struggled valiantly, and toward the end, he looked up at me from his bed and said, "You're older than me. You shouldn't outlive me." I replied, "You're younger than me. You shouldn't attain salvation before me." Yet he did.

Needless to say, on that night back in Bloomington so many years ago, the Baron did not die. After returning from New York, we all joined in working for his recovery. His spirits were buoyant. The first thing he said to me upon my return was, "Fire the secretary." Admittedly, she was a difficult woman. A call was made from Washington by Senator Pat Moynihan, promising the Baron help with any experimental medication he might need. But it was going to take many months for the Baron to recover. I recall one grim morning that I, with my life-long friend Al Somers, a swimmer on the 1960 Olympic team and an accomplished neurologist, spent with the Baron. Suddenly, he began to throw up. There was blood mixed with God knows what else in his discharge. The doctors and Al hustled me out of the Baron's room. Later, as we drove home, Al and I agreed: The Baron should not be suffering this way. His death would be a blessing. Yet he survived. In the months ahead, he gained strength, and he did more than survive. He went on to become the chief fundraiser for the largest foundation on our side, the multimillion-dollar Heritage Foundation.

There is one more story about the Baron I should relate. Malcolm Muggeridge was staying in Bloomington at our house, unbeknownst to the Baron, who was convalescing in an Indianapolis hospital. Malcolm was a fitful sleeper, being tormented by his past demons. He joined me and my children, P. D. and Katy, in going to the 7:00 a.m. mass to pray for the Baron's recovery. Malcolm was very devout, though he did not take the Holy Eucharist, for he had not yet decided to become a Catholic. Later that morning, we surprised the Baron with Malcolm's unannounced visit to his bedside. They had become friends when we were putting together *The Future That Doesn't Work*. The surprise of Malcolm's visit touched the Baron deeply. A couple of years later, a letter came to me from Malcolm. He wrote that he had become a Catholic. Seeing my two little children receiving Holy Communion, he wrote, had convinced him and Kitty to convert. Well, maybe, but I will bet that several others got similar letters.

It was about this time that I became friendly with two people who were to influence me enormously. One was Bill Casey, soon to be Governor Ronald Reagan's campaign manager and the head of the Central Intelligence Agency. That might have been expected. The other was Meg Greenfield, the editorial page editor of *The Washington Post*. Meg seemed an unlikely influence. According to my diary, my friendship with Meg began first. It started in 1976 when I began conferring with her on the telephone and with an occasional visit. Meg was smart, lively, independent, and she had a sense of humor, a somewhat bawdy sense of humor. She would send me outré clippings for "The Continuing Crisis," which she obviously read. The most outré that I recall was a newspaper report about a young man who passed away unceremoniously while committing an act of autoerotic asphyxia, which in those days before sex education became widely taught in our public schools was almost unheard of. I ran the clipping, but until now I have kept Meg's name out of it.

Over dinner one night, probably in June 1978, she asked me why I had not begun a syndicated column. I answered that if I did begin a column, would she run it? She assented. I look back on it now as one of my most consequential decisions. Writing a weekly column assured me that I would stay au courant with the daily news. Before I began my column, I would not always be attentive to current events. Now I had to be.

Meg's offer was probably all of a piece with the surprising attention that I, an outlier from the rolling hills of Indiana, was then receiving in New York, Washington, and other cosmopolitan centers. I began the column in the autumn of 1978, and Don Graham, the *Post*'s publisher, gave my column his blessing the following spring with a dinner party for me, including Pat and Liz Moynihan, and the Keystone State's Senator John Heinz and his wife, the fated Teresa—after Senator Heinz had perished in an airplane accident, she married the Bay State's Senator John Kerry, making him a millionaire after Senator Heinz had made Teresa a millionaire. Meg was also there and Joe Califano, the former secretary of health, education, and welfare whom President Jimmy Carter had recently fired for, as far as I could tell, Joe's singular competence in Jimmy's cabinet. Upon meeting Califano, my wife said rather breathlessly, "Bob wrote about you in his new book." Joe asked what the name of the book might be. My wife replied, "*Public Nuisances.*" Whether she said that from guilelessness or disdain, I never asked, though she was pretty hard core as we conservatives were given to saying. For years thereafter, Califano and I maintained a mutual if limited friendship. I never understood fully why. Possibly it was owing to our low regard for Jimmy Carter.

The column got off to a good start. It was carried in the major cities, Los Angeles, New York, and San Francisco, but not in my hometown of Chicago where the dominant newspaper, the famously conservative *Chicago Tribune*, resisted—curious. Naturally, the column was carried in Indianapolis. Though in Washington, things were dicey from the start. The problem was that Meg felt that the *Washington Post* was considered in foreign parts to be the national newspaper of the United States. To some, especially those living in what was then called the Third World, the *Washington Post* spoke for the government. Then, too, her telephone would begin ringing off the hook by late Monday morning after my Monday column appeared. Liberals were famous then, as they are today, for closing down conservatives. They often speak of their yearning for dialogue, but that usually means they and their allies are free to speak; we conservatives are free to listen. Whether it be in the news media or on what is now called social media, their goal is to silence those on the right.

One week, Meg told me that Rowland Evans and Bob Novak were no longer her most controversial columnists. I had gained that prominence and I noted a hint of defiant pride in her voice. She seemed to me to want to let an unruly voice be heard. Yet, on another occasion, she asked me to please not mention Ralph Nader, the famously liberal advocate of consumerism, because he had his agents burning the wires about me whenever I wrote about him. Alex Cockburn, too, the British Marxist, had caused a stink, and, of course, my column's appearance in the same newspaper where George Will was a columnist could not sit well with the prof. By 1985, I was becoming Meg's burden. True, I would reserve a Christmas column every year to highlight some Communist hellhole, for instance, on December 24, 1979, when I did "Christmas Time in Cambodia." She never objected to such columns. Yet, I had to be watched. There was the 1984 Olympics when—with Al Somers, the 1960 Olympian at my side—I wrote of the chemically and medically engineered "Soviet stallions and geldings." An editor rushed in to change it to "the Soviet bloc's state-owned athletes," lest the Cold War heat up.[5] By the late 1980s, I was reduced to a biweekly schedule, then an occasional appearance. The final curtain came down on me with the *Post* on October 20, 1990, when I saluted Newt Gingrich as "our staunch champion of economic growth."[6]

Bystanders had watched the increasing censorship and imagined my calling in every week to Meg's office with compensatory edits, but they would be wrong. I hardly ever did. Meg had given me a chance. I proved that the First Amendment had its limits with the liberals, and besides, I knew of a happier place to land, the *Washington Times*, known to the civilized minority as the *Good Times*. The editors there have never changed a word in my column, even when I used such words as "ichthyosaurus."

The other person I met about this time who was to influence me for even longer than Meg was the prominent New York lawyer and former chairman of the Securities and Exchange Commission, Bill Casey. He arrived at my office in Bloomington unannounced on a September morning in 1978. After my morning ritual of reading the newspapers over coffee, I rode down to the office to be told by my secretary, Debbie Grubb, that a large man was waiting for me in my office. I opened my office door, and sure enough there I found a large man in a rumpled suit sitting *on* my desk. Bill told me he was to be at the law school for a lecture that day, but he wanted to meet the editor of *The American Spectator* first. It was the beginning of a friendship that was to last for almost a decade until his dramatic expiry occasioning a controversy that should have attracted more attention at the time, for it cast doubt on the honesty of what was then the legendary reporter Bob Woodward.

The controversy began with the Iran-Contra scandal which was making headlines in late November 1986. The Democrats were trying to implicate Bill, then the head of the CIA, in the Iran-Contra skullduggery. As luck would have it, I was with Bill at Sunday Mass on December 14, a day before he collapsed at his desk and was rushed to Georgetown University Hospital where the diagnosis was a cancerous tumor on his brain. At Mass that Sunday, I asked him about the charges against him. He said, "I'm as clean as a hound's tooth." I had no doubt that he was, given his superb legal mind. He would, however, never recover. He was paralyzed and could not speak. I know this because I visited his bedside, and in my diary, there is an affecting notation from his secretary, Betty Murphy, which I made shortly after his hospitalization: "Bill Casey having trouble getting out what he wants to say. Can't write…frustrating."[7]

His wife and daughter were at his side almost constantly. His security detail was there, along with his doctors and nurses. Yet now while Bill was under treatment in the hospital, Woodward was preparing to come out with his book *Veil: The Secret Wars of the CIA, 1981–1987,* in which he said that Bill had cooperated with him. Woodward had finished the book or was about to finish the book, and there was not a word about Iran-Contra in it. Bill had told me weeks before that he was talking to Woodward, though he said with a smile that he had divulged nothing of consequence. Apparently, he had not.

So, Woodward slapped together a last chapter in which he claimed to have appeared in Bill's hospital room and asked him about his involvement in Iran-Contra. Despite Bill's security detail, his family's presence at his bedside, and people like me who have testified that his speech was unintelligible owing to his paralyzed tongue and the paralysis of the right side of his neck, Woodward somehow entered Bill's hospital room and asked him about Iran-Contra. Bill supposedly summoned the strength to utter his response to Woodward, "I believed. I believed." What nonsensical melodrama! I have never believed Bob Woodward. I wrote about Woodward's faked last chapter when the book finally came out in 1987. I have never heard a word of complaint from him. By the way, is there not something obsessive about a man claiming to have inveigled his way into the hospital room of a terminally ill patient, hoping against all odds to wrest some momentous corpus delicti from a dying man? Most people would be afraid of the harm that they might do, for instance, by disrupting a life support system or causing such alarm to the patient as to cause pain or even death.

As I have said, I believe that Meg's interest in my column was of a piece with the unanticipated interest in me during the late 1970s. As I shall explain, there were inklings of a cultural shift in the late 1970s up through the 1980s. Some liberals at center stage and even conservatives on the sidelines sensed that something was in the air. One of the great, if underestimated, triggers of history was about to be activated. That would be mass boredom. Americans were simply bored with the tumult of the 1960s. The decade was over. Something different was coming, but what? Meg, I think, sensed it. Even *Time* magazine sensed it, as we shall see. Could I be part of it? Some liberals and some establishment figures seemed to be anticipating a change, but what?

In a matter of just a few years, I—who never had gone to Harvard except in the late 1970s to lecture and to leave the name of a serial killer, Richard Speck, in the guest book at Winthrop House where JFK spent his senior year—was the recipient of a rush of national awards and accolades. In 1975, I won the Jefferson Award for the Greatest Public Service Performed by an American 35 Years or Under. I beat out Richard Ben-Veniste, special prosecutor at the Watergate hearings, who probably thought *The American Spectator* was a sports magazine or possibly a magazine for nudists. Another runner-up was Julie Nixon Eisenhower, who assuredly deserved the award more than I did that year. Also, I copped the American Eagle Award from the Invest-in-America National Council. Then in 1978, came the Ten Outstanding Young Men of America's glorification. In those days, the award was highly prized, having, as I have said, been awarded to the likes of Henry Kissinger, Richard Nixon, the three Kennedy brothers, and, for true American esthetes, Elvis Presley. Also, in 1979, *Time* made me one of "The 50 Future Leaders of America," along with Bill Clinton and the Reverend Jesse L. Jackson, all the ingredients necessary for amusing years ahead.

Nor was the print media immune to my charms. The March 7, 1977, issue of *Time* appraised *The American Spectator* as "one of the nation's most energetic and sprightly journals of opinion..." If the *Spectator* "has a guiding philosophy, it is little more than a disgust for hypocrisy, utopian social engineering and bad writing."[8] In the July 27, 1979, *Washington Post*, Henry Mitchell rolled on:

> R. Emmett Tyrrell Jr. is one of the most luminous young gadflies now singing in the American wilderness, and I can only describe an afternoon spent with him as joyful and zany.... He edits a monthly opinion paper, *The American Spectator*, where you will not, perhaps, find anything so gentle as Addison and Steele, but will find at least short sentences, literate vocabulary and a monthly ration of vitriol.[9]

The November 5, 1979, issue of *People* did a spread on us,[10] and *The Washington Star* noted my "masterworks of image demolition."[11] There was *The New Yorker*, admiring "A garland of diatribes and jeremiads."[12] *The Wall Street Journal* spoke of "Mr. Tyrrell's feistier fulminations,"[13] while *Commentary* found me "entertaining, and often devastating"[14]—and I could go on, but you get the idea. All were satisfied customers. On December 31, 1980, *The Washington Post* designated *The American Spectator* as Washington's "in" magazine.[15]

What had caused the stir? Well, some of it had to be caused by President Jimmy Carter, whom I called the "Wonder Boy." He was elected over President Gerald Ford in a surprisingly close race in 1976. Jimmy began with a healthy lead owing to Ford's unpopular pardon of President Nixon, but as the average American got to know the Wonder Boy better, his lead faded. In fact, had the race continued a few more weeks, Jimmy would undoubtedly have lost the election, and had it lasted a few more months, he might have been institutionalized. His campaign was that weird, and his goofball presidency gave even Democrats reason to review their first principles, for instance: his insistence that he never lied to the American people. Some liberals blamed Jimmy's performance on his gimcrack conservatism. Others blamed it on his ineptitude. But those who could face the facts squarely blamed it on his attempt to embody the whole liberal agenda, including its diktats about keeping the thermostats down and the air-conditioning off. Jimmy presided over the first glimmers of the liberal crack-up.

The Wonder Boy had been puttering around the White House, fussing with the thermostats, to the amazement of his National Security Council and his economic advisors. The potentates in Washington were becoming anxious when the economy went into a tailspin while Jimmy monitored his staff's use of the White House tennis court and prowled up and down the halls of the Old Executive Office Building in search of errant television sets. At the end of his four years of officious dithering, unemployment was at 7.5 percent, inflation was at 11.8 percent, and GDP was growing at the astounding annual rate of

0 percent. The misery index stood at 19.3. Abroad, the Soviet Union was active in Asia, Africa, and Latin America, and the Shah had left Iran for good, his place to be taken by Ayatollah Khomeini. Jimmy had entered the White House with six years of experience in state government. On Inauguration Day, *Who's Who* still listed his occupation as "farmer and warehouseman." On his last day in office, there was still no reason to change his occupation.

The Wonder Boy had attracted my attention, too, particularly when he was attacked by an amphibious rabbit while canoeing in some godforsaken creek, or so he boasted. Then there was the time that he sat down to memorize every page of the IRS code. I have characterized the fifty-plus years of my adult life as a period of calm punctuated by spells of Episodic Chaos. Jimmy's presidency witnessed little calm, and it reached a crescendo *di bravura* of Episodic Chaos in 1979 when fifty-two American citizens were taken hostage in Tehran and the oil crisis turned America's service stations into war zones. The chaos lasted a year, until January 20, 1981, when Ronald Reagan took residence in the White House. Then the hostages were miraculously released, and Episodic Calm ensued at least until the new president was launched into his own period of Episodic Chaos with the Iran-Contra uproar.

The presidency that the Wonder Boy began on January 20, 1977, was the most bizarre that the world had beheld in modern times. President Warren Gamaliel Harding was redeemed. He was no longer our worst president. All around the world, people were scratching their heads. Even in remote Bangladesh, there must have been a lowly peasant who, after plodding through furrows, his face impassively set toward the undulating hindquarters of a mortgaged bovine, would rush home to inquire, "Hey, what's the latest with the Washington yokel, eh?" Today, decades later, the Carter presidency appears on calendars in capitals around the world as a great black hole. Almost nothing of importance got done. Jimmy's defenders pound the table and remind us of "Camp David," but in truth, Egypt's Anwar Sadat and Israel's Menachem Begin watched the greenhorn from Plains, Georgia, dithering madly for days and decided that they had better cut a deal before the winter snows, and so on September 17, 1978, they did, and Jimmy grinned with that toothy rictus of his.

How did it all begin? How did a peanut farmer from the Georgia outback get to sleep in Warren Harding's bathtub? Well, Jimmy was a proficient juggler. He could keep the likes of former governor Lester Maddox and the local Klan in the very same air that he juggled state courts and state legislatures. The Klan and Maddox quickly receded into the vapor that followed the Wonder Boy everywhere, but they would be replaced by the NAACP and the Democratic National Committee as he ventured ever upwards. He made admirable use of whoever was at hand, liberals, conservatives, the virulently racist White Citizens' Council of Georgia, even the "Ku Klux Konspiracy." A matter he has buried with the utmost care. But facts are facts. He ran with the support of racists, blacks, and anyone who could vote. What is more, he was a colossal liar.

For instance, on November 30, 1975, during the national television program *Face the Nation*, the Wonder Boy was asked about campaign finance reform. He responded, "I favor the law. I've been a member of Common Cause for a long time and participated in the evolution of the ideas that led to that law." As it happened, syndicated columnist Bob Novak was watching the show in his Maryland home and he doubted that the governor of a conservative state such as Georgia would be a member of that "liberal do-gooder organization," Common Cause. At his office the next day, Bob discovered that he was right. Jimmy had never been a member of Common Cause. Very much aware of how Jimmy at every campaign stop invariably reiterated: "If I ever lie to you, don't vote for me," Bob began to look for verification of what other things Jimmy had said on *Face the Nation* and at a December 2 Godfrey Sperling breakfast for Washington journalists. Bob revealed the contents of his research in a January 6, 1976, column, toting up "nine separate untruths," and thus began Bob's years of following Jimmy's mendacity. Not many others in the press paid attention. Most agreed, the Wonder Boy was "enigmatic," and Norman Mailer even labeled him a "political genius." So, it was to go with the nation's journalistic colossi and its later-day Hemingway. The Wonder Boy was "enigmatic" and a "political genius" to the nation's elites, but the presidency of such a born blank left them uneasy.

Essentially, Jimmy Carter was a simple dope-fetcher and a flagrant poseur. However, he was a useful model for the Clintons. And his presidency did set one precedent. Owing to recent civil rights laws, his state was in important ways governed by the federal judiciary, not by its governor. This gave him plenty of time to do what he wanted to do anyway, run for the presidency. He campaigned day and night for months. In this, he was much like Senator Barack Obama. Both men spent their time running for the presidency. While Jimmy's prospective opponents were at work in the Senate or the House of Representatives, Jimmy was swatting flies and promising crowds of hillbillies that under no circumstances would he ever lie to them. Further, he had studied the reform laws from the 1972 Democratic Convention and so he was as well versed as George McGovern had been on how to achieve the presidential nomination. Thus, he had the esoteric knowledge to win a Democratic convention. He had plenty of time to campaign. Finally, he had hordes of spellbound yokels pulling for him. Consequently, he won the nomination.

The one thing he lacked was any knowledge whatsoever of how to *be* president. He could run for office; he just could not hold office. In 1980, he proved it. Jimmy Carter began the postwar decline of the presidency and one other thing. He was the first president to be memorialized with a presidential portrait by a Pulitzer Prize-winning cartoonist. The artiste was Jeff MacNelly. *The American Spectator* awarded this priceless piece of art to Jimmy on April 1, 1981, as fortune would have it that was April Fools' Day. We have never heard back from President Carter. He was the first president to be a poor loser in public, though it bears noting that he was followed by Al Gore in 2000, John Kerry in

2004, and Hillary Clinton in 2016—all Democrats. Though in 2020, Donald J. Trump got in on the act.

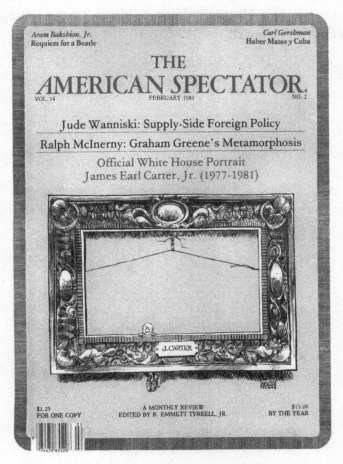

Pulitzer Prize–winning cartoonist Jeff MacNelly's presidential portrait of Jimmy Carter.

Jimmy's last days in office were spent in the Oval Office. What he did there is, for the most part, unrecorded. There were few leaks; but then again, there was very little to leak. Jimmy always took great pride in reading everything put on his desk. His aides were careful to keep his in-basket full. Once, some lout left an open Washington, DC, telephone directory there. Our president was dutifully advancing through the *R*'s when the evening janitorial detail came across him and sent him to his quarters. His aides down in Plains, Georgia, have never tried to refute this report.

Chapter VI

EXPLICATING THE KULTURSMOG, AND THE CULTURE WAR BEGINS

*I*t was in Rome in the summer of 1979 that Luigi Barzini proclaimed to me rather theatrically: "*This* is your moment in history." Luigi was standing in his doorway. My taxi was squalling off into the night, kicking up stones as it exited Luigi's long cypress-lined drive. Frankly, I was nonplussed. I was not dressed for the occasion, and I had not anticipated a "moment in history." Would I be called upon to make public appearances? What would my wife say? Actually, all I was looking for that night at *Onorevole*, Barzini's home, was a chilled glass of Pinot Grigio Santa Margherita—his favorite—and an evening of convivial conversation with one of the era's great raconteurs, the author of *The Italians*, *The Europeans*, and, recently, several terrific pieces for *The American Spectator*.

Yet Luigi did not exactly have me in mind. He was thinking about larger matters. A constant reader, he had been following the growth of the conservative movement in America and the attendant decline of the liberalism that he had grown up with. He had in mind, to be precise, the former governor of California, Ronald Reagan. As Luigi saw it, it was Reagan's moment in history. As the political leader of the American conservative movement, Reagan would inevitably bring people like me along. However, it was he in the summer of 1979 who was headed for the Republican nomination in 1980 and for a victory that fall. What a relief! I could now have a second glass of wine.

I had met the California governor only three times before. The first time was in 1968, after Bob Kennedy's assassination as I related in Chapter I. Then again, I interviewed him at his home in Los Angeles in 1978 while I was getting my column underway and creating somewhat of a ruckus at the *Washington Post*. I was under the impression that, as a *Post* columnist, I had to ask the *tough question*, though I actually liked the former governor already. He was different from most politicians I knew. The sense of him that I got that day, I never lost. Ronald Reagan was a regular guy with one added ingredient. It turned out that he was a great man, as Franklin D. Roosevelt was a great man— not always to my liking, but a great man nonetheless—and Lincoln and Washington. Though General Washington, it now turns out, once owned slaves before freeing them upon his wife's death, a matter overlooked by today's critics.

The former governor came to the door, beckoned me into his living room, and asked me to sit down on the couch while he attended to his wife Nancy's latest exigency in the other room. Sitting alone, I prepared some tough questions. When he returned, he plumped himself down on the same couch I had chosen. Unfortunately, Ronald Reagan was roughly fifty pounds heavier than me, and when he settled into the couch, its cushion inflated, lifting me up and landing me snuggly at his side. He was oblivious. I was embarrassed. For the next hour or so, I was in no position to put the *tough question* to my host. Indeed, I hardly asked any questions. I mostly listened, and what I heard was his policy proposals for limiting government and dealing with the Soviet Union, all of which sounded perfectly sensible.

Only when my interview was about over did I ask the *tough question*. I noted that as a sixty-seven-year-old man, his age was bound to be an issue in the upcoming election. How would he handle it? He gave me a surprised look, cocked his head, and related how he had spent the weekend splitting wood and repairing fences on his ranch. As I recall, he clenched his arms in front of him as if he were wrestling with a post. He demonstrated how he carried the wood and asked me to join him on the ranch the next time I came to California. I never visited him again in California until his retirement years later. Then he moved more slowly, but he still looked trim enough to wrestle with those fence posts.

A year later, my friend Peter Hannaford whose firm, Deaver & Hannaford, handled Reagan's public relations efforts between races called me and asked me to put together a dinner for the former governor that would bring out some new recruits to the conservative movement, the neoconservatives. We met at New York's Union League Club, just off Park Avenue. Among the guests were Harvard's Nathan Glazer and his wife as well as Norman Podhoretz and his wife, Midge Decter, my editor at Basic Books. One person who was glaringly absent was Irving Kristol, the godfather of the neocon movement. He had told me that he thought the former governor of California was "vulgar." There was also another reason. He wanted Representative Jack Kemp from New York to run for president. Jack was a promising candidate espousing supply-side economics and the revival of decaying cities, two of Irving's pet projects. Unfortunately, Irving had overlooked one thing. It was now Ronald Reagan's moment in history. He would bring us along, of course, but our role would be minor. Reagan would be the most conservative president since Calvin Coolidge and, unlike Cal, Reagan brought a movement with him. Calvin Coolidge in the 1920s represented America as it was and had been for years. Ronald Reagan represented America as we conservatives wanted it to be again.

The discussion that evening extended from graffiti (Nat had written a sociological piece on it in a recent issue of *The Public Interest*) to urban problems (the Podhoretzes were avid city dwellers) to the California system of higher education. As governor, Reagan had taken strong measures against campus disorder, to the neocons' delight. I, too, participated. When the club's air conditioner insisted on belching arctic blasts at Nancy Reagan, I, very gallantly, draped my blazer around her shoulders. The evening was a success.

Today it is a matter of the historical record that Reagan was by 1979 headed for the White House in what would be one of the greatest landslides in American history, but there is a mystery about the 1980 election. Though Jimmy Carter had failed with practically every initiative he undertook, I cannot think of one of our sagacious national pundits who picked Reagan to win. One would think that if Carter was not picked to win, some observers would tap Reagan to win. That did not happen. The mainstream media was resistant to a Reagan victory. The race was judged a toss-up.

That should have been a harbinger of things to come, strange things, such as the unwavering judgment by the pundits that Reagan was a boob. Despite improving the economy and winning the Cold War, he remained a boob in the eyes of the sages. Almost no one was prepared for a Reagan victory. Even many conservatives were unprepared for his election. Hannaford, chronicling his experiences in the Reagan campaign, writes: "Up to the night before the election, the networks and the major polling organizations had a near consensus that it was 'too close to call.'"[1] Then came the deluge.

So far as I know, the strangeness of this election has never been noted. If Jimmy was going to lose, then his opponent was going to win, correct? Not in 1980. Moreover, Jimmy distinguished himself as a very poor loser. The Democrats grumbled that the Reaganites had fashioned an October surprise; Bill Casey supposedly had colluded with the mullahs of Iran. There was no evidence to support the charge. Then time and again in the years ahead, the Wonder Boy groused about his defeat, even when on foreign soil. That was a first for an American ex-president.

Usually, an American president, either defeated (George H. W. Bush in 1992) or victorious (Barack Obama in 2008), speaks politely about a sitting president, or he speaks not at all. Jimmy thwarted this precedent. Since his 1980 defeat, Carter has felt free to disparage a sitting president, most notably Reagan, from foreign soil repeatedly.[2] For that matter, Al Gore, John Kerry, and Hillary Clinton followed the Wonder Boy's precedent-shattering behavior by disparaging a sitting president while on foreign soil.[3] Even former Democratic presidents now break the precedent of abstaining from criticizing an incumbent while on foreign soil. Bill Clinton did it to President George W. Bush on November 13, 2007, and Barack Obama did it to President Donald Trump on December 2, 2017.[4] All have criticized their Republican adversaries while abroad. It is another example of the Democrats' political libido crashing ahead and establishing new precedents while the Republicans remain perfect gentlemen and ladies. Their political libido remains almost Victorian—while the Democrats' political libido takes on the character of a sex maniac. As for Donald Trump, we shall deal with him in Chapter XIII.

The only pundit I knew in 1980 who predicted Reagan's victory did so with me over coffee on the morning of October 28. That would be Richard Nixon. What is more, on this occasion the "disgraced" former president successfully picked every Senate race but two. Then he added that Reagan would be a successful president. RN said that Reagan had an advantage that few candidates could command: "He is always underestimated."[5] We would see that on election night. RN had already, in a conversation with me years earlier, said that the Wonder Boy would be a failed president because "he is too arrogant to learn from his mistakes."[6]

Possibly a few pages back, when I played down Luigi Barzini's announcement that the early 1980s might be *my* moment in history, I was making yet another failed attempt at playing the humility card. Though I do not know why, I would don the shawl of humility with Luigi. He never struck me as being particularly humble. As for me, of all the virtues, humility is the one that I have never quite gotten the hang of. I mean, what could possibly be in it for me? And though I resided in the Midwest, I was frequently traveling to Washington now, for I had been picked by Bill Casey and others to nominate people to staff the Reagan administration. During the election, Casey had asked me to set up some meetings for the candidate with my European writers, which I did to the discomfiture of the Reagan campaign staff. As a matter of fact, President Nixon had asked me to put in a good word for Alexander Haig as secretary of state, which I did.

At some point, something like forty associates of *The American Spectator* joined the administration. Even I was under consideration, though I intended to remain a literary guy. One thing was certain: Writers such as Ken Adelman, Martin Anderson, Bill Bennett, and Jeane Kirkpatrick would be in demand. This was to be a *conservative* government, and I knew most of the young players and a dozen or so older players, most of whom had been writing for *Commentary*, *Human Events*, *National Review*, and *The American Spectator*. Never before had conservative academics and writers played such a role in Republican politics.

Dr. Fred Iklé, a scholarly foreign policy adviser to the Reagan campaign who was about to become undersecretary of defense for policy, was one of the first to ask me for the names of fellow *The American Spectator* writers and what their expertise might be. He also wanted to submit my name for consideration as chairman of the board of directors of the Corporation for Public Broadcasting. I have always kicked myself for not allowing my name to be floated across the glabrous heads over at National Public Radio. I have in my long life been asked precisely once to appear on NPR's "All Things Considered," and apparently, I caused sufficient acid reflux among the evening's listeners to be permanently banned. What would the NPR potentates make of me being their boss? Mass defenestrations? A drinking of the hemlock? Eventually, I settled for a seat on the board of a bilateral Japanese American initiative, which allowed me to travel back and forth to Japan, becoming aware of issues facing the two countries and also becoming aware of a new culinary enthusiasm—sushi washed down with sake.

Bill Casey also sought enlistments from the world of intellectual magazines. I gave him a list with Elliott Abrams at the top of it. Elliott has since had a distinguished career in government, albeit marred by controversies—all being controversies of which I approve. Then there was Charles Horner and his wife Connie, both of whom served the Reagan administration well. Elliott and the Horners were all former Democrats, which was the case with many Reaganites. For years, Casey had worked with Leo Cherne on the International Rescue Committee, an organization formed in the 1930s to protect intellectuals from tyrants—for instance, Hitler, Mussolini, and even Stalin, to mention a tyrant rarely included with the others. I have often wondered why. Do Democrats still call this murderer of millions of innocents Uncle Joe, as FDR once did? Thus, Bill was familiar with the role that intellectuals can play in politics. Bill was comfortable with intellectuals and thoroughly capable of being one himself.

One evening just before the inauguration, Bill, the president-elect's campaign chairman and soon-to-be director of Central Intelligence, strode into a small party at my Hay-Adams suite wearing a tuxedo. He reassured me that this was his first stop in a busy night that would end with the president-elect. He wanted to see my list of prospective appointees. To the astonishment of my guests, who included, according to my records, Adelman, Aram Bakshian, Suzi Garment, John Coyne, Tom Bethell, *The American Spectator*'s Washington correspondent, and John Lehman (about to be chosen as the next secretary of the navy). Bill flung his vast frame down among us and opened a

Coors. This was to be an administration characterized by its critics as inert to the life of the mind, but that evening the talk turned to post-World War II history, Arthur Koestler, and Hannah Arendt. It is not often that a cabinet officer from either party has been able to hold his own on such topics with learned intellectuals, but Casey could. And he was seeing to it that the conservative movement was emptying its think tanks and intellectual reviews for government service.

Bill was an old man with a young man's imagination. He was the rare individual who, full of age and honors and ready for retirement, had yet to begin the most illustrious chapter of a long life. Ronald Reagan, too, had a similar last chapter to his life. America has, since the Kennedys, been a nation engaged in a mad celebration of youth, but in the Reagan years, it was often the old men and women who made a difference. I, with a theatrical sweep, presented Bill with my list and off he went into the night. My guests were impressed. I was, of course, humble, as was my wont.

Suddenly, the world was moving for us conservatives *allegro con brio*. The conservative movement was finding its place in government. A sense was spreading throughout the country that something as momentous as the New Deal of the 1930s was taking hold in our nation's capital. Then on March 30, shots rang out at the Washington Hilton and the president was hit in the chest. He was rushed to George Washington University Hospital. Back in Bloomington, a cold wind whipped through town. What added to the bleakness of the day was the media's coverage, particularly by the airheads at CBS. I wrote in "The Continuing Crisis," that "[e]ven before it was known whether the President would live or die, loutish television journalists were duteously reminding ideologues that the President had opposed gun control."[7] Imagine! Ronald Reagan had opposed gun control! My secretary, Lou Ann Sabatier, reminded me that I had to be in Washington, DC, to deliver a speech on April 2, three days after the president was shot. "Where was I speaking," I asked. Why, at the national headquarters of the National Rifle Association. Egad! Would I go? Well, a gentleman keeps his word. Then, within twenty-four hours, the sun was out and shining again.

Word was coming out that the president had been launching a host of witticisms without the benefit of a teleprompter. With a bullet lodged near his heart, he looked up at Nancy and quipped, "Honey, I forgot to duck." Already having suffered serious breathing impairment and a serious loss of blood, he looked up at his surgeons sharpening their blades and inquired, "Please tell me you're Republicans." His good spirits continued throughout the night and into the morning when he signed a dairy price support bill. Then upon being notified that the government was "running normally" he responded: "What makes you think I would be happy about that." In "The Continuing Crisis," I pronounced: "Ronald Reagan is the greatest showman of all. On with the Administration!"[8]

Through all the excitement of the 1980 election, the inauguration, and the conservative takeover of government, back in Bloomington, changes were taking place, too. Our precocious managing editor, Erich Eichman, was leaving for *Harper's* magazine. This was an early instance of a migration that has continued for decades. Young writers and editors begin their careers at *The American Spectator* and graduate ever onwards to places like *The Washington Post*, *The Wall Street Journal* (where we presently have three alumni), and the White House.

Erich had begun as a dishwasher, graduated from the renowned Indiana University Jacobs School of Music, and joined the staff of the magazine. Now he was moving on, though he surprised me when he said that we already had a likely prospect to replace him among our proofreaders. The replacement was a graduate student in IU's respected Robert F. Byrnes Russian and East European Institute, Wladyslaw Pleszczynski. I remember meeting Wlady for the first time at one of our bibulous Saturday Evening Club meetings in September 1980. He was pleasant, learned, and one other thing. I could tell from his reticence that he hated me. Yet, what was I to do? We needed someone to manage the production of the magazine, and so I hired a man who hated me. That was more than forty years ago. Obviously, I failed to take Wlady's full measure.

Wlady turned out to be the easiest man to work with I have ever known. I never had to train him. He could write—and he writes very elegantly to this day. He could edit—and by now he is a master of the English language. Moreover, Wlady shared the magazine's big picture of the world, starting with the realization that culture is more important to politics than politics is to politics, and humor is more important to understanding the world than sober facts. What is more, his intellectual inheritance is about the best that a Western intellectual can be endowed with. His mother was Jewish. His father was Roman Catholic. They were born in pre-World War II Poland, and they met after having made a hasty exit from Nazi concentration camps that were about to go out of business thanks to the Allied army under General Dwight David Eisenhower. They were deposited in a British camp for displaced persons and six weeks later, they married.

Wlady is not completely sound. He has never enjoyed a cocktail, not even a shot and a beer, but otherwise, he is a perfect gent. After the discovery of our IRS incorporation letter smoldering atop a garbage heap in front of our rural Indiana farmhouse back in the 1960s, I would say that finding Wlady amongst our proofreaders was the second great miracle handed down to me from the heavens. In the more than four decades that we have worked together, we have had only two arguments. The first was over a piece that the British writer Ambrose Evans-Pritchard did during the *Spectator*'s pursuit of the Clintons. The piece was about the deputy White House counsel, Vince Foster's demise, and Wlady was opposed to it. I thought of it as another nail for Bill Clinton's coffin. We agreed to let another very sensible man on the staff decide, Marc Carnegie. Marc thought the piece was sound and even amusing. We ran it. Our second argument was over drug running at Mena airport, as will be discussed later. After huffing and puffing at home for a night, Wlady was back the next morning. Peace was restored to the *Spectator* for another forty years. Wlady and I have never even argued about Donald Trump. At first, Wlady's approval was muted—again, he is always sensible. I was full of hope. In time, we both came to admire Donald, particularly for his cosmopolitan charm.

Such calm is not the norm at other intellectual reviews. *The New Republic* was always a famous center for violence and even foul language. Hendrik Hertzberg, a man suffering an apparent "anger management" disorder, reminisced publicly once about his open warfare with the magazine's erstwhile owner, Martin Peretz. "One setting for such arguments was the office hallways" recalls Hendrik; and he continues as his blood begins to boil, "another was the weekly staff meeting"—both being locales that Wlady and I would steer clear of if we were on *The New Republic*'s staff.

Trigger warning!

The following exchange may not be suitable for all audiences.

Hendrik elaborates on a particularly violent confrontation where things grew heated over what he calls "the nation and the world." Here is how they concluded:

MARTY: "Fuck you, Rick!" (*slams door*)

ME: "Fuck you, Marty!" (*slams door*)

Marty, reappearing a few minutes later: "Mmm, I feel much better now."[9]

That reminds me: I have never known Wlady to employ the F-word in anger, much less in friendly wordplay.

This is not to say that conservatives do not become emotional about each other's editorial judgments. About the time that we were making changes to our staff, I received the following letter from my old friend Christopher Buckley, the only son of Bill Buckley, whom I had inadvertently provoked by referring to John Lennon's death as a "sad expiry" and I did it *in print*! I mean, I was as devastated as the next guy by the death of the composer of "Sgt. Pepper's Lonely Hearts Club Band," *but* four months after John Lennon's death, I had finally pulled myself together. Not Chris. On March 7, 1981, he wrote:

> Dear Bob,
>
> The remarks about John Lennon—"sad expiry" etc.— were disturbing. I am suppressing a lot of anger when I say that. I've sent gift subs of the *Spectator* to a lot of friends, liberal friends, not one of whom has appreciated the gift, all of whom have asked why it must be so smug, snide, kooky. Up to now I have defended your magazine. I am truly sorry that I will no longer be able to.
>
> Sincerely,
> Christopher[10]

As for choosing Wlady as our next managing editor, I gained confidence within months that I had raised the right proofreader to a sensitive editorial position. Then in 2009, all doubts vanished when he wrote of Christopher in our June issue: "As long as I've known of him, Christopher Buckley has struck me as an odd piece of work. In early 1981, shortly after I joined this magazine, Bob Tyrrell received a letter from him. Christopher was very upset. Much as he had liked *The American Spectator*, he would no longer be able to recommend it to friends or purchase gift subscriptions. Bob's sin? He'd apparently made light of former Beatle John Lennon's death."[11]

Yet back to 1981, and the White House three months after the president's brush with a would-be assassin's bullet. It is a festive occasion, one of the earliest state dinners of the Reagan presidency, honoring Malcolm Fraser, the prime minister of Australia; and Ronald Reagan, the oldest man ever to be elected president of the United States, has just swirled across the floor of the White House's grand foyer and will ascend to the executive quarters overhead. In recent years, journalists such as David Broder and Lou Cannon, have been writing about the Republican Party as being on its deathbed dominated by, in the words of MIT's professor Walter Dean Burnham, "extreme tendencies."[12] On this evening at the White House, "extreme tendencies" are everywhere. Conservatives of all varieties have filled that stately old mansion as never before. The guest list includes eminences from *two* conservative think tanks; one of the Coors beer barons; Lt. General Daniel O. Graham, US Army, retired, a Star Wars prophet; Edwin Meese, now a counselor to the president; Richard Allen, one of the conservative movement's preeminent strategic thinkers; William Simon, former secretary of the Treasury and destined with Allen to find a seat on the board of *The American Spectator*. I am in attendance with my wife, Judy, having had our youngest daughter Annie two weeks before via C-section so Judy could attend the dinner. We claim Annie to this day as a presidential baby, and she, seven years from this evening, will introduce herself to the president at our dinner table in McLean, Virginia. Unlike his Republican predecessors, Ronald Reagan was not coy about bringing his ideological allies right into the White House to enjoy the usufructs of victory. They had another distinguishing feature. All were driven by a sense of mission.

It has been a dazzling evening. The guests—craving one last handclasp with him—startle me. After all, our fortieth president has surely had a long day. The pomp and clatter of this dinner for the Australian prime minister has been enough to tire me, and I can always rely on the restorative power of a nocturnal cocktail, even at state dinners. Ronald Reagan does not betake of this "coping mechanism" as the shrinks now call it. He is only a mild tippler. Now as he crosses the red carpet to the elevator that launches him and Nancy, the love of his life, homeward, he remains as genial as the morning sun.

A few pages back, when I introduced Wlady Pleszczynski, I spoke of *The American Spectator*'s "big picture" that included the notion that culture is more important to politics than politics is to politics. At least during my lifetime, political struggles usually have begun with cultural struggles. Maybe this was not true in Aristotle's time when the Greek philosopher was writing *The Politics*, or in Machiavelli's time when the Florentine was at work on *The Prince*. Yet, for certitude in modern times, what is to be decided today in politics was decided yesterday in culture, especially pop culture, often by illiterate adolescents. For instance, the values of rock 'n' roll steamrolled the values of "The Hit Parade" decades ago. Or when the values of nihilism replaced the values of the Broadway musical long before any election had taken place, and most emphatically before the values of a 1960s ithyphallic draft dodger replaced those of war heroes such as George H. W. Bush, Bob Dole, or John McCain. In these instances, one sees how culture preempts politics in modern times.

The stirrings that accompanied the rise of Ronald Reagan put political observers in mind of the stirrings that accompanied the rise of FDR and perhaps JFK. We know that Ronald Reagan had three political goals: the defeat of the Soviets, the lowering of taxes, and the restoration of American greatness. Yet we also know that he was disturbed by the coarsening of American culture. Conservatives saw his election as a way to revive American culture. I saw it as an opportunity at least to dilute the nihilism that was poisoning our education system and our entertainment. I noted the stirrings of the late 1970s as an opportunity to influence the culture, and I believed that the president saw it that way, too. He was unhappy with the recent Hollywood emphasis on zoo sex and violence. On several occasions, I saw him demonstrate with his hands how the famous director Ernst Lubitsch would dramatize an intimate love scene for his actors using only his hands. The former actor would reproduce Lubitsch's scene by hanging an imagined "Do Not Disturb" sign outside an imagined hotel room door. The president and Nancy watched movies, but for the most part, the movies they watched were a product of the past, not the tawdry present.

My scheme to bring conservative values into the 1980s began on the afternoon of August 6, 1982. I had just entered my home office soaking wet from a noon handball match. As I was recording my game, I was interrupted by a call from the White House. A silken voice told me the president wanted a word with me. Ever since the age of fourteen, I have made room practically every day for a workout: in a pool during my competitive swimming days or in a gym from my early twenties on—weights one day, handball the next. I am what is called type A, and a workout calms me down even more effectively than a martini and with fewer side effects. So, standing in my home office dripping with perspiration, I was perfectly calm as the president questioned me from the White House.

I had a column in the *Washington Post* the week before arguing that the White House's assistant presidents were undercutting the president's plans for tax cuts and causing a rift within the conservative community. He insisted that a tax increase, then being pressed upon him by congressional Democrats, would ensure three dollars of congressional budget cuts for every additional tax dollar. He disputed the news stories that the assistant presidents were conspiring to enfeeble conservatives and asked how a rift with them could be avoided. It would take six years and the publication of assistant president Mike Deaver's egregious memoirs before any of the others would come clean and validate my claim that some of his staff had committed various acts of betrayal. As for Congress's promises of budget cuts, the Hill never made good on them. We did, however, end the rift dividing the president from his friends. Our solution was lunch. Reminding the president that he stayed in touch with conservative economists by holding a series of luncheons with them, I suggested a similar series of luncheons with conservative editors to keep the president and the conservative editors au courant with one another and, à la FDR and JFK, to put the presidential seal on our attempts to create a conservative counterculture—a counterculture to the *Kultursmog* was what we needed, as I shall explain in due course.

On September 22, 1982, we lunched in the cabinet room with the president. All was going well, though I was somewhat startled by the retinue that accompanied him. I had editors from the major conservative publications: *Commentary*, *National Review*, *Policy Review*, and *The Public Interest*. The president had his chief of staff, James A. Baker; his national security advisor, Bill Clark; his deputy chief of staff, Mike Deaver; his chief counsel, Ed Meese; his director of the Office of Management and Budget (OMB), David Stockman; and David Gergen, then serving as his director of communications and planning. Irving Kristol, who was one of my guests, had convinced me that Gergen was one of us. He would help us do with conservatives what FDR and JFK had done with liberals, to wit, lend presidential prestige to political culture.

With the midday sun enhaloing his head and shoulders, the president bid me sit across from him in the vice president's chair, saying something to the effect of "This is your show, after all." The president's disposition was as sunny as the Rose Garden behind him, though the assistant presidents sitting on either side of him did not appear to share his good cheer. I thought we were just going to ventilate some of the conservatives' concerns about the state of the nation and share some ideas about how to build a conservative counterculture. But the assistant presidents were edgy. They sensed that the arrival of these writers portended a full-scale coup. History might remember it as a takeover by the Writers Junta, and there would be pictures of Irving Kristol leading all the assistant presidents out of the White House in handcuffs.

Unfortunately, we were not in cerebral New York circa, say, 1969. This was political Washington in the 1980s, and the assistant presidents were on the alert. Few believed that we editors were in the cabinet room of the White House merely for lunch and to establish something as amorphous as an informal relationship with our friend, the president, that might have a cultural content. Surely, we were there for a power grab, a coup de main against them. The president seemed to be leaning our way!

The most insecure of the assistant presidents, which is to say the most inveterate schemer, had been obsequiously telephoning me for a week to reassure me that he was a genuine conservative and a faithful reader of *The American Spectator*. His name was Richard Darman and now he had caught me just as I was leaving my hotel room for the White House to pledge that he was not only an admirer but also an "intellectual." Yes, Darman, assistant to the president and deputy to the chief of staff, was a conservative intellectual, and he assured me that *The Public Interest*'s executive editor, Mark Lilla, would vouch for his bona fides. "Stop by the office after lunch for coffee," he insisted. Espresso? Cappuccino? What do such intellectuals drink in the early afternoon? Bourbon and branch? No, that would be the LBJ White House.

The lunch was very agreeable, except when I would accidentally lock eyes with one of these grim assistant presidents. For his part, the president was in fine fettle. So, I was emboldened to proclaim to the leader of the free world:

> You have won the political campaigns. The intellectual
> battles have been won, too. Your adversaries have no
> spellbinding dreams or revivifying policy initiatives
> that have not been tried. The terms of political debate
> have become conservative. No longer do we hear
> calls to limit economic growth, radically redistribute
> income, or to negotiate with every hostile country.
> Now is your (dare I say it?) Moment in History. It is
> time to implement the policies of limited government,
> economic growth, deregulation, and a strong foreign
> policy. You have the ideas and the power.

Wow, I still remember the thrill. I had lived to deliver a stirring exhortation to the president of the United States in the privacy of his own home, and I delivered it while seated in the very spot in which Vice President Calvin Coolidge had slept while President Warren

Harding had droned on. This was history in the making. The beginning of Ronald Reagan's conservative counterculture.

From the other side of the table, five pairs of dilated eyes focused on my beaming face. Only the president shared my enthusiasm, and in his cheerful, can-do demeanor, he asked Dave Gergen to schedule a series of these pleasant and fruitful luncheons. Apparently, we were going to have regular access to the president. The conservative counterculture's future was assured. Everyone on my side of the table understood that if the media was to change and the left-wing tilt of the universities was to be challenged, we had to start at the top. Starting with the president on our side, as the New Dealers and the New Frontiersmen had started with FDR and JFK on their side, was the way to go. The president obviously thought so, too. His interest was evident. In a follow-up letter to his friend Bill Rusher, the publisher of *National Review* and another of my guests that day, the president wrote: "I agree with you [with Rusher] about doing this more often."[13]

After the luncheon, Gergen came shivering toward me (Wlady always called him Mr. Potato Head), and, to my amazement, blurted out that I probably would be more comfortable dealing with a staff member "friendlier" than he. *Friendlier* than he? Irving had assured me that Dave, who had worked at the conservative American Enterprise Institute before joining the White House, was friendly to all of us conservatives. But Dave was a bit of an oaf. He could not keep his hostility under wraps, even when there was no reason to admit his hostility. Yet, why would he reveal it? Well, I do not know, but suddenly things did not look so auspicious for our conservative counterculture.

Dave had obviously thrown in with the assistant presidents, and they had no appetite for a conservative counterculture. All my talk of "ideas" and "culture" was only seen by them as menacing. Dave told me that he would enlist the overworked but "friendly"—that is to say conservative—Ed Meese to schedule further meetings. Alas, our project was about to become lost in Ed's congested attaché case. Our group never met in the White House again. The White House had averted another coup. As the 1980s passed, the only reliable member of the conservative counterculture on daily duty at 1600 Pennsylvania Avenue was the president, and he was not getting any younger.

There was a cordon sanitaire taking shape around the chief executive, certainly by 1982. Lou Cannon, a leading biographer of the president, writes in his biography *The Role of a Lifetime*, how the assistant presidents, such as Mike Deaver and Gergen, tried with only limited success to keep the conservative tabloid *Human Events* out of the old cowboy's hands. They saw it as too conservative. Another Reagan biographer, Richard Reeves, makes the same point. Apparently, the assistant presidents now wanted to distance the White House from the conservative publications, though the real president, the one elected by the voters, had demonstrated his affinity for us. Larry Speakes in his memoir *Speaking Out* testifies that *The American Spectator* was among the president's favorite publications and that I was one of his four favorite syndicated columnists. The president had demonstrated his friendship with me by inviting me to an early state dinner, and he was about to have me and my conservative associates in for a luncheon. Nonetheless, the assistant presidents were active on all fronts, and as Dave Gergen artlessly admitted, they were not friendly.

Between the state dinner and my luncheon with the president, I got a call from Peter Rusthoven, associate counsel to the president. If ever anyone could say "I got my job through *The American Spectator*," it was Peter. He had written a regular column for us while at Harvard after Pat Moynihan had introduced us. He was a native of Indiana, and while he was still writing for us, Peter Hannaford commissioned a memo from him that became a prominent ingredient in the Republican presidential nominee's acceptance speech. What is more, he was on my list of potential appointees that I had given to Bill Casey.

So, what was Peter calling me for? He was calling, in his official capacity, to ask that we cease claiming the president as a reader. In the magazine's house advertisement, which listed famous subscribers, we regularly reproduced a photograph of Ronald Reagan's old address label from his Pacific Palisades residence. There were, Rusthoven said, complaints from the public. The advertisement was neither illegal nor in dubious taste. However, some among the assistant presidents wanted to avoid controversy over the president's conservative ties. Recently, the *Washington Post* had named *The American Spectator* Washington's new "in" magazine. So, how was the editor in chief of Washington's new "in" magazine going to respond to Rusthoven, my former writer's request? I complied with his wishes! It was one of the stupidest decisions I have ever made. The establishment of a conservative counterculture had become a prized goal of mine. I thought it was within my reach. I believe that the president had already demonstrated that he at least wanted us to get started on its rudiments. Now I began to realize that it was not going to be easy.

In writing his installment of the Oxford History of the United States, which covered the period of time from Watergate through *Bush v. Gore*, an old history professor of mine, James T. Patterson, notes that while "the GOP had advanced dramatically between 1974 and 1984," there were limits. The GOP's growth was not as "dramatic" as observers might have expected. Ronald Reagan's landslide election "had not realigned American politics in the dramatic way that FDR's triumphs had done in the 1930s."[14] In a word, the GOP had not touched the culture, which was moving steadily to the left. If the assistant presidents around President Reagan had taken testosterone injections to supplement their listless political libidos, the outcome might have been different, and if they had had a robust counterculture to fumigate the *Kultursmog*, it would have helped. But then they would not be assistant presidents. Some might even have presented themselves as presidential candidates in 1980. Yet they would probably lose to the man whose moment in history was at hand, the fortieth president of the United States, Ronald Reagan. He was old, but only he had the political libido of a winner.

Once again, we saw that the Republican political libido was no match for the Democratic political libido. The only man in the White

House with the capacity to oppose the Democratic political libido in the 1980s was an ex-Democrat, Ronald Reagan. What is more, when I made my case for a counterculture in 1982, only the president and his national security advisor, Bill Clark, favored it. The fumes of the *Kultursmog* had made their way into the White House long before I arrived. That was apparent when I presented the need for a conservative counterculture to oppose the *Kultursmog*. It is time to explicate the *Kultursmog*.

At *The American Spectator* in the late 1970s, we became increasingly aware that American culture was filled with alien politics. First, it was the politics of the liberals. Later, it became the politics of the Progressives. In the distant future, it may become the politics of the radical nudists. The New Dealers had begun this evolution in the 1930s when they merged their ideological world into the world of culture. Eventually, the cultural world and the ideological world became one world. At *The American Spectator*, we recognized it as *Kultursmog*. It is today wholly polluted with politics, the politics of the Left. It is the only pollution that the Left approves of and even spreads. Though ordinary Americans have been blissfully unaware of this dreadful transmogrification of their values. Now *Kultursmog* pervades the education system at every level. It dominates the government bureaucracies. It pollutes the offices and the boardrooms of giant corporations. It is everywhere. No one has developed a way to fumigate it or even deodorize it.

Affirmative action has only speeded up the spread of this noxious pollution, taking up the cause of feminism and every species of identity politics. It can even be found in zoos, especially where endangered species are housed. Someday, affirmative action will probably even promote people with eating disorders and others living in as yet unimaginable circumstances. All in the pursuit of that exalted misnomer: *diversity*.

Kultursmog pollutes schoolrooms at every level. Think of the controversy over pronouns. Is, say, little George a "he" or a "she" or an "it"?

Think of the controversy that a schoolgirl creates merely by wanting to go to the bathroom in a room free of troubled boys. She might have to wait in the hallway for days before the Supreme Court takes action. Or imagine the hostility facing the normal boys who thought their locker room would be free of tomboys. Or think of the production of a Shakespeare play with the players appearing in the nude or dressed up as 1930s gangsters, complete with machine guns. I have never seen, say, the Royal Shakespeare Company perform Shakespeare in the nude, but doubtless, the day will come. On the other hand, I have seen *Macbeth* cast in gangster garb. It was twenty years ago, and I was either in New York or London (after a few drinks, I get the two confused). I suppose the outré casting of *Macbeth* was supposed to make the audience *think*.

One of the conceits of the *Kultursmog* is that Americans do not think very intently about anything. So, the smog's sacrosanct duty is to make us think, and the way to make us think is by disturbing us, by making us want to tear down the theater, by giving us a nosebleed or by making us really nauseous. It is another example of the left-winger's goal of disturbing his neighbor, though on a macro scale. As for me, I have never gotten even mildly uncomfortable at a high culture event or even a low culture event. I have laughed out loud but never fallen ill; not even over the art of Andy Warhol or Robert Mapplethorpe or this modern clown of the plastic arts, Jeff Koons. Incidentally, yet another of the *Kultursmog*'s false assumptions is that high art, if it is great art, has always disturbed its audience, especially on opening night. You know, at the premiere of Beethoven's Third Symphony, or Michelangelo's unveiling of the Sistine Chapel ceiling, or Rodin's *The Thinker*. In truth, if Beethoven's or Michelangelo's or Rodin's artistic goals were to disturb their audiences or annoy their patrons, they would be out of work in a flash and quite possibly jailed by Prince Esterházy or the crown prince or the emperor—whoever was footing the bill.

Kultursmog may be laughable and trivial and childish, but it is all around us. Americans cannot escape it. Even Europeans and Asians cannot escape it, which is one of the reasons why *The American Spectator* has survived for more than fifty years. It has been one laugh after another, usually at the expense of the *Kultursmog*, its pollutants, and its polluters. We began by laughing at the *Kultursmog* when the liberals were pumping it out of their venerable smokestacks at the universities and in the media. There was, for instance, the Alger Hiss sham. It went on for decades. At *The Nation*, it doubtless still is going on. There, Alger remains innocent. One of the magazine's most persuasive arguments adduced by one of his credulous sons is that Hiss could not possibly have been a Communist because he once caught his male member in the zipper of his trousers while indulging in some noncommunist activity, possibly the solitary vice as promoted in sex education class or possibly just out of Alger's endless curiosity. This example is no joke. Google it, and if you are incredulous by nature, you will doubtless feel some sympathy for Alger.

We continued laughing at the purveyors of the smog's insistence that Ronald Reagan was a dunce, while Al Gore invented the internet and John-François Kerry bicycled his way across Europe. Of course, the creations of the *Kultursmog* slowed down a bit around 2009 just as the *New York Times'* Sam Tanenhaus came up with his unfortunately timed book *The Death of Conservatism*. The book came out only fourteen months before the conservatives won a wave election. By then, *Kultursmog* ceased to be dependent on liberalism for its fantasies. After all, liberalism was dead. But *Kultursmog* had found a new source of inspiration—progressivism—and progressivism took on such new fantasies as, for instance, the *New York Times'* 1619 Project and the Green New Deal. What will replace progressivism as a wellspring for *Kultursmog*? Maybe nothing. Possibly the end of the world will come to pass.

The *Kultursmog* is created in two ways: (1) the endless repetition of falsehoods and (2) either the complete neglect of those with whom the smog disagrees or the utter misrepresentation of them and their views. Judge Robert Bork is a case in point, as we shall soon see. Perhaps for a succinct definition of the *Kultursmog* that you can carry around with you or have tattooed on your person, use the abbreviated definition devised by the philosopher James Piereson. He has said: "*Kultursmog* is the liberal understanding of events ratified as a matter of morals and etiquette." That sounds right to me.

At some point in 1982, I was becoming tired of all the travel back and forth to Bloomington. Then, too, there was the sight of IU professors who once dressed in handsome tweeds now passing my breakfast window dressed like little boys. Some even affected a backpack rather than carrying a briefcase like an adult. Thus, I asked my wife and Wlady to consider a move to the East Coast, following the Baron, who had taken a job in Washington at the Heritage Foundation some years earlier. We considered New York City, Washington, DC, and northern New Jersey before settling on the DC area. On the advice of President Nixon's old aide, Pat Buchanan, we focused on Northern Virginia, specifically the suburb of McLean. After reconnoitering the region, I found an unspoiled tract of land just fifteen minutes from the White House via the George Washington Memorial Parkway. The lot was at the end of a cul-de-sac, enshrouded by trees, and abutting a national forest that ran a mile or so to the Potomac River. It ensured our privacy and allowed my children to grow up surrounded by nature: deer, wild birds, woodland animals, such as foxes and raccoons, and even an occasional eagle, plus all the amenities of suburban life.

After showing the lot to my wife, we put up a home as impressive as we had in Indiana, and now all I watched out my breakfast window were the deer munching on my azaleas. A local hunter testified to me that azalea-fed deer made a stupendous meal, and we were to share his delicacy with such luminaries as Bill Casey and his wife, Secretary of the Navy John Lehman and his wife, and the legendary Clare Boothe Luce, among others in the years ahead. I hated to leave behind good friends, such as Tom Tarzian and Al Somers, but I could call them whenever I wanted, and to this day, they always answer the telephone, usually with the latest Midwestern joke about the bungling in Washington.

The construction of our house went with hardly a hitch because my secretary, Lou Ann Sabatier, was coming with us and bringing her husband, the son of a Hoosier contractor who kept an eye on the construction. Most of our staff was young and eager to come out with us, too, and they all arrived to set up our office while my children finished school in Indiana and our house was being completed. The only problem, as I recall, was one night I received a call from Lou Ann's husband telling me that the bricks, which by then were halfway up the walls of our house, were the wrong color. How to explain it to my wife? At first, our contractor insisted that the right bricks were going up. When I proved him wrong, he was more persuasive, claiming that the bricks were more attractive than the original bricks we had chosen. My wife agreed. There was a final problem. When we moved in, my children came down with poison ivy repeatedly. We only put an end to the pox when a gardener discovered a poison ivy plant growing up one of the trees that stood on our front lawn. It ran straight up the tree and had a stalk as big as my wrist. It took months to subdue it, but finally, we got Mother Nature before she got us.

Through all this moving of our offices from halfway across America and building a new home far from where I had been raising a family, I continued my attempts to thwart the assistant presidents in the White House and to build a counterculture to clear the atmosphere of the *Kultursmog*. Working with Reaganite loyalists at the United States Information Agency (USIA), Wlady and I arranged funding for trips that sent young American intellectuals to Europe to meet their counterparts there and to bring them to Washington and New York in the hope of establishing enduring relationships. For instance, Lou Ann arranged for us to meet with the Europeans in our respective European embassies, and then for them to meet with us in New York and Washington. In New York, we met with Al Haig at the

Essex House on Central Park South and with President Nixon at his offices in Manhattan's Federal Plaza. In Washington, we met with Bill Clark in the White House.

I reported back to the president as I would continue to do throughout his presidency relating news of our success. He replied in a letter saying, "I like your idea about having your European counterparts here in June and having them get together with Bill [Clark, his national security advisor]." And then he added "I hope I'm not out somewhere in the hustings at the time. I'd like to meet them myself." And finally, "When you have the dates write me (through Kathy), that way I'd be sure to get it and we can set something up."[15] Kathy was Kathy Osborne, his personal secretary. The old cowboy knew how to thwart his assistant presidents when he was serious about something, and I can only conclude that he was serious about helping me in my efforts to thwart the *Kultursmog*.

Looking back on the project, I find that we were amazingly prescient in our selection of participants. The Americans that we sent to Rome, Paris, and London became prominent voices in the years ahead. For instance, Bill McGurn in the Bush II White House and at the *Wall Street Journal*, and Bill Kristol in the office of Vice President Dan Quayle and later at *The Weekly Standard*, until he was felled by Trump derangement syndrome. What is more, we were bipartisan, bringing from *The New Republic* the magazine's literary editor Jack Beatty, who went on to work at *The Atlantic* as a senior editor and at National Public Radio as a news analyst. The young European intellectuals that we introduced to America had even more impressive careers. For instance, from Rome came Antonio Martino, the economist who rose to become Italy's minister of foreign affairs and later its minister of defense, from London we invited Frank Johnson one of the major journalists of his generation, and Charles Moore, who became editor of the London *Spectator*, the *Daily Telegraph*, the *Sunday Telegraph*, and Lady Thatcher's official biographer, and from

Paris, we chose the public intellectuals Jean-Marie Benoist and Michel Gurfinkiel, founder of the Jean-Jacques Rousseau Institute.

The president, Bill Clark, and Ed Meese were the serious conservatives in the White House in those days, but that was not enough to oppose the assistant presidents. President Reagan had his three major goals to pursue: winning the Cold War, lowering taxes, and the restoration of American greatness. That was pretty much a full-time effort. I had numerous meetings with Meese and Clark throughout their White House years, but somehow, we never got back to discussing how we might delouse the *Kultursmog*. As for the assistant presidents, they proceeded along their way to meretricious fame and fortune. Some years after Deaver left the White House, he sat down to chronicle all he had learned while serving President Reagan at the center of the free world. He mingled on holidays with playwrights such as Lillian Hellman, a die-hard Stalinist, and novelists such as William Styron, a ritualistic leftist, in the Hamptons. What did Deaver learn? In his memoir, he wrote: "Sometimes I think we need more artistic people in government service. They are often eccentric, but their virtue is that, unlike generals, they want to blow up only themselves."[16] What would Deaver have thought of that Austrian painter, Adolf Hitler?

**The editor-in-chief (left), the commander-in-chief
(right), and the future monarch (center).**

The editor-in-chief in repose.

President Donald Trump tries to make a point.

President George W. Bush greets R. Emmett Tyrrell Jr. at the White House luncheon honoring British historian Andrew Roberts on February 28, 2007.

**Introducing the next president of the United States.
Then vice president George H. W. Bush at *The American
Spectator*'s twentieth anniversary gala, November 4, 1987.**

**Barbara Bush, President George H. W.
Bush, and the mysterious stranger.**

**Tom Wolfe and the Tyrrells at the 2007 *American
Spectator* Gala in which he pronounced Troopergate
"the most important article of the 20th century."**

**Another president tries to make a point with
The American Spectator's editor-in-chief.**

Smiles all around.

Finally, the editor-in-chief is silenced.

R. Emmett Tyrrell Jr.'s presentation of Reagan on the Rock—the Rock being Mount Rushmore. The gifting took place at the Tyrrell residence, July 26, 1988.

R. Emmett Tyrrell Jr., his wife Jeanne Hauch, and still more Bushes.

It all began with Bob Kennedy.
Robert F. Kennedy
November 20, 1925–June 6, 1968
R.I.P.

Chapter VII

INTRODUCING RONALD REAGAN TO THE MUSIC OF FREDERICK THE GREAT

*T*hrough all of this activity—back and forth to Europe, back and forth to the East Coast, *The American Spectator*'s assaults on the *Kultursmog*, and the *Kultursmog*'s assaults on us—there was an ongoing sense of excitement that lasted for years. It would come and go. People on our side were winning their first Pulitzer Prizes: in 1977, George Will, in 1980, the *Wall Street Journal*'s Bob Bartley, a man for whom I was to grow in admiration and gratitude in the decades ahead (he came aboard as our senior editorial advisor in the autumn of 2003 upon his retirement from the *Wall Street Journal* and despite battling cancer), and in 1987, Pulitzer Prize–winning columnist Charles Krauthammer. We could get our books published. We would be invited on television.

Sure, there were warning signs that all was not as auspicious as we thought. There was Rusthoven's call from the White House. There was Gergen's stammering chat with me at the end of our luncheon with the president. There were other signs that conservatives were just not sufficiently interested in the battle for cultural values. Several times I approached my friend, Bill Buckley, still the leader of the conservative movement, to suggest that we build a counterculture. Always he was negative. On one occasion, when I urged that we take an interest in each other's work—not a hagiographic interest but simply an interest—he was almost insulting. "Oh," he said in the comfort of his 73rd Street pied-à-terre in Manhattan, "*that* would be *boring.*" *National Review*'s circulation never got over 269,512. Before we were ambushed by the Clinton Justice Department, *The American Spectator*'s circulation approached three hundred fifty thousand.

As we arrived at our agreeably dumpy offices in Arlington, just across the Potomac from Washington, we held a couple of festive receptions. One was at our offices, where the staff and various writers met with Boone Pickens, the folksy oil tycoon, and Tony Dolan, the president's speechwriter, and Bill Casey, followed by an impressive squad of security men. Bill also brought along Bill Simon, who he thought would be a resourceful board member, and he was.

A second reception was held at the toney Jockey Club, a now-defunct night spot that in the 1980s offered what nightlife there was in Washington, and it was destined to be the scene of my first encounter with Bill Clinton a decade later.

Bill was more interested in my fourteen-year-old daughter than me, at least until I asked him what he thought of my Mena airport piece published a few days earlier. It was a piece about the surreptitious flight of arms and drugs through a remote Arkansas airport. Then his tantrum would not subside. I, being but a country boy from Indiana, had to direct him, the president of the United States, back to his seat. For some reason, the Secret Service did not object. As I left the restaurant, I inquired as to why the Secret Service had allowed me such access to the president. The agent smiled somewhat sheepishly. I took his smile as more evidence of a conclusion that I had already arrived at, to wit: The Secret Service, like the Arkansas State Police, did not hold the first family in high regard. The Clintons introduced something new to the American presidency. I called it their pastoral charms.

At our Jockey Club reception in the mid-'80s, we had Bill Simon, soon to be the chairman of our board, and the inevitable Bill Casey, who rarely failed to attend an *American Spectator* affair. (It is curious that no one in the press ever accused *The American Spectator* of fronting for the CIA. After all, I knew some significant members of the CIA hierarchy in Bill's day.) Fred Barnes, a rising talent, also attended, along with Brit Hume, Fred's equal in television journalism, and from across the pond, the infamous rastaquouère Taki, our European correspondent. Lou Ann saw to it that such luminaries of print as E. J. Dionne of the *Washington Post* were present and Michael Kinsley of *The New Republic* and the fluent Christopher Hitchens, who then wrote for *The Nation*. Possibly they were present because of Lou Ann's charms, but I believe it was also something else.

I think they sensed what the historian James T. Patterson sensed when he assessed the achievements of the Reagan administration, as mentioned in the previous chapter. Reagan represented such a clear break with the old order, its collectivism, and its growing list of entitlements. He rolled over his opposition in two landslides in 1980 and 1984. Patterson expected, as did many others, conservative reverberations within American culture, but the reverberations never amounted to much. The media that Reagan had to deal with was more insular than the diffuse media of FDR's day. As Patterson, a perceptive historian noted, Reagan's arrival "had not realigned American politics in the dramatic way that FDR's triumphs had done in the 1930s."[1] Reagan's distinct break with the past and his two landslides might have been expected to bring with them a cultural shift, but it did not happen. The explanation for this is that the media had changed. They were more insular in Reagan's day, more resistant to change. By the late 1980s, people such as those ritualistic liberals Kinsley and Dionne had caught on. There was no reason to fear us, if you did not mind being laughed at by *The American Spectator*, and apparently, they did not. Polarization had begun, and by the 1990s, it was going to get worse.

For now, the storm clouds had passed. Our sense of excitement also had abated, at least for a while. I continued seeing the president off and on, though only one more time did I mention the derelictions of his assistant presidents. That would be on March 30, 1987. I went to the Oval Office charged with reassuring the president about the Iran-Contra affair, but before I went into his office, I encountered one of his speechwriters, who told me that the speech writing staff, composed of solid conservatives, had been barred from quoting conservative intellectuals and public figures in the president's speeches. The assistant presidents were being vigilant. I was urged to mention this censorship when I sat down with him. Well, I tried, but the commander in chief had other things on his mind. I never brought up the disloyal assistant presidents again. He would have none of it. His mind was burdened with something else.

Of course, there were other things to do at the magazine, too. Senator Christopher J. Dodd, a Democrat from Connecticut, had given a widely celebrated rebuttal to President Reagan's recent speech on Central America, and though it is today utterly forgotten, back then the speech was ranked right up there with the Gettysburg Address, at least by Democrats and the mainstream media. Only one thing about it really stung my conscience. The senator claimed that when he was in the Peace Corps, he had visited numerous backward countries and seen for himself how poverty breeds revolution. Had anyone in his audience ever been to backward regions and witnessed the conditions prevailing there? Well, he had me on that one. When I visited impoverished regions, it was always for their dazzling beaches, and I usually stayed safely behind the stout walls of an elegant hotel, for instance, in Barbados or Antigua. Stung by the Senator's Peace Corps revelations,

I made my mind up on the spot to rectify the situation. It was almost June 1983, and I, with my legendary decisiveness, called *The American Spectator*'s foreign correspondent, Taki Theodoracopulos, whom I reached somewhere in the Swiss Alps. I told him to pack all the requisite travel equipment: ointments, tonics, antimalarials, and aspirin. Together we would travel to one of those backward lands, where as a Peace Corps volunteer the senator had learned the elements of New Age statecraft, namely empathy. I selected Monaco.

There was a grand prix motor race being held in Monaco, and we flew down to see firsthand how the guerrilla movement was faring. I got *Car and Driver* magazine to pick up the tab, as its editor, David E. Davis, knew I was a car enthusiast and I promised to bring Taki along. Once in Monaco, Taki, after observing the yachts in the harbor and the Bentleys in the streets, noted that the conditions there supported Senator Dodd's thesis 100 percent. There was very little poverty in Monaco and almost no guerrilla activity, except at the bar in the Hôtel de Paris after 12:00 a.m. Perhaps the left-wing Democrats, then crippling our foreign policy in Central America, could arrange a grand prix race for Nicaragua that would be as successful as the one held annually in Monaco. Of course, Nicaragua was a Marxist paradise, and in the Grand Prix of Nicaragua, the Ferraris and Renaults barreling down the straightaway would have to be stripped of all the frivolous capitalistic advertisements in favor of wholesome revolutionary exhortations. Yet I looked forward to 1984 and the Grand Prix of Nicaragua with Senator Christopher Dodd as the honorary grand marshal. It has yet to take place.

As for our stay in Monaco, it had its ups and downs. Taki's father ran some of his vast shipping concerns out of the port, and he maintained lordly quarters in the Hôtel de Paris where all the employees knew Taki. The liveried staff spied the name Tyrrell on my luggage and spirited us to the head of the line at the front desk, thinking we were from the famous Tyrrell Formula One team. The hotel manager personally escorted us to an enormous suite overlooking the racetrack, Taki having assured the desk clerk that his famous father had reserved the room well in advance. Alas, Taki had *forgotten* to reserve *any* room, and shortly after our triumphal entry into the lobby of the Hôtel de Paris where tout le monde observed our impressive arrival, we were ignominiously booted from the premises. Taki caused such disasters frequently. We got rooms down the road at Cap-Ferrat. I retired at a sensible hour. Taki retired at 3:00 a.m. having met a bartender loaded with war stories about how he had served in World War II in the Luftwaffe or the Spanish Civil War or some other heroic service. The two of them had put away a lot of muscadets. The next morning, we got up at the crack of dawn and spent a glorious day at the track after a long, languorous lunch with acquaintances of his from all over Europe. One, a delectable young beauty from Colombia, became convinced that I was a CIA operative, and she was visibly distressed when I told her I had a wife back in Washington. So, Monaco ended well for us, and we forgot Senator Dodd halfway through a good bottle of claret at lunch. Keke Rosberg won the race in a Williams Cosworth, and, incidentally, Taki is still going strong well into his eighties.

As luck would have it, I was not finished with the Caribbee in 1983. In fact, I was just beginning a stint that would last for years and leave me with a multiracial household. On October 25, 1983, the world found out that Ronald Reagan's military buildup was not just for show. The US intelligence agencies had been apprising him that in Grenada, a tiny isle floating atop turquoise and blue waters and exuding the fragrances of exquisite spices that grow from its mountainsides, there were also Cuban engineers completing a huge airport that could serve as a strategically placed aircraft carrier capable of hosting Soviet bombers and missile silos. President Reagan gave the command, and the island was liberated in a matter of days. I had been kept informed of the militarization of the island by Luigi Barzini and his friend Contessa Vivi Crespi, for they visited the island every winter. A few months after the invasion and just after Luigi's death from lung cancer, my wife and I flew down to the island and checked into the

Spice Island Beach Resort, a very high-toned hostelry on the Grand Anse Beach, whose walls still bore evidence of heavy gunfire and whose beach had been mangled by two downed American helicopters.

The scene was grim, but not as grim as it had been in October. Then, people such as Walter Mondale were warning that the president's decision "undermines our ability to effectively criticize what the Soviets have done in their brutal intervention in Afghanistan, in Poland and elsewhere."[2] The Reverend Jesse Jackson declaimed that Americans "should all feel a sense of outrage and disgrace."[3] Well not me, comrades; I sided with the large Grenadian who startled me on the Grand Anse Beach by walking up and bellowing with a thumbs-up gesture: "America, number *one*," or another who confided in me that "Uncle Reagan" is "loved" in Grenada. In the rollicking calypso-English of the island, he continued, "If he cum down here we poot heem on our shoulders." Ronald Reagan did come down to Grenada in February 1986, though without the ceremonial procession.

Judy and I went on long skin diving expeditions with a splendid local boat owner, Captain Denham Peters. Denham also took us fishing and boating, and he advised us on where to taste the island's very good cuisine. He, too, had become a Reaganite, and I told him if he expressed his gratitude in a letter to the president, I would take it back to the White House. When I showed it to the president and told him that the island was abundant with goodwill toward him, he insisted on writing Denham. It was a typical Reagan gesture. I saw the president's letter hanging from the wall of Captain Peters's tiny home when I returned the next year. A few months before, when I had learned of Luigi's terminal illness, I mentioned to the president that a great friend of America, Luigi Barzini, was dying. From the Oval Office, he sent a get-well note to Rome, which arrived just weeks before Luigi passed away. Luigi never heard from the Italian president. But this friend of America heard from Ronald Reagan before he died.

I continued to visit Grenada through the 1980s, as Vivi Crespi had built a home there, and I became acquainted with more of the

R. EMMETT TYRRELL JR.

islanders, perhaps the most interesting being the slightly dotty Right Honorable Sir Eric Gairy. He had become *the Right Honorable* Sir Eric when Queen Elizabeth II asked him into her Privy Council in 1977 before his fall from power. When I met him, he was living in retirement in a radiant pink house high above the port city of St. George's. There he dreamily plotted his comeback and the return of his "electric vibrating chair," which had been taken from him when the revolution overthrew him in 1979. Aside from his absorption with "the electric vibrating chair," he was an expert on UFOs and God. In fact, he lectured twice at the United Nations on UFOs and God. He had exchanged materials on the subject with world leaders, among them Jimmy Carter, who responded by telling Sir Eric that he had had a UFO experience back in 1969. Eric even inaugurated the First World Congress on UFOs in Acapulco. There does not appear to have been a second conclave. When I knew him, he was given to reminiscing, and with surprising frequency repeating, "What manner of man is this?" He was referring to himself, not me. Believe it or not, I would be in need of him a few years later.

By then, the year was 1988, and I was confronted by an event that too many Americans have experienced: an impending divorce. Mine was a prosaic kind of divorce, despite my wife's excitement. It is the kind of process that destroys a marriage when one spouse or the other becomes successful or, even worse, achieves some sort of celebrity status. Often, the disgruntled one cannot live with the other's sudden success. Of course, in my case, I attracted attention from about the age of twenty-four, and there was no reason to conclude that I was going to subside anytime soon. Moreover, my wife was not discomfited by the state dinners or the splashy life we led. She, like so many in our situation, just did not like to enter a room where everyone was interested in my ideas and not hers. After a few more festive occasions in the late 1980s and one presidential dinner at our home—whose arrangements I made with the help of Bill Buckley's wife, Pat—Judy took the bewildered children and vamoosed to a town house a mile or two away. I was suddenly in need of a cook, a laundress, a housekeeper, and, as it turned out, a full-time babysitter. Judy was not particularly comfortable with children. Upon Vivi Crespi's advice, I called Sir Eric. He asked a few pertinent questions, the most memorable being one that I still recall today. In his deep, rich baritone voice, he rumbled, "Do you want double duty?"

It was a good thing I demurred, for a few weeks later Doreen Gibbs landed at Dulles International Airport, weighing 240 pounds and carrying in her luggage a machete. Later, her young daughter, Nikki, joined her and the two lived in my guest room, never giving me a moment's grief. Nikki was my daughter Annie's age, and they made a very contemporary twosome, playing the diversity card without any idea of how much virtue it signaled. Annie was rather petite and quite white. Nikki was elegant, very black, and at least a foot taller than my daughter. In the years they spent growing up together, the question of race came up only once.

That was when a virtue-flaunting Roman Catholic priest decided to lecture his flock—including Annie, Nikki, Doreen, and me—on the matter of American racism, which he found omnipresent, despite the Civil Rights Act of 1964, the Voting Rights Act of 1965, and the War on Poverty programs. At Mass one Sunday morning, standing at the base of his church's amphitheater seating arrangement and being able to see all his congregants—white, black, and Asian—the priest droned on and on about racism. Throughout his tirade, Nikki looked clueless and Annie, too. Both were eight years old. On our drive home, an obviously troubled Nikki asked us what was meant by the word racism. I cannot recall if even Doreen knew. Racism was a word not widely used in Grenada in those days, and there was never a need to use it in the Tyrrell household. For that matter, neither was there a need to use the term affirmative action.

No-fault divorce is one of those easily argued policies adopted by Americans in the 1960s because, well, who was going to argue against it? After all, no one is going to be faulted and that is a good thing, is it not? Well, I shall argue against it. Economically, sociologically, and for the sake of the fatherless children, no-fault divorce has proven to be a disaster. The presence of a strong father in the home, to say nothing of a strong mother, has been sorely missing in America for generations now, and America has suffered in so many ways because of it. I cannot imagine how America can ever recapture the security that was lost when family life became embattled. Earlier in this book, I said that "these fifty chaotic years were the consequence of an ongoing breakdown of authority from the late 1960s through to the 2020s with every moral certitude being challenged, many moral certitudes discarded..." Then I added, "Whatever was the cause, during my life, I have seen a near-total collapse of the moral authority of institutions..." The breakdown of the family was perhaps the most critical breakdown.

I am not saying that divorce should always be impossible, but it should be difficult to obtain, as a death certificate is difficult to obtain. Okay, I exaggerate. But only a little. After Judy vacated the premises, I began ten unexpected years of a second bachelorhood. My children lived nearby, and Annie pretty much lived with me. Judy informed me as she left that "No woman will ever look at you." It was another miscalculation on her part. My bachelorhood began about a month later, and I rarely had a quarrel with what turned out to be a very pleasant experience with the opposite sex. I never had an unhappy experience with anyone I dated. Of course, I never took liberties with any of them, but then, I never had to. Supposedly, the battle of the sexes was roaring in those days, and when I look at the likes of Harvey Weinstein and Bill Cosby and Charlie Rose, I can understand that the battle got pretty rough at times. Surely some of these women were cruelly used, but others should have had better taste. Incidentally, Rose once turned up at my office in Bloomington to interview me. I believe he was then employed by the Reverend Bill Moyers. At the end of the interview, I agreed to guide him out of town in my car. Leading him up to a stoplight, I had the disagreeable experience of his trying to bully me off the road so he could make a red light. He did not make it.

Needless to say, in the battle of the sexes, I was a full-time pacifist. And after a decade of very sweet women, I found the one for me. Or I should say that an extraordinary woman found the woman for me. It was 1995, and the indefatigable Barbara Olson, celebrating her fortieth birthday, seated me with a garrulous gasbag on my right and what was to become the light of my life on my left. Her name remains Jeanne Hauch, and I have been married to her for more than twenty-five rewarding years. Barbara Olson was a bridesmaid at our wedding and her husband was the best man. September 11, 2001, is a bitterly sad day for us both, for that is the day Barbara died heroically when American Airlines Flight 77 plowed into the Pentagon. She had delayed her departure a day so she could awaken with her husband, the solicitor general, Ted Olson, on his birthday. The two talked to each other on their cell phones until the very end. Their last words only Ted knows.

One of the things that I have never gotten used to, as an editor, is dealing with an aggrieved complainant. Why do they not just write a letter to the editor or, better yet, an article? We have printed lively articles taking an adversarial position to *The American Spectator*. I am, however, much more patient than Bill Buckley, who upon hearing from a complainant who ordered him to "Cancel my subscription" replied, "Cancel *your own* goddamn subscription." I avoid such strong language.

The American Spectator has always been a staunchly conservative libertarian magazine, but we also publish pieces that do not slavishly follow the party line, which gets us into trouble with some true believers. At the end of 1983, we published a piece by Joseph W. Bishop Jr. of Yale Law School. Joe was a neocon, and he took a conventional view of Wisconsin's Senator Joe McCarthy, the famous anti-Communist. Still, Bishop wrote and argued with verve. Nonetheless, all hell broke out when his review appeared. He had not only attacked the senator, but he took several swipes at the lawyer Roy Cohn, who had worked for the senator. For almost six months, the reverberations were being

heard. One rebuke came from Roy himself, a man I had met occasionally at conservative gatherings and who possessed a reputation for
vindictiveness. When he called, he was mostly polite, though there
was an air of menace in his voice. He seemed to be complaining that
Bishop had called him a homosexual—which all agreed he was—and
that the charge was libelous—which it was not. If I recall, I told him he
had committed a "double negative." That was the last I heard of him,
but it was probably the most threatening complaint I have received in
more than fifty years of editing *The American Spectator*. If Roy Cohn
had sued me for libel, it would be in keeping with what was emerging as a perverse finding at the magazine. Though we were staunchly
conservative, it was troublemakers on the right that caused us more
damage than troublemakers on the left. We could always deal with
the Left, for instance, the Clintons. It was the people on the right that
caused the most trouble.

The only threat to me that I sensed might be more dangerous than
Cohn's came a few years later from a writer who was diagnosed as a
paranoid schizophrenic, and who is now safely deceased. He showed
up at our Arlington, Virginia, offices in the late 1980s and insisted
on talking to me in language that suggested to my secretary, Jenny
Woodward, that he had ulterior motives. I was not in the office, though
a couple of young staffers were, and one, Greg Gutfeld, who would
make his name on Fox News years later, rose to the occasion. After
telling Jenny to call the police, he prudently offered the suspected
assassin a drink at a local bar, the Keyhole Inn. It was another occasion
when, contrary to popular opinion, a strong drink proved to be a welcome alternative to violence. Gutfeld mollified our guest with literary
praise for his talent and a few more drinks. Then he directed him to
Capitol Hill. Later, when Gutfeld checked with the police, he discovered that the would-be assassin could not be arrested until he took a
shot at me. Yet if he merely threatened a congressman, he would be
marched off to the calaboose. So, presumably, Gutfeld did the humane
thing when he directed our friend to Capitol Hill, though I was uneasy

about Gutfeld's interview with the police. At any rate, we never saw the suspected assassin again.

It was at about this time—the mid-eighties—that the magazine got into a kerfuffle with the Catholic hierarchy in Indianapolis, headed by a pompous archbishop named Edward T. O'Meara. At IU, there was a much-beloved priest presiding over the Newman Club, Father Jim Higgins, a close friend of the great basketball coach Bob Knight and Baron Von Kannon. He was my friend, too. You might recall that I mentioned Father Higgins earlier on in our joint operation against the Bloomington Hospital. Without any regard for the IU community or Father Higgins, O'Meara yanked him from his parish and replaced him with two, utterly foolish, arrested adolescents whose idea of Sunday Mass was some sort of a séance. Eventually, both left the priesthood, though one made his plans known from the pulpit. He told the faithful that he was leaving the priesthood to become a massage therapist (!) and invited them to join his clientele.

Our first line of attack was, of course, ridicule; and in our April 1984 issue, we launched the "Find the Fattest Bishop Contest." To enter, all that was necessary was that a prospective sponsor find a bishop who was violently opposed to the economic system that enriched his bishopric, which is to say, capitalism. Also, the candidate must be a shameless hedonist as measured by his girth on a scale certified by the National Livestock Producers Association. I thought that last detail would limit participation, but it did not. The "Find the Fattest Bishop Contest" was a worldwide success. One gentleman sent his entry all the way from Tokyo, signing it merely, "A Tokyo Spectator." His candidate was Patriarch Pimen of Moscow, who our Japanese friend said provided anti-capitalist quotes throughout the English-language edition of the monthly *Journal of the Moscow Patriarchate*. Well, we could not afford the airfare to either Tokyo or Moscow, so we thanked our loyal Japanese reader but gave the award to Archbishop O'Meara and forgot about it until the night of March 19, 1985, President Ronald Reagan's state dinner for Argentine president Raúl Alfonsín.

I was invited, and, in fact, I was featured in the second paragraph of the *Washington Post*'s report on the dinner along with Gina Lollobrigida. There was, however, someone else at the White House that night who fetched my attention even more than Gina. That would be Archbishop Pio Laghi, pro-nuncio of the Holy See. Archbishop O'Meara had not been very grateful to us for our generous award to him, and now was my opportunity to bring instances of the fat bishop's boorishness right to the Pope. Archbishop Pio Laghi was Pope John Paul's ambassador to Washington. As the original George Washington Plunkitt might say, "I seen my opportunities and I took 'em."

Shortly after my visit with Laghi at the White House, we arranged to meet at Laghi's embassy on Massachusetts Avenue across from the vice president's residence. He was a very pleasant man, easy to talk with, and so I was not diffident about raising questions about our worldly archbishop, his disruptive appointment of two roués for a traditional priest at the Newman Club, and about rumors of sexual errancy in the American Catholic Church. His answers seemed candid. He said the Pope was aware of the rumors. The Holy Father was pursuing them, and, with regard to Archbishop O'Meara, that his days were numbered. I left the embassy confident I had made my point. Now, decades later, I am not so sure.

Traversing more than fifty years of public life during a time of ongoing tumult, I have come across a few extraordinary figures, particularly when it came to the peaceful ending of the Cold War. One was Roger Scruton, the British philosopher and Cold Warrior, who bravely slipped behind the Iron Curtain time and again to reenforce the message of freedom, most notably to the people of the former Czechoslovakia, now the Czech Republic. When I arrived there at the end of the Cold War, some young freedom fighters showed me around. Stopping on the historic Charles Bridge in Prague with tourists scurrying about us, they showed me where, before the fall of Communism, they had been lured by pretty girls and beaten to a pulp by the police. Then one fellow asked why I had not followed Scruton and come to Prague before the fall. Actually, it never had occurred to me that I could. Would not our government object, and, by the way, what if I caused an international incident? I have never spent even a night in jail.

As for Roger, I always thought of him as a lonely evangelist of freedom, and I got to know him pretty well before he died in 2020. He showed up frequently at the Travellers Club in London where I often stayed, and where I got him to write for *The American Spectator*. He participated in our 1983 USIA event at the American embassy in London. Somewhere along the way, he pleased me immensely by remarking that my coinage for feminists, "the women of the fevered brow," would stick. It did not, but at least the term *Kultursmog* has been attributed to me in the Urban Dictionary.

Even braver than the Westerners who defied the Iron Curtain's masters were the victims of Communism who challenged Communism every day. As I have mentioned, I became friendly with Czechs such as Pavel Bratinka, who was trained as a scientist but was handed a shovel by the Communists and ordered to spend his days shoveling coal. Fortunately, Pavel recognized how low the productivity standards were under Czech Communism and so he polished off his quota each day in an hour or so and could spend the rest of the day reading writers such as Hayek, Voegelin, our own Michael Novak, and creators of other forbidden works, preparing him for Communism's fall. He became a great friend of mine from the time I met him in 1991. On one of my first visits to Prague, he directed me to a section of the old city where moth-eaten Red Army uniforms were being sold. Fearing disease, I did not buy a uniform, though I did buy several red stars to wear on my lapel during television performances when I got home. I believe I claimed that with the fall of the Berlin Wall, I had become a Communist. Through the years, our friendship endured. He became a member of the Czech Chamber of Deputies and later undertook the ultimate transition from government service to the private sector. He founded a consulting firm in Prague.

Then there was Vladimir Bukovsky, the famous Soviet dissident who began writing for us in 1980, four years after he was heaved out of the Soviet Union. He was almost exactly a year older than me and spent twelve of his first thirty-four years in prison. He, too, was a man of science, though from high school on he became a ward of the state, being incarcerated in psychiatric hospitals, labor camps, and prisons. It was in those places that he received his real education, which was far superior to mine.

He wrote brilliantly. His great work was *To Build a Castle—My Life as a Dissenter*, but for a sense of how wicked his wit was, here is an excerpt from his article in our October 1984 issue, "America's Crack-Up." He tells his readers that he had been reading Twain and Melville, searching in vain for a precursor to the modern American liberal whom he obviously finds quite looney. From his room at Stanford University, he looks out and eureka:

> [J]ust as I was fishing for an appropriate passage in the old books, I happened to look down to the street—and there he was, our symbol in flesh and blood. Speeding recklessly along on roller skates was a middle-aged Californian (about 45 years old, I'd say, judging by his grayish beard) in defiantly red swimming trunks, mouth chewing gum and steadily making bubbles, ears plugged safely by Walkman earphones. His eyes seemed to be the only part of his body not entirely pleased with their occupation. They expressed total amazement, as if repeating that favorite American phrase: "What's going on here?"

Bukovsky, the Soviet expatriate, concludes, "Irrespective of their age, Americans are supposed to be 'kids,' and the ultimate objective of their lives is to have 'fun.'"

How could Bukovsky write like that when his education was in the prisons and psychiatric hospitals of the Soviet Union? He was made for *The American Spectator*, though, alas, when the Cold War ended, our audience's interests moved on rather rapidly.

Vladimir was staying with me in my McLean home in early February 1987, when I was asked to appear on television. Though he obviously scorned television, he agreed to watch me as I was appearing with the first secretary of the Soviet embassy in Washington, Vitaly Churkin—he being broadcast from his embassy; I being broadcast from the ABC studio. Apparently, ABC had previously broadcast a fictional drama, *Amerika*, portraying our country's sorry plight after being taken over by the Soviet Union. The Kremlin was indignant with ABC's portrayal, and Churkin's task that night was to enlighten Americans as to how benign the Soviets really were and how the present American establishment was a mere tool of, as Churkin put it, "cultural fascism."

Well, Churkin was not a very nice man, and he hardly had begun his spiel when I told him we defeated Hitlerism in 1945, and now we would defeat the closest approximation to Hitlerism extant, Soviet Communism. I began ticking off the similarities, starting with state-supported anti-Semitism, when the television screen abruptly went dark. The airheaded ABC anchor started questioning his studio's engineers about the provenance of the problem when I gently told him the Soviet embassy had "pulled the plug." While the ABC people were still looking around for the unplugged cord or whatever the source of their darkened screen might be, I left for McLean and my friend Bukovsky, who informed me that the diplomat, Churkin, was a colonel in the KGB. Ah, now I understood his rudeness. Incidentally, during the post-Communist regime, Vitaly popped up as Russia's permanent representative to the United Nations. An unemployed KGB agent can always find work in Vladimir Putin's Russian Federation.

As the 1980s lengthened, there seemed to be a renewed interest in the magazine by the media and even by Hollywood. We were publishing conservatives, libertarians, neoconservatives, and evangelicals, all the components of the conservative movement. We even published

Cold War liberals who eventually blended in with us. There was also growth among the liberals with writers splitting off from liberalism to call themselves neoliberals. Of course, there was an ongoing debate between those on the right and the left, but it was relatively civilized by today's standards, and it was usually intelligent, unlike nowadays.

A milestone of this renewed interest in us or at least awareness of us came in November 1984 when I was invited to *The New Republic*'s seventieth-anniversary celebration held in the stately National Portrait Gallery. The invitation came despite certain rude remarks I had recently filed in my scholarly study, *The Liberal Crack-Up*. Perhaps I was invited because I expressed in my November 30, 1984, column that *The New Republic* was one of the intellectual reviews "that boldly faces a changing world and attempts to maintain both high intellectual standards and essential liberal values..."[4] I thought back then—and I still hold this view today—that intellectual reviews, such as *The New Republic* on the sensible left and *The American Spectator* on the sensible right, enrich the life of the mind in the Great Republic. Yet those reviews have declined drastically in importance, having been replaced by, by what? There has been no replacement for the intellectual reviews of the past, and their high-tech replacements are no match for the hard copy issues of yesteryear.

At any rate, *The New Republic*'s seventieth-anniversary dinner was a pleasant evening. Hundreds of people were in attendance, many of them politicians, many more of them writers. Michael Kinsley, then presumed to be the godfather of rising neoliberalism, much as Irving Kristol was the godfather of neoconservatism, was everywhere that night with his ho-ho-ho style and smarty-pants demeanor. The erudite British sage Christopher Hitchens still had twenty-seven years to live, write, and drain scotch bottles or almost any other bottle that caught his eye. Happily, I caught his eye, and he playfully insisted to my wife that I was about to go berserk in the presence of so many left-wingers that night. At the end of the evening, we left with Penn Kemble, a longtime handball partner of mine, and his wife.

Penn, during the late 1960s, had opted for the most principled and austere form of radicalism. He had become a social democrat. The rest of his biography provides a snapshot into life as lived by a principled man on the left in the sixties, seventies, eighties, and nineties—he died in 2005. Wlady and I attended his service at St. John's Episcopal Church in Georgetown. In the pew in front of us was the woebegone former associate attorney general to then president Bill Clinton, Webb Hubbell. He had spent a stretch in the calaboose for Bill, but he was the better man than Bill and also a better man than Hillary.

In the late 1960s, Penn fell out of favor with the liberals by opposing violence on campus and favoring effective prosecution of the Vietnam War. He was to suffer their further disapproval in the 1980s by opposing the Sandinistas' dictatorship in Nicaragua and supporting aid to the Contras. Being a good liberal as life progressed became less a matter of adhering to timeless principles and more a matter of conforming to an exacting, if ever-changing, etiquette. Penn was not a proper conformist, and he eventually would become a neoconservative.

We left with him that night, but first, we had to sit through the evening's keynote speaker, Betty Friedan, the era's leading screamer for feminism. There she stood, bellowing as we sipped our espresso and longed for home: "...have it all...we've come a long way...still a long way to go...but now, feminism's *second stage*!" Duck! I feared she was about to start throwing things. No, no, she regained her control. In the distant future, when America's war between the sexes is looked back on as but another chapter in human folly, equal in futility to, say, Prohibition or militant vegetarianism or Napoleon's invasion of Russia, Ms. Friedan's excretions of cant will be wholly incomprehensible.

As Betty was accepting the applause of the audience, I looked across the dinner table to exchange smiles with my wife, but to my surprise, she was not amused. Rather, she appeared to be in some sort of turmoil. When the speeches shut down, I hastened to her side. By then she had recovered and was, in fact, just a little pleased. She had been seated with an anurous little man on the far side of middle age who was *Newsweek*'s Washington bureau chief, the respected Mel Elfin. As soon as Friedan had piped up about raised consciousness and how far women had come, Elfin began playing pizzicato with his hand up my wife's leg, apparently impervious to Ms. Friedan's message. During dinner, he had won my wife's admiration by telling her how highly he esteemed me, having followed my career from its earliest triumphs. Well, that night he allowed his interest in my career to go too far, and I looked around for him, but Mel had departed, and I had missed my opportunity to validate Hitch's assessment of me.

More evidence of interest in us came over the next year. *The American Spectator* had readers in Hollywood, though not many. One was Charlton Heston, who corresponded with me for years and invited me to his performance of *A Man for All Seasons* when I was in London. We also spent a day over lunch at his home high on a promontory above Coldwater, California. He was a great gentleman and a marvelous storyteller. Another prominent actor was John Wayne, who never passed up an opportunity to chide me and my disrelish for violence in the movies. I actually was a fan of his Westerns and did not mind the rough stuff, which never seemed gratuitous. Yet I remain critical of the fanciful and brutal violence that increasingly has taken over Hollywood's productions and apparently thrills the country's low-grade morons.

I have through the years become familiar with other Hollywood figures through the work I did helping my friend, Steve Tesich, to film his movie, *Breaking Away*, in Bloomington, and other Hollywood figures whom Vivi Crespi introduced to me, for instance, Pamela Mason, the wife of James Mason, and her family. Also, I spent time in Dublin where, through my friend, the actress Jeananne Crowley, I came into contact with actors and actresses associated with the famed Gate Theatre. In Dublin, the indigenous Irish often assumed that I was one of their countrymen until I began to speak and revealed my Yankee roots. I even found a Dubliner from the theater troop to play handball with me at Dublin's Croke Park.

That the editor in chief of *The American Spectator* would establish relations with the likes of Charlton Heston and John Wayne should come as no surprise, but I received a jolt at Christmastime 1985 when I received a seasonal card from Jane Fonda and her husband Tom Hayden. Actually, I received the card from their whole family. Tom, I had met in broadcast studios from time to time, and he was always strangely subdued. Would Jane share her husband's timorousness? We two fitness enthusiasts could talk about physical fitness, though it would be just like me to bring up her various friendly encounters with the North Vietnamese or her infatuation with the barbarous Reverend Jim Jones of the Jonestown massacre in Guyana.

A few months later, I was taken aback when I received a postcard from a Hollywood figure with obvious literary ambitions: Madonna, the entertainer, not the religious figure. There she was, appearing on the photo side of the postcard, looking at me seductively, wearing a bustier, and adorned with a surfeit of jewelry. Above her heaving right breast were the words "MADONNA—like a virgin." Well, she would have fooled me! On the other side of the card, she wrote in the boxy handwriting of a young girl: "Hi Dude," and she proceeded with "You got something in for me? I mean, every time I read the *Spectator* I'm the editorial. Look, if I weren't married I'd do a number on you in the women's room at Danceteria. But sorry now, you can try and you can die, but I won't let you play! Bye—Madonna." The postcard had all the hallmarks of a young girl smitten by the literary itch right down to the stamp. It commemorated America's first Nobel Prize winner in literature, Sinclair Lewis. I had to admire her industriousness and responded promptly with "If you want to be published in *The American Spectator*, I suggest you send us your poetry through conventional channels where it will be judged on its merits independent of your salacious suggestions." Perhaps I should have added that I am a well-known hypochondriac and any variation of sexual congress with me was off limits, no matter how raunchy her poetry or limericks or whatever she had in mind.

Whatever the case, sexual congress or simply a friendly tête-à-tête over tea with this troubled woman was, at this point, impossible. The winds of history were about to pick up. First, there was Iran-Contra, then the first stirrings of the conservative crack-up, and finally the early stages of what was to become the polarization of American politics. Ronald Reagan's "Morning in America" was about to be undone by what has become a theme of these fifty or so years, Episodic Chaos. It began on November 3, 1986. A Lebanese magazine, *Al-Shiraa*, had just run a story alleging that the United States government had engaged in an arms-for-hostages deal with the Islamist mullahs then running Iran. Seven Americans were being held hostage in Lebanon by Hezbollah, a paramilitary terror group with ties to Iran's Revolutionary Guard. The alleged deal would have been in violation of the US arms embargo. The Iran-Contra affair had begun. Even a chat with Madonna on the telephone was now out of the question.

Working in the White House at the time was a man who was to become a close associate to me at the magazine three decades later, Jeff Lord. He was then serving in the Reagan White House's Political Affairs office, and he was with the president the day the *Al-Shiraa* story broke. He and his colleagues were standing around the president at the famous Resolute desk for a photo session. When the pictures had been taken, they attempted to leave, but the president bid them to wait. Amidst the chaos of the day, he raised his hand, and looking at them squarely, said: "I want you to know. I have done nothing wrong." Jeff was startled and spoke up, assuring the president that they all knew that. Then Jeff recalls that the president "smiled a bit."

When Jeff told me this story, I was immediately reminded of my own meeting with the president, some months after Jeff's meeting, as the Iran-Contra story was coming to a full boil. By then, on March 30, 1987, he had admitted to transferring in his words, "defensive weapons and spare parts for defensive systems to Iran" for the purpose of easing tensions and opening a dialogue with Iran. He had appointed Attorney General Ed Meese to complete an investigation and discover if wrongdoing had been committed. He admitted that the National Security Council erred in implementing his foreign policy. Ollie North was fired, and Admiral John Poindexter resigned. An independent counsel was hired. The Tower Commission was convened, and on March 4, 1987, in a televised address, the president took "full responsibility for my own actions and for those of my administration," but he added that he was not previously aware of the money transfers to the Contras.[5]

So it was that on March 30, I met with the president in the Oval Office, precisely six years to the day and the hour that an assassin tried to kill him. I was with Ken Cribbs, an old friend who before his White House stint headed the Intercollegiate Studies Institute. Washington was abuzz with Iran-Contra rumors, one of which was that the president was hopelessly out of touch with the daily details of the government. Not a bad position to be in from my point of view, given the fact that President Reagan's predecessor, Jimmy Carter, had engorged himself on the esoterica of government, starting with the policing of the White House thermostats to presiding over the government's foreign and domestic policy. Yet the president's assistant presidents had cowed him into memorizing facts and figures and every aspect of the Iran-Contra controversy. At one point, I think I said, "Hey, Mr. President, I'm on your side." Like Jeff Lord, I believed that President Reagan had "done nothing wrong." History has seemed to agree with the old cowboy—and with me and Jeff Lord.

Yet there were other problems out there. The conservative movement that Ronald Reagan had captured America with was revealing signs of stress. Even more ominous, the comparative feebleness of the conservative political libido, which provided us at *The American Spectator* with so much amusement, was about to reveal its unfunny side. It was about to allow the defeat of a nominee to the Supreme Court. On July 1, 1987, Ronald Reagan stepped to the microphones and, with ill-considered joviality, announced that Judge Robert H. Bork of the United States Court of Appeals for the District of Columbia was his nominee to replace Justice Lewis F. Powell. The first problem was what we at the *Spectator* called the conservative crack-up. I wrote a book about it, and it has been vindicated. A later book by me was titled *The Death of Liberalism*. It, too, has been vindicated. The second problem had no formal title, but as the years rolled on, it was recognized as polarization, *political* polarization, and it grew into a critical problem facing the country.

The failure of the Bork nomination highlighted both the conservative crack-up and the conservatives' weak political libido that allowed the country's eventual political polarization. It was a major historic event and deserves more attention, for by the twenty-first century, the political polarization of the parties had reached a crisis.

Wlady noticed the stress on the conservative movement before I did. At the beginning of this memoir, I chronicled the attention that we early members of the conservative movement paid to each other. I was going to New York and Washington frequently, and conservative leaders were visiting us and other conservatives in their haunts and on their campuses, too. Yet by the mid-1980s we were all too busy, as Wlady noted, and there was something else. We were all avid for fame, and the itch for fame got worse. A younger generation had joined the movement, bringing their huge self-regard to it. What is more, there was the sense that fame afforded conservatives too few outlets. We suffered from a well-known condition. Sociologists of the Caribbean call it "crab antics." When one tips forward a pail of crabs, the crabs at the bottom of the pail pull the crabs that are about to escape back into the pail. Eric Hoffer, the longshoreman philosopher of the 1950s came at it from a different perspective when he wrote in *Temper of Our Time*, "What starts out here as a mass movement ends up as a racket, a cult, or a corporation."[6] Either way, the unity of purpose that we saw in the early years of the Reagan administration was slipping away. The conservative libido was too weak to preserve our common sense of winning. The Left rarely has such problems.

We at *The American Spectator* had our first taste of crab antics and, for that matter, a foretaste of the conservative crack-up in 1985 when a reporter came out to Bloomington from *Vanity Fair* magazine to immortalize me. He followed me around in what for him was apparently foreign territory, a Middle American town—somehow, he lost sight of the university that was nearby. Then he attended with me a Washington meeting of the Committee for the Free World—more foreign territory. Jeane Kirkpatrick and Sidney Hook and other conservative luminaries were there—foreign territory to the utmost. As he progressed in his project, I received alarming calls from friends claiming that the *Vanity Fair* chap had become panicky. No one whom he interviewed had anything negative to say about me! What was he to do? Reporting an accurate depiction of me was unthinkable.

Yet he finally struck pay dirt. We had an intern from the early 1980s who now produced fine movie reviews for us. I knew his parents very well. I admired them and so I put up with his pretensions. His name was Johnny Podhoretz. He was perfectly capable of describing me as a "relative you have to tolerate." Or "He's provincial…" Or "Bob would attract young talent and then he would make their lives miserable, because Bob is one of these people that needs sycophants." All of the above quotes I have lifted from *Vanity Fair*'s final product. I thought of firing him after I discovered his disloyalty, yet his mother interceded on his behalf, quite properly I would say. I have had a mother too. She said I should punch him in the nose but lay off his career. And his brother-in-law, who had gotten his start at *The American Spectator*, warned him to cut it out, which he did until *Time* magazine did a piece on me, but by that time, we had another movie critic.

It was, however, an alarming sign. Johnny came from the bosom of our movement. I do not believe a left-winger would act that way, and I have known a lot of left-wingers. What is more, the crack-up continued, though we at *The American Spectator* became inured to it. In fact, the embarrassment of some conservatives at our stories about Bill's sex life often amused us. We were headed for a world where every sexual transgressor was exposed, not just Bill Clinton. We were at the end of the sexual revolution. It was reassuring to know that *The American Spectator* had broken another scoop, though this scoop was not as jarring as the Troopergate stories. With the arrival of the #MeToo movement, the sexual revolution was dead. We at *The American Spectator* were among the first to notice it.

Podhoretz's disloyalty, and the disloyalty of other mostly younger conservatives that followed, was the weakness of spoiled brats who did not understand politics. The crack-up of conservatism on display during Bob Bork's nomination was something more serious. It was to hamstring conservatives for years to come. It began with President Reagan's July announcement. The Reaganites had no idea of the massive force being mounted against them. Their response was puny when compared to the left-wing fury. Some conservatives were simply complacent. Others thought a political campaign for a Supreme Court nomination was unseemly. Withal, it was a failure to act politically. The conservatives did not seem to realize that the struggle for the Court had become political and would last for years. There was, for instance, the Democrats' "lynching" of Clarence Thomas, their mendacious character assassination of Brett Kavanaugh, and their attempt to banish Amy Coney Barrett, who, I thought, pretty much buried the Senate's miscreants.

Which of these proceedings was more barbaric, I shall leave to historians who specialize in social decay. It is enough to say that objectivity, truth, and good manners were never in any Democratic senator's playbook. It was also an astonishing display of cultural domination, in this case, the domination of the *Kultursmog*. Judge Bork, a highly educated scholar, a graduate of the University of Chicago, a former professor at Yale Law School, whose nomination to a lower court but five years before had easily been accepted, now sat alone before a Senate panel that included a plagiarist who was to become president of the United States, two campus cheats, various drunks, and a famed womanizer who left a woman to drown in his submerged vehicle while he went back to his hotel room to call family advisors and get some sleep.

Said the senator who left the corpse in his car back in 1969, the Honorable Edward Kennedy, also known as the Lion of the Senate:

> Robert Bork's America is a land in which women would be forced into back-alley abortions, blacks would sit at segregated lunch counters, rogue police could break down citizens' doors in midnight raids, and school children could not be taught about evolution, writers and artists would be censored at the whim of government, and the doors of the federal courts would be shut on the fingers of millions of citizens.

There were other indignities that the Judge had to endure. For instance, the outburst of Senator Howell Heflin, who actually queried the judge about his beard and later commented that Judge Bork had "a strange lifestyle" and was "some kind of right-wing freak."[7] Heflin grew up in Alabama during an era when animals such as him still lynched blacks. He and fifty-seven other senators rejected Judge Bork's nomination on October 23, 1987.

For now, the era of Episodic Chaos was adjourned. A period of Episodic Calm ensued. Ever since 1981, when President Reagan reopened disarmament talks with the Soviet Union and floated a "zero-zero" proposal for mutual destruction of all intermediate-range nuclear missiles on either side, he was steadily inching toward an end to hostilities with the Soviets. Indeed, as the commentator Paul Lettow has claimed, Reagan is more properly called a "nuclear abolitionist" than a warmonger, as his critics on the left do.[8] In 1983, he placed intermediate-range ballistic missiles (IRBMs) in Europe, hoping to deter the SS-20s, which the Soviets had put in Europe, though Reagan's IRBMs were used as bargaining chips. When in 1983, he announced his Strategic Defense Initiative (SDI) and offered it to the Soviets, it was in keeping with his long-range goal. He believed it would render nuclear missiles "impotent and obsolete." In November 1985, when he met Mikhail Gorbachev for the first time in Geneva, a major topic for discussion was SDI. Gorbachev was against it. He feared his country could not keep up with the United States. He was as adamant when next they met in October 1986 in Reykjavík. Yet, Reagan and Gorbachev were making genuine headway toward peace. When next they met on December 8, 1987, they signed the INF Treaty eliminating an entire category of nuclear weapons for the first time and laying the foundation for President George H. W. Bush to complete the first Strategic Arms Reduction Treaty. President Reagan's critics continued to call him a warmonger, and conservatives such as Howard Phillips called him "a useful idiot for Soviet propaganda," but the Cold War was almost over thanks to Ronald Reagan's perseverance.[9]

I was invited to a question-and-answer session for a small group of journalists with the president two days after the historic signing. We were among the first journalists to meet with him. Waiting with me outside the Oval Office that day was Georgie Anne Geyer, a syndicated columnist, Philip Geyelin of the *Washington Post*, and Ben Wattenberg, an old friend who had crossed over from the liberal camp years before. Ben sat down next to me and earnestly asked what I intended to ask the president. I was reminded of an old joke of Evelyn Waugh's, and I said, "Ben I intend to ask the president, 'Mr. President, precisely what evidence have you that President Gorbachev is not a woman?'" Ben was horrified. He pleaded with me not to do it. He rightly believed that I was about to hog all the publicity. I relented. Upon entering the Oval Office, Ben asked the president, "Have we won the Cold War?" His answer was unfocused. I then pushed harder, "Well, have we?"[10] The president nodded, yes. The media was giving Gorbachev all the credit for reaching an agreement that was mostly confected by the old cowboy. Now Reagan had weighed in with his side of the story, albeit with a little help from *The American Spectator*.

In the early spring of 1988, the president accepted an invitation from me to dine at my home in Northern Virginia. He had had me in and out of his house for almost eight years, so I thought it was time to reciprocate. When I sent my invitation to him, the Tyrrell household was relatively peaceful, but by the time he had accepted, my wife had begun her divorce proceedings. Given that the president traveled with an ample Secret Service detail and, I was told, he brought his own White House bartender, I thought it would be safe for him at my home, at least, for a few hours. Surely the Secret Service when in my house at least carried Tasers. So, we settled on July 26, despite the fact that down in Havana, Fidel Castro reserved that night to celebrate his 26 de Julio movement, the one that left Cuba as such a hellhole. Aside from the president, his wife, and 250 or so security agents, I invited ten of my most promising young conservatives, conservatives likely to leave a mark on the future. Several of them, like the president, had been liberals in their early years. But only one of my guests had clung to, at least, parts of the liberal political libido, Ronald Reagan. As mentioned earlier, that explains how he remained focused on his trinity of goals: defeating the Soviets, cutting taxes, and reviving American greatness.

A week before the president's arrival, the Secret Service stopped by the house with a dozen White House personnel to arrange communications, security, and the president's cocktail. Then the Secret Service ingratiated me to my neighbors by interviewing every one of them about their personal arms caches. Next, the Secret Service sent a swarm of helicopters overhead to photograph the neighbors' yards for random missile silos and perhaps to get a shot of a nude yuppie sunning herself by the pool—even the scar from her appendectomy would not be missed by their powerful cameras. A sobering note was struck when the Secret Service asked me for the location of the nearest hospital capable of landing a helicopter. For a week, unexpected visitors would ride through the neighborhood, and a day or so before "D-day," the telephone company began putting in extra wires with

R. EMMETT TYRRELL JR.

the assistance of White House communications experts—twelve lines were needed.

The day of the dinner, a team of cooks, waiters, and butlers flew down from New York, for by this time my wife had forsaken home and hearth for the tennis court—the formidable Pat Buckley arranged the caterers for me. She sent down New York's finest, Glorious Foods! An hour after the caterers' late-morning flight, LaGuardia was socked in by a furious rainstorm that was moving in on the entire East Coast. As the hours passed, Teddy Forstmann, chairman of *The American Spectator* board of directors, reported worsening climatic conditions that will bar him from flying our New York guests down on his private jet. Teddy was a fiercely determined fellow; if he cannot get his plane into the air, the weather in New York must be ghastly. Soon came word that Nancy Reagan, too, was stranded in the Manhattan deluge. I scrambled to find suitable standby guests, as a last-minute flight from New York seemed improbable.

The action picked up steadily through the afternoon. A military buildup was taking place in my neighborhood. By four o'clock, twenty-five security cars filled with cops and police dogs have parked along the streets by my home, serving as barricades lest terrorists aim an armored personnel carrier at my living room at the end of our cul-de-sac. Checkpoints have been set up to bar the unauthorized from the neighborhood. My house is evacuated as dogs search for bombs—completely missing my son's arsenal of fireworks. But they do not miss my houseguest, John O'Sullivan, who is hustled out onto the lawn in the middle of shaving. John's presence made history, for on this day, he became the only man known to have begun his day in London taking morning coffee with Prime Minister Thatcher and ending it three thousand miles away in McLean, Virginia, over dinner with President

Reagan—a feat made possible by the technology of the supersonic Concorde and the politics of a spreading conservative movement.*

By five o'clock, radar and lights have been strung around the house and in the forest behind it. Seventy sharpshooters, Secret Service agents, and local police are in and out of our walk-in basement, where we have set up a buffet, and where the sharpshooters talk endlessly about the same topics, then favored by university profs, to wit, real estate prices and personal incomes. The communications center is in the garage. The twelve telephones are there, in the library and in the guest room, which is also fitted out for the "football," an attaché case with the codes to activate the US nuclear arsenal. Yes, I got *that* close to our nuclear codes. (Later, the ubiquitous Greg Gutfeld got even closer, and as a result, a Secret Service agent put him up against a wall. Greg was nonetheless rewarded after dinner by being allowed to eat President Reagan's leftovers. Or, as he was to put it through the years, "I shared a dinner with Ronald Reagan on July 26, 1988.") Guests, rain-soaked and bewildered, are now passing a security check and entering through the garage. Soon I shall greet the president in this same inelegant room amongst bicycles and gardening equipment—our front door is deemed too exposed for use by the president of the United States.

Trying to relax, my guests have drinks in the living room where I have arranged appropriate background music as we await the president. There are supercilious devotees of serious music who sniff at the idea of it being used as background music. They insist that it was written to be wept over and otherwise to exacerbate neurosis. This

---

* John had arrived to become editor of *National Review*, and *The Washington Post*'s story about him is an illuminating example of how the *Kultursmog* obscures a reality of which it disapproves. The *Post*'s Sidney Blumenthal was frequently reporting on conservatives in those days. In fact, it seemed that conservatism had become his beat. Here is how he keeps the dimensions of conservatism's ascendency manageable: "On Tuesday morning, O'Sullivan has a long chat with British Prime Minister Margaret Thatcher in London…. In the evening he dined with President Reagan in Washington…" Where did he dine, Sidney? Was it at McDonald's?

notion is, if you allow me, doltish. Haydn wrote music, much of it in symphonic form, to be played while listeners performed such normal bodily functions as eating, drinking, and gossiping. Other composers did the same. I had laid hands on the perfect background music for dinner with the liberator of Grenada and the pacifier of Libya, symphonies and flute concerti composed by Frederick the Great, king of Prussia. Two years earlier, when I had Bill Casey and his wife for dinner to observe May Day, my twelve-year-old daughter Katy found an exquisite record to help us solemnize the economic miracles of Marxist-Leninism, a recording of wolf calls titled *The Music and Language of the Wolves*. I think Robert Redford narrated it or he should have narrated it. Now, in honor of Fidel Castro, we turned to the music of an enlightened despot, Frederick the Great.

As the sough of the orchestra radiated softly from the living room speakers, an importunate White House aide began popping in, announcing the president's progress toward my house. "The president has left the White House," she announces. O'Sullivan orders his first American-made cocktail of the day. "The president is coming up the George Washington Parkway, Mr. Tyrrell," the officious lady continues. My guest, Lally Weymouth, is becoming visibly distressed, not about the president's progress, but by the music. "He is fifteen minutes away, Mr. Tyrrell." "He is five minutes…" "Please," I say, "you are unnerving my guests"; whereupon the entire front of the house lights up. Helicopters thrash overhead. My wife and I hasten into the garage, where through a steady downpour, we see Acting White House Press Secretary Marlin Fitzwater and Chief of Staff Ken Duberstein holding umbrellas above a bemused Ronald Reagan. Rain splattering at their feet, all three are illuminated in a mysterious shaft of light. Behind them, the presidential seal is resplendent on the door of a huge White House limousine. A similar car purrs behind it, that being a dummy to dupe would-be assassins. The caravan includes motorcycles (twelve of them, my son P. D. later reports). Two ambulances, two vans with Secret Service agents, a van containing the night's press pool ("the death watch") and overhead the source of that shaft of light, a helicopter, perhaps two.

In a Washington rush hour made more impossible, still, by a monsoon, the cops have blocked traffic on the George Washington Memorial Parkway, the Capital Beltway, and a nearby congested country road. All this so that I can introduce the president of our democratic republic to the music of Frederick the Great. My driveway is a chaos of police lights and revving engines from which I now extricate my distinguished guest. Into the serenity of my garage, he comes with only half a dozen aides, including the White House doctor, the White House bartender (carrying the president's vodka and orange juice), and an Air Force officer (carrying "the football"). The other one hundred or so cops stationed from the checkpoint down the road to my front door and the seventy other security personnel in and around the house itself are not invited. Over a grease spot, we shake hands, and President Reagan says, "Bob, I apologize for all this."

We deposit the president's retinue in the family room, and I lead the president through double doors that open down into a sunken living room. The doors slam shut. There is a hush of quiet. The president is standing among us. The melodies of a Prussian emperor insulate us from the pandemonium outside. The president smiles at my guests, but before he can sit down, there is alarm in his eyes, and hastily he retreats through the double doors. Had the Secret Service noticed something amiss? Was my wife becoming agitated?

As it turns out, my apprehensions were unwarranted. Within minutes, the president reemerges, explaining that his doctor had replaced a failing hearing aid battery—now he can really enjoy the music! The White House bartender brings him the presidential cocktail, a screwdriver. Frederick the Great's orchestra saws away from behind a bookshelf. And the conversation begins, along with photographs—an American president goes no place without White House photographers. My wife was fine. In fact, she was splendid, a reprise of days gone by. It was Lally who imposed on me to turn the music down.

A final guest, *The American Spectator*'s assistant managing editor, Andy Ferguson, sloshed into the room. He was one of our most gifted writers with a knack for the woebegone drollery. At the last minute, he was drafted to take the place of our grounded New Yorkers (Forstmann was still indignant and calling in about every half hour to denounce the clouds). The congestion caused by the presidential caravan has forced Andy to walk half a mile through the rain. He makes his ordeal sound like the Italian army's retreat from Caporetto, as imagined in Hemingway's *A Farewell to Arms*. I hint to the president that we are slightly behind schedule, and that is all this most agreeable guest of honor needs; he hastily downs his second screwdriver, and we enter the dining room, where the palaver about politics continues.

The president's first concern is the Soviet Union, whose leader, Mikhail Gorbachev, has recently signed a historic treaty with him. The president, despite critics such as Howard Phillips, is convinced that change is in the air in Moscow. The president believes that the people of the Godless Soviet Union now long for God in Russia. On this subject, he turns pensive, almost distracted. But back to politics. He is eager to get on the campaign trail for George Bush, though the pundits doubt his sincerity. The president insists that the Democratic candidate, Massachusetts' Governor Michael Dukakis, is wrecking his state's economy. What is more, he is incensed by Dukakis's recent charges that the Republican Party is the instrument of the rich. He believes that his policies have made it the party of the mainstream while the Democrats have moved off to exotic parts. "I didn't leave them," he claims, "they left me." It is a revelation he has uttered before and will utter again. But then he observes that "It's hard for people to give up party allegiance." He himself did not become a Republican until 1962. He ran for the governorship reluctantly, but then he adds "five or six months into the governorship, I realized politics is more exciting than anything I'd ever done before."

The evening is winding down. My seven-year-old daughter Annie squeezes past the legs of Secret Service Agent Shanahan and says,

"Now, Daddy?" I growl, "Autographs come later," but the president overrules me, saying, "Let her get her autograph," and merrily he takes her under his arm. Then he signs autographs for Katy and P. D., too. I have already given him our pièce de résistance, an artist's conception of *Reagan on the Rock.* That is to say, a drawing of how we envision he will look once we launch our campaign for "Ronald Reagan on Mount Rushmore." Actually, we had no such campaign planned, but over the next few days, it had roused so much interest in us from the media that we immediately convened "The Committee for Monumental Progress." In fact, anytime I wanted to draw attention to *The American Spectator*, we announced some new initiative by the Committee. It worked for several years. Such nonsense comported with the media's sense of conservativism. It took an amazingly long time before the media realized that we were pulling their legs.

As I headed off to bed that evening, I thought of the remnants of Ronald Reagan's liberal past that he had brought to conservatism, his surviving political libido. We saw it in his tenacity for focusing on the Soviet Union, tax cuts, and renewing the promise of America. I personally saw it in his efforts to create a conservative culture to oppose the *Kultursmog.* That was one goal too many for him, and anyway, there were not enough conservatives who shared his unique political libido. Of course, the president was no ideologue, much less a utopian; those values were buried long ago in his liberal past.

Ronald Reagan, in his maturity, was a man governed not by the ideology of a liberal but by the *disposition* of a conservative. Au fond, he was governed by the disposition to delight in what is present rather than what is not or what may not even be. He, like all my guests on the evening of July 26 stood with the conservative Michael Oakeshott when he wrote: "To be conservative, then, is to prefer the familiar to the unknown, to prefer the tried to the untried, fact to mystery, the actual to the possible, the limited to the unbounded, the near to the distant, the sufficient to the superabundant, the convenient to the perfect, present laughter to utopian bliss."[11]

That night in Virginia, we had an abundance of laughter.

Chapter VIII

THE END OF THE COLD WAR, AND NORMAN MAILER MEETS THE CIA'S DEPUTY SECRETARY

*O*n June 12, 1987, President Ronald Reagan, with the Brandenburg Gate as a historic backdrop, enunciated words that resonated for years to come. He said, "Mr. Gorbachev, tear down this wall." The wall was the Berlin Wall, and for more than twenty-five years, Germans had tried to escape the wall's confines. A few made it, but many perished in trying. Interestingly, despite the incidence of Marxism in the West, especially on college campuses, no one ever tried to undertake the surreptitious journey in reverse, from West to East. Not even a chuckleheaded Western Marxist would attempt it, for instance, say, Theodor Adorno. He was the celebrated Marxist mesmerizer at the Frankfurt School in West Germany. Yet even he knew that it was too dangerous, but then, he deemed a lot of things dangerous. Do you remember his lonely expiry a few months after he was mobbed in his classroom by Teutonic beauties stripped to the waist, armed with flowers, and in an inordinate state of excitement?

Then a couple of years later on the evening of November 9, 1989, after a day of comic indecision by East German authorities, the wall's destruction began, not at Gorbachev's insistence, but at the insistence of ordinary German citizens from both sides of the barricade. They used sledgehammers, chisels, and whatever tools they could get their hands on—a great moment in the history of human freedom was taking place. The Berlin Wall was rubble, and rather surprisingly, within a month, the Iron Curtain was no more. On December 2, George H. W. Bush, the newly elected president, and Mikhail Gorbachev, the Soviet president, met in Valletta, Malta, to discuss nuclear disarmament and ways to strengthen trade relations between their two nations.

As it happened, I appeared that evening on CNN's *Capital Gang*, allegedly to participate in a battle royal with Patrick Buchanan, Al Hunt, and Mark Shields. Bob Novak, the show's dominant voice, was broadcasting from Moscow. It was to be a curious evening. Before the show, sources told me that the Cold War was over, as the Red Army was convinced that it could not machine parts to keep its defenses competitive with our forces. They feared that continuing the Cold War would bankrupt the Soviet Union just as the old cowboy had predicted when he launched the arms race earlier in the decade. Coming on the show that night, I was in a cheerful humor, and I expected the same from my colleagues, both conservative and liberal. Here was something we could agree on. Winning the Cold War was good news, no?

To my amazement, Pat Buchanan, the conservative, and Hunt and Shields, the liberals, were quite gloomy and full of doubt that the Cold War was, in fact, over. From Moscow, Bob was curiously diffident. I kept hammering away at my colleagues' obduracy. We had won! The next morning—though perhaps one had to read the newspapers with care—it was obvious that Bush and Gorbachev were in agreement: The Cold War was over. The December 4, 1989, *New York Times* quoted Gorbachev as saying that he and President Bush agreed that "many things that were characteristic of the Cold War should be abandoned."[1] A few days later, Bob Novak came to my home for dinner and to reprise our show. Bob had some vague idea about making me a regular or at least a semi-regular. Alas, he left me that night burdened with doubts. He feared I would never make it on *The Capital Gang*. His reason? I had not been sufficiently polite to *The Capital Gang*'s ruffians, and they were never roughed up by me again.

In my library back in McLean, in those days, I had almost an entire wall of books absorbed with one aspect or another of that parlous feud that had divided the West and the Soviet bloc for four decades. Haunting private life and dominating all sense of national purpose. Not one of these books, learned as they were, envisaged the dissolution of totalitarianism about to be undertaken by Gorbachev and Bush. Thus, I suppose it ought not to surprise us that about the only world leader who possessed the words to do justice to this historic event was West Germany's Helmut Kohl. He picked up the telephone and called President Bush to acknowledge that the peaceful end of the Cold War was made possible only by a resolute United States.

For more than forty years, the United States had waged a cold war despite ceaseless deprecation from many who benefited from American sacrifices without ever pausing to say thanks. Sophisticated Europeans made us out to be reckless one minute and faithless the next. Through the decades, we had been portrayed as inept diplomats, trigger-happy brutes, power-hungry imperialists, and, in the 1980s, cowboys—Hollywood cowboys, not even real cowboys! Now Chancellor Kohl had expressed his gratitude. Gratitude is a wondrously appropriate sentiment, and we, who were about to enjoy the benefits of peace, ought to be grateful, though, as we shall see, in the aftermath of the Cold War, many people were not grateful. Many liberals had come to the conclusion that the Cold War was a waste of money. Communism's "internal contradictions" would doom it eventually, not American statesmanship.

For four decades, others living on both sides of the Atlantic and both sides of the Berlin Wall saw things differently.

There were the writers who braved abuse and poverty by exposing the brutal nature of Communism. When my English friend, Malcolm Muggeridge, returned from Russia in the 1930s to refute such celebrated defenders of Joseph Stalin as the Nobel Prize–winning playwright George Bernard Shaw, Malcolm lost his job, leaving his wife and four children on hard times. George Orwell was not accorded a much friendlier reception for blowing the whistle on the Communists in the Spanish Civil War and for satirizing Communist totalitarianism. Thanks might be expressed to Arthur Koestler, whose *Darkness at Noon* exposed Stalin's show trials, and to Whittaker Chambers, who in *Witness* exposed Communism's versatile evil. Chambers died in despair for the West. The prose of those writers and others like them paved the way for the deeds of the Cold Warriors.

To my mind, the greatest of the Cold Warriors for what he did in warning us of the Nazis and later of the Soviets was Winston Churchill. The great Englishman, whose mother, of course, was American, spent years on the firing line, first as the widely derided Jeremiah of the Nazis in the 1930s. Then as the wartime prime minister who saved his country and possibly our civilization. At age seventy-one, he still had the grit to notify the world in his 1946 speech in Fulton, Missouri, of the Iron Curtain recently descended over Europe and of the dangers that lay ahead. Then there was Dean Acheson, one of America's greatest secretaries of state, whose diplomatic career was crucial to the establishment of the Truman Doctrine, the Point Four Program, the Marshall Plan, NATO, the end of the Berlin Airlift, and the execution of the Korean War. There were farsighted presidents who contributed to the Cold War, such as Harry Truman and Dwight David Eisenhower, who kept us on an internationalist course and free from the slumbers of isolationism. The academic treatise of George Kennan gave the United States a schema for pursuing the East-West conflict to victory, namely: "containment."

Through the years, every president from Truman to Richard Nixon and even to Jimmy Carter in his last year of office paid a high price for waging the Cold War. Then, in the 1980s, Ronald Reagan faced the renewed challenge of Leonid Brezhnev and his successors and demonstrated that an arms race was a race that the United States could win. If there was one politician who brought the Cold War to an end, it was Reagan. And if there was one writer who roused the West to a final awareness of the horrors that existed behind the Iron Curtain, it was Aleksandr Solzhenitsyn, whose pitiless *One Day in the Life of Ivan Denisovich* began tolling the bell on Marxism.

But, of course, no one person can be cited for bringing to an end so epic a conflict. Millions deserve gratitude, for instance: the voters, who supported the aforementioned leaders and paid the bills; the intelligence agents and military personnel, some of whom paid the ultimate price, such as US Army Major Arthur D. Nicholson, Jr., who on March 24, 1985, was shot in cold blood while unarmed and on duty in East Germany. He was left to bleed to death, and he was probably America's last Cold War casualty. His killer was a Russian sentry named Aleksandr Ryabtsev. There were others, such dissidents as my friends Pavel Bratinka in Prague and Vladimir Bukovsky in Moscow, and dissidents in Warsaw and Budapest, whose names I have long forgotten.

At the end of this ghastly conflict, we should have paused in a prayer of thanks to Providence for keeping everyone's hands off the nuclear devices that are still lying out there. Moreover, we should have celebrated. Certainly, at *The American Spectator*, we did celebrate, but I have forgotten most of the details after taking aboard a drink or two. It was that rollicking a party. Though in London, Taki outdid me. A year after Bush and Gorbachev met in Malta, Taki invited hundreds of his closest friends to celebrate at the historic Savoy Hotel with black tie, evening gowns, and plenty of champagne. Then, at the end of 1990, he had his usual New Year's Eve bash at Mortimer's on New York's Upper

East Side. I could not make his London bash, but I did attend his year-end celebration in New York.

My guest that evening was the very pretty Deputy Secretary of Transportation Elaine Chao, who was destined to hold an even higher position in the cabinet of President Donald Trump and to marry the leader of the US Senate, Mitch McConnell. Upon entering the restaurant, I took Elaine's coat and got us a couple of drinks at the bar where I encountered my old friend Norman Mailer, who told me he was finishing a book on the CIA eventually to be entitled *Harlot's Ghost*. "Norman, this is your lucky night," I told him. "My date just happens to be the CIA's deputy secretary." Norman could not wait, and I put the two together, introducing Elaine as Madam Secretary. For the next couple of hours, I flitted back and forth among Norman, the astounded Madam Secretary, and the rest of Taki's guests. Norman never caught on, and if Madam Secretary ever caught on, she remained mum. Possibly she really was with the agency. By the way, the CIA had no deputy secretary in 1990.

Yet, as I said earlier, the movement of intellectuals and of the pols from left to right that had livened up the late 1970s and early 1980s had by the late 1980s pretty much petered out. Though it took a while for us at *The American Spectator* to recognize the cessation. People such as Jeane Kirkpatrick, who began her life as a socialist and ended up being a Reagan Republican, were now part of the conservative movement. In fact, she was about to join *The American Spectator*'s board of directors. We at the magazine saw no reason for the intellectual migration not to continue. Free market economics had led to widespread prosperity in the late 1980s. Now the Berlin Wall had come down. To this day, we keep a chunk of it on display in our office, barbed wire and all.

On December 25, 1991, Gorbachev resigned, the Soviet Union dissolved, and Boris Yeltsin, who had been elected president of Russia in June 1991, fully assumed the presidency of the Commonwealth of Independent States—all without the benefit of a mushroom cloud. Why did we not hear more champagne corks popping? What is more, why did we not hear the boos of disapproval from Americans on both the left and the right after the Nobel Prize Committee gave its Peace Prize to Gorbachev, leaving President Reagan on the sidelines? Did the Committee not know that Gorbachev initially *opposed* tearing down the wall when Reagan publicly called on him to tear it down on that gray and gloomy day in Berlin?

Part of the answer for the silence was that increasing multitudes of liberals had grown gloomy. Indeed, they had grown absolutely agelastic. That is to say, they never laughed. They rarely smiled. They took as their role model Malvolio from Shakespeare's *Twelfth Night*, not a heroic figure as might be expected but, truth to tell, a comic figure. The party of hope, optimism, and good cheer that extended from the New Deal to the New Frontier was increasingly the party of sourpusses and sanctimony. They never laughed, unless it was over some misfortune that befell one of their enemies, usually a Republican. After they defeated Bob Bork, doubtless Senators Biden and Kennedy retired to their chambers and had a good laugh. They may have anticipated more laughter when they set out to unhorse Clarence Thomas's nomination. Yet he saved his Supreme Court appointment with an eloquent speech about his "high-tech lynching" by the Senate. After that, with Malvolio as their model, the liberals found less and less to laugh about and more and more to bemoan.

The increasing grimness of the liberals is a historic fact. By the time of the Cold War's culmination, the prospect of celebrating with Ronald Reagan, whom the liberals had dismissed for eight years, was out of the question. The liberals had to come up with another explanation for the end of the Cold War, other than President Reagan's intention of bankrupting the USSR. They did. It was pithily put by Strobe Talbott, *Time* magazine's resident Sovietologist, who would soon bejewel Bill Clinton's State Department. He explained on the television show *Inside Washington* that "[t]he Cold War ended... because of *internal contradictions* [italics added] and pressure within the Soviet Union.... And even if Jimmy Carter had been reelected and been followed by Walter Mondale, something like what we have seen probably would have happened."[2] Internal contradictions became the liberals' preferred sophistication for how the Cold War ended, though Eleanor Clift gave a slightly more sinister version of it when she said on *The McLaughlin Group* that "[p]eople who want to give Ronald Reagan the entire credit for the collapse of the Soviet Union ignore the fact that the Soviet economy was collapsing and the Reagan administration covered it up."[3] The end of the Cold War was a cover-up!

So, at the end of the Cold War, the liberals were neither going to celebrate with us nor were they going to give Reagan credit for nearly bankrupting the Soviet Union. However, Gorbachev did. He did so on October 8, 1986, when he said: "The United States has an interest in keeping the negotiations machine running idle, while the arms race overburdens our economy. That is why we need a breakthrough…" And he went on to say, "If they impose a second round of arms race upon us, we will lose!"[4] Years later, Ambassador Vladimir Lukin who had been chairman of the Supreme Soviet Foreign Relations Committee in the 1980s was even more emphatic. When asked in 1993 by the American diplomat Bud McFarlane "what role U.S. policy in general and the Strategic Defense Initiative in particular played in the Soviet Union's collapse," Mr. Lukin answered, 'You accelerated our catastrophe by about five years.'"[5]

Of course, how could liberals congratulate a man whom they had for years called a fool, and an idiot, or, to quote the Democratic elder statesman, Clark Clifford, just an "amiable dunce?" To the liberal mind, Reagan had done everything wrong.

For instance, on March 8, 1983, Reagan called the Soviet Union an "evil empire." A sampling of the liberals' reaction comes from Anthony Lewis in the *New York Times*: "outrageous," "simplistic," and in conclusion, "Primitive: that is the only word for it."[6] Or from the *Washington Post*'s Richard Cohen: "Question: What does Ronald Reagan have in common with my grandmother? Answer: They are both religious bigots."[7] Or from Columbia University's historian, Henry Steele

Commager: "It was the worst presidential speech in American history, and I've read them all." Commager went on to explain that it was because of the president's "gross appeal to religious prejudice."[8]

Then there was the liberals' criticism of the president's Strategic Defense Initiative (SDI). Teddy Kennedy derided SDI as "Star Wars" the day that Reagan gave the speech, March 23, 1983. The next day Kennedy went to the Senate floor to denounce the president's "misleading Red-scare tactics and reckless Star Wars schemes."[9]

Finally, there was the liberals' dissatisfaction with Reagan's prediction that communism would end up on the "ash heap of history," which he made in London at Westminster Hall on June 8, 1982. Lou Cannon, Reagan's biographer, sums up the Western press's dissatisfaction with Reagan's prediction as being "wishful thinking, bordering on delusional."[10] Yet, looking back on that prediction in writing his biography, Cannon, almost ten years later, recalls that the Westminster speech "stands the test of time as the most farsighted and encompassing of Reagan's anti-communist messages."[11]

Well, Soviet Communism did end up on the "ash heap" of history. SDI was a contributing factor in ending the Cold War. In fact, General Makhmut Gareev, who headed the Department of Strategic Analysis of the Soviet Ministry of Defense, later revealed his assessment to the Soviet politburo: "Not only could we not defeat SDI, SDI defeated all our possible countermeasures."[12] Finally, the Soviet Union was indeed an "evil empire." Ronald Reagan was right about Communism, and toward the end of the Cold War, the liberals were obviously wrong. Communism was unlikely to self-implode without a push. Reagan obliged, and he should have shared the Nobel Peace Prize with the man he beat.

Actually, in the late 1980s, even many conservatives were in the mulligrubs, and though it is not remembered today, many were surprisingly critical of the president. I thought about this after getting a rare "off the record" call from Richard Nixon on December 15, 1986. Off the record? Was RN going to impart to me a new version of his famed Eisenhower martini? He asked me about how things "were going down in Washington." We discussed how "adrift" things had become. I was, at the time, somewhat gloomy myself. RN was less so. When I mentioned that Don Regan, the White House chief of staff, "ought to go," RN corrected me, saying, "The animals would not be satisfied." Well put, though, I complained that the president "should at least get together with his old friends. We were stronger in years past than today thanks to his lack of support." RN replied that "not even I hear from the White House." Incidentally, the isolation of almost any White House sets in by the second term. After a few more observations about Washington, RN ended with "Merry Christmas and Happy New Year," adding, in a typical Nixonian coda, "I never say 'Happy Holidays.' It's not religious or anything. It's just that I prefer 'Merry Christmas and Happy New Year.'" [13]

It is mostly forgotten today that even movement conservatives were impatient with the White House in the late 1980s. As the old cowboy was directing America toward a peaceful conclusion of the Cold War, I got over my impatience with him. I wonder how long it took *The Capital Gang* members to get over their impatience with him. On July 10, 1987, Henry Kissinger expressed his impatience with the president over breakfast at New York's River Club, startling me by saying that the administration had "destroyed" conservatism with Reagan's foreign policy. He "urged" the magazine to "resist" the administration's "zero-zero" option, as it was then called. Henry assured me that we would be vindicated within five years.

Henry and RN went on to express their disagreement with the president in an April 27, 1987, essay for the *Los Angeles Times*. Movement conservatives were even more ardently opposed to the president. Tom Bethell, our Washington correspondent, exploded in his monthly column: "What a terrible disappointment President Reagan has turned out to be. He's a nice enough fellow, of course, but that is hardly what is needed in the Oval Office. What is needed is someone who knows what he wants..." [14] Well, I think at the very time that Tom was tapping out those words, President Reagan knew precisely what he wanted. Moreover, he was about to get it. Or I should say, President Bush was about to get the peace that Reagan had worked so hard for and against such odds here and abroad.

There were other memorable events for me in 1987, one being particularly troubling to me. It involved a leading member of the conservative movement, Clare Boothe Luce. We dined alone at the elegant Il Giardino restaurant in Washington on March 21, 1987. I had for the last few years been socializing with Clare, the widow of Henry Luce, who founded *Time* magazine. In her long lifetime—she was now in her mid-eighties—Clare had been a playwright, a congresswoman, the US ambassador to Italy, and now she was a member of the president's Foreign Intelligence Advisory Board. Still radiant and soigné, she had a discerning mind and a wicked wit. The Baron and I took her around a bit, and I had had her to my home as recently as November 1985 with the Baron and the Lehmans. John Lehman was then secretary of the navy, charged by the president with bringing the fleet up to six hundred ships.

In the morning, my wife had taken the children back to Indiana for a week, and so I asked Clare to join me for dinner that night. The evening was off to a good start with Clare telling stories about literary figures I would be familiar with. There was the very handsome George Jean Nathan, Mencken's old buddy, whom she pronounced a "wimp." How startling! She also mentioned Luigi Barzini, whom she knew when she was our ambassador to Italy. She pronounced him a gentleman and a storyteller. What a relief. Since World War II, she thought the quality of the gentleman, especially in America, had declined. I assured her she was in "good hands tonight." That was definitely the wrong thing to say. She announced that during the postwar period, she had been raped twice, once in Karachi in the late 1940s by a Brit and once in Honolulu in the early 1960s by an American. My diary note that night stopped abruptly at "Honolulu." As I recall, I changed the subject.

Two days later, immediately after dinner, Clare called my home and was very distressed. She claimed that her after-dinner drink on Saturday night had looked like water, though it was sambuca, and it had hit her hard. I assured her that I had no recollection of the incident. A week later, at something like 2:00 a.m., Judge Bill Clark, her lawyer, called from California. I had known him from the Reagan White House. He said that Clare was indeed still distressed and asked that I give her a call. I did, and we were back to normal, though I never saw her alive again. She passed away on October 9 of that year from cancer. Clare was one tough lady.

Years later, an acquaintance, Sylvia Jukes Morris, called me asking about my friendship with Clare. She was writing Clare's biography. What could I tell her about Clare? I thought back to our evening in the spring of 1987 and of her summary judgment of George Jean Nathan. I said that Clare was a strong woman, and little else. Sylvia seemed to be looking for something else. When her two-volume biography came out, it contained no mention of rape or even sexual abuse, but then it contained no mention of George Jean Nathan either.

Less troubling was a roisterous adventure I had in London with my English friend, Andrew Roberts. Actually, it was the first of several high-spirited adventures I have had with him through the years. I first met Andrew at the 1984 Republican Convention in Dallas, where he was serving as an intern for Senator Jesse Helms. Andrew was to become a superb historian, writing such books as *A History of the English-Speaking Peoples Since 1900*, the best biography of Winston Churchill, *Churchill: Walking with Destiny*, and a biography of Napoleon, whom he rather admires. I detest the Corsican homunculus and consider him the nineteenth century's preview of Hitler, though Napoleon did wear more colorful uniforms. After Dallas, we stayed in touch, and in 1987, when Prime Minister Margaret Thatcher was up for reelection, I told him I was coming over to observe the bloodbath. Both she and Vice President George H. W. Bush, who was running in 1988, were running on their administrations' conservative records and I predicted that she would win in 1987 and that the vice president would prevail in 1988. It was a conservative tide on both sides of the Atlantic.

On election night, June 11, when I thought that we were just going to have a beer together, Andrew surprised me by including me in a group of young Englishmen who were destined to make their mark in the world, including the budding young historian Simon Sebag Montefiore, the author of *Jerusalem: The Biography*; a young man studying for the priesthood; several investment bankers; and four very pretty blondes plus one brunette. We were to spread out in the posh purlieus of Chelsea and to "canvas" for Mrs. T. We went door-to-door campaigning for her. It was a lot of fun and, given my accent or lack of an accent, we displayed what would now be boomed as "diversity." I was forty-three years old and obviously a Yank. My colleagues were twenty years younger—still more diversity. Then we were off to the ballroom of the Savoy Hotel for a delicious meal, compliments of the media tycoon Conrad Black. Among his holdings were the *Telegraph* newspapers and the *Spectator* of London. Moreover, he would prove to be a friend for years to come. Mrs. T., of course, was there, and the celebration was euphoric. She had now won three victories in a row!

Five years later, I reciprocated Andrew's invitation to an election night celebration of Mrs. T. with an invitation to the Balkans where we would see ghastly scenes and for the first time in our lives we would come under enemy fire. Putting us both in mind of Churchill's quip that "Nothing is so exhilarating in life as to be shot at without result." Though Andrew did complain about getting bits of plaster in his hair.

In autumn 1992, Teddy Forstmann, the immensely successful chairman of the board of *The American Spectator*, asked me to accompany him to war-torn Bosnia-Herzegovina and to bring along a historian. Teddy had a sense of history, to say nothing of a sense of drama. He might also have asked for a camera crew. We were going to fly in one of his Gulfstream IVs—he then owned the company—to London, then to Zagreb, and then to drive to our destination, Mostar

in Bosnia-Herzegovina, where Teddy was going to dispense something like a million dollars to the refugees of the Bosnian War. I asked
the great historian, Paul Johnson, to join us, but he had commitments.
So I asked Andrew, the Paul Johnson of his generation. We landed in
Zagreb and were met by the city's mayor and various dignitaries on
the tarmac, who seemed to think that Teddy's largesse was meant for
them. Actually, Teddy had made some sort of arrangement to help
the International Rescue Committee relieve the suffering in Mostar.
(Interestingly, Bill Casey, too, had participated in charitable work with
the International Rescue Committee after World War II.) So, Teddy
thanked the mayor and proceeded to the Esplanade Hotel, Zagreb's
equivalent to the Ritz.

After dinner, Teddy headed for the casino atop the Esplanade with
his friend, the Croatian-American tennis player Suad Yitzanbegovich,
who would be our interpreter in the days ahead. I prudently went to
bed, and Andrew went off to taste the delights of the town. The next
morning, we assembled in front of the hotel, where Teddy assured us
there would be an armored convoy to take us safely through what was
an active war zone. Apparently, the mayor's ardor for Teddy had cooled
since our meeting at the airport, and where Teddy had expected several armored vehicles to be waiting, there was a lone and quite shabby
Volkswagen Passat with a lanky driver leaning on its fender smoking
a cigarette. Croats share many mannerisms with their Italian neighbors across the Adriatic. What is more, the letters "HMO" could be
seen on his dashboard, those being the initials of the local Croatian
fascists. It was not an auspicious beginning, and the Passat lacked
air-conditioning.

Suad rode shotgun, the better to interpret. Andrew and I climbed
into the back seat with an increasingly irritated Teddy, and off we went
down the Dalmatian coast. Within an hour, we were lost. Our driver
stopped at a police station, and now we were lost and possibly in police
custody. What is more, Teddy was coming to a boil. If the cops ever

figured out how much Teddy was worth, our stay at the police station might be long and perilous.

Suad got us out of police custody, or so he said, and we proceeded through a countryside that reminded me of Tennessee, except for one troubling difference. As we passed through the villages, we saw rows of perfectly tidy homes interrupted by a house or two that were utterly gutted by fire. Apparently, the area in which we were heading was what American Progressives would today proudly proclaim the epitome of diversity. Serbs lived next to Croats. There were Bosniaks mixed in with Herzegovinians, and as soon as the war broke out, they set upon their neighbors ferociously. Hence, the gutted homes in otherwise peaceful neighborhoods. The destruction increased as we drove south through Medjugorje, a Catholic shrine, past bombed-out mosques, and ruined Serbian Orthodox churches. Once again, diversity had gone horribly wrong. Soon we would be seeing grisly scenes: body bags by the roadside, freshly dug graves, automobiles overturned, and bombed-out buildings, some still smoldering.

We had made it to Mostar, a city that once abounded with diversity. The sixteenth-century Ottoman bridge that separated Croats from Bosniaks lay in ruins. Now the town was eerily silent. In the center of town, makeshift graves spoiled the scene of the village green. We slept that night either in the mayor's office or in the office of the city council. There was no place else fit to sleep, but before we did get to sleep, we hazarded a walk by what once had been a modern hospital. Unfortunately, the Serbs across the valley had liquored themselves up with slivovitz and they began firing at us. Their aim was off, but it was the first time that either Andrew or I had been fired upon in anger—or at least fired upon under the influence of slivovitz—and all we wanted to do was to drop off a million dollars of Teddy's money and go back to London after a little R & R in Venice.

The next day, we visited the refugee camp outside Mostar, where Teddy completed his donation. He also gave a shivering girl his athletic jacket before departing for Split on the Croatian coast for dinner with

Franjo Tudjman, Croatia's president, in one of Tito's thirty-six palaces that he had acquired as the postwar leader of Communist Yugoslavia, doubtless from a grateful citizenry. After Split, we flew back to Venice to decompress and to London and then on to Washington.

But I have gotten ahead of myself. Upon returning to Washington after celebrating Mrs. Thatcher's victory, it was time to celebrate ourselves. On November 4, 1987, the magazine celebrated its twentieth anniversary with a gala party, provoking *The New Republic* on its December 7 "Washington Diarist" page to sneer at us, to depreciate us, and in so doing to mislead *The New Republic*'s readers once again. Their reporter, James Glassman, chronicled the remarks of one of our speakers, Midge Decter, but Glassman did not mention the evening's main speaker at all. That would be the vice president of the United States, George Bush, soon to be the president. This would be another example of how *Kultursmog* is created. When the smog does not mischaracterize those with whom it disagrees, it neglects them. George was completely ignored. So was Mrs. Bush, for that matter. Yet George was elected president anyway.

My next adventure was well underway by the time of our twentieth-anniversary dinner. It began on April 13, 1987, when Gary Hart, then a senator from Colorado, announced his presidential campaign, or should I say his first presidential campaign of the 1988 nominating season? There would be a second presidential campaign for him. The first campaign lasted for three weeks, whereupon a mob of journalists surrounded him in his Washington town house during a sleepover with a woman who was not his wife. He withdrew from the race on May 8, complaining about the journalists' acts of "character assassination." Then he reentered the race on December 15, full of lunatic hope. Unfortunately for him, about this time, I had written my syndicated column in which I revealed that "Gary Hart, of course, wears a toupee." I was mobbed. *Parade* magazine asked me if it was true. The *Washington Post*'s Chuck Conconi sought my confirmation. Hart's campaign vehemently denied his having worn a hairpiece. I, being nonchalant as ever, responded to Conconi with a cool, "Who do you trust, Gary Hart or me?" I like to think that my column finished him off, and in fact on March 11, after a pathetic showing on Super Tuesday, he did, in fact, pull out of the race for a second and final time. He has never run again, though I could have been more thorough in my research. I could have interviewed his barber. Four years later, Gary Hart, if he were to keep on lying, might have been the comeback kid, though by that time there was an even more prodigious liar in the Democratic field.

It was about this time that I began many of my days counseling with two men a generation older than me whom I had known for years, Vic Gold and Professor Kenneth Lynn, who was on the faculty at Johns Hopkins University. Kenneth was a wide-ranging scholar with a weakness for politics. Vic was a political advisor and friend of George H. W. Bush. His literary skills were superb. Both men were helpful to me with ideas, and both contributed pieces to the magazine. Both were a little flinty, and often they started a telephone call to me with an exasperated outburst. For instance, one objected when I replaced my name on the cover of our February 1987 issue with "A Monthly Review Edited by R. Elmer Tyrrell." Alas, those days are gone forever. Occasionally, they had a point.

Of the two, Vic had known me longest and provided a steady stream of pieces and advice. We met years before when I was traveling with Vice President Spiro Agnew and Vic was his press secretary. I was a couple of cars back behind the veep in a motorcade and we were at a stoplight when Vic rather maniacally jumped into my car to introduce himself. Most things that Vic did had a touch of the maniacal to them, though we were to remain friends for at least two decades. Kenneth never jumped in a motorcade to greet me, but we, too, remained friends for at least as long as Vic remained my friend. I owe these men a lot.

During the 1980s, both men assisted me with editorial advice and, if memory serves, Vic came up with the idea of giving President

Reagan, on the night he came to my home for dinner, a picture of how he might look on Mount Rushmore. As the 1988 election approached, it became obvious that both Vic and I had our candidate: George I. Kenneth came aboard, too. George Bush was the closest approximation to President Reagan in the 1988 field. He had been the president's loyal vice president for eight years, and we assumed that he would continue Reaganism after Reagan retired. Moreover, he was a gent. George was especially fond of Vic, whose combustible personality amused him. During his administration, I communicated amiably with him, particularly about Vic, and I have several notes from him written on Camp David stationery commenting on Vic's eccentricities. I also have a warm note from him written from Camp David in appreciation of my support. He was very good about thanking his supporters. As I said, he was a gent.

Even before the 1988 campaign got underway, the pundits and the pollsters were against Bush, which only proved their bias. After all, from the Reagan era on, the media seemed to be against the Republican nominee with ever greater intensity. George Bush was a war hero, successful businessman, and he held a wide range of government offices. He had served in an administration that was a success domestically and in foreign policy, so I concluded that the nomination was his if he wanted it, and he did. I had known him since the mid-1970s when he spoke at a private dinner at New York's Union League Club and showed he could handle a joke. He was then the head of the CIA, and the agency was under fire for, among other things, surreptitiously subsidizing intellectual magazines. As I had just started an intellectual magazine, I asked him to promise not to discontinue supporting such endeavors. As I recall, he said he would take my request into consideration.

Now ten years later, Bush was running behind in the polls, behind his Democratic opponent, Governor Michael Dukakis of Massachusetts, and he was not even running well against the Republican field. As Vic wrote in *The American Spectator*'s May issue: "Indeed, next to Reagan,

Bush has been the most mis-stereotyped, underrated national candidate of modern times."[15] Yet like Reagan, he tightened up his campaign in the late spring. President Reagan endorsed him in May. Then Bush allowed Lee Atwater a free hand to run his campaign and by midsummer, Bush had erased a seventeen-point deficit, and in the fall, he would beat Dukakis by eight points. The *Wall Street Journal* wrote on November 11 that "George Bush's come-from-behind victory to capture the presidency will be hailed as a model campaign."[16] Perhaps, but curiously the media still were not heaving flowers in his path. On November 10, the *New York Times* concluded that

> Mr. Bush's victory was a triumph of tenacity. It cannot fairly be called a mandate. His agenda is unformed, and Congress remains ever more firmly—and perhaps angrily—in Democratic hands. Mr. Bush's task now will be to learn the difference between bashing the Democrats and working with them.[17]

The media maintained its frosty tone toward the president for the next four years.

With George Bush winning 426 votes in the Electoral College, we thought he, who had been our keynote speaker as vice president at our 1987 Washington Club dinner, would be an even better choice as president at our 1989 dinner, even if the dinner had to be postponed until early 1990. Here is how President Bush handled the matter at our gala on January 22, 1990: "I understand that this is actually *The American Spectator*'s 1989 annual dinner. [Laughter] Now, that's true conservatism, you see. Wait until the year's over—completely over—until you decide whether it's worth celebrating. [Laughter]" The president was in good form and he went on to observe, "I'm very pleased to be on Bob Tyrrell's kinder, gentler side. [Laughter] That's his right side, if there's any question about that."[18] The president was very amusing that evening and a good friend in the months ahead, though not always a good conservative. He was, however, often a crafty politician as he showed himself to be in the following kerfuffle with Dan Quayle, his vice president.

The kerfuffle began in late March 1989 when Dan got into a row with me and the magazine that never quite made sense to us aside from the possibility that Dan, then a good conservative, was suddenly chloroformed by the *Kultursmog*. Now, after so many years of prudent silence, I shall reveal the role that President Bush played in Dan Quayle's discomfort.

Dan and I went back years to Indiana where he was finishing law school and I had just started *The American Spectator*. We would meet regularly with M. Stanton Evans, the staunchly conservative editor of *The Indianapolis News*, for his monthly meeting with the Beer & Pizza Marching Society, a rowdy group of middle-aged men harboring political aspirations but very little political acumen. As we were almost a generation younger, Dan and I were often the target of lighthearted jokes, often lighter for Dan than for me. Dan's family owned the city's two newspapers and perhaps a dozen more nationwide. We both ended up in Washington, I through journalism, Dan through politics, first the House of Representatives, then the Senate, and finally as George Bush's vice president. It was there that the kerfuffle occurred.

The American Spectator's Washington correspondent, Tom Bethell, somehow wangled the assignment to interview Vice President Quayle for the *Wall Street Journal*, which should have presented no problem as Dan was as conservative as we were. What is more, there had never been any animus between us. Moreover, Dan never drank before sundown and then in moderation, so far as I knew. Yet something went off in Dan's brain when Tom asked him which magazines he read. As I have said, I suspect that Dan suddenly could no longer resist the *Kultursmog's* allures. Perhaps he thought there was a future for him on the left. Maybe he was planning to move to Manhattan or strap on his Birkenstocks and move to Berkeley.

At any rate, Dan answered Tom's question about the magazines he read by insulting major components of the conservative journalistic community and paying obeisance to *The New Republic.* Said Dan: "I used to, I've read, I read *National Review*—some. I used to read *Human Events.* Don't read it as much as I used to. *The American Spectator*—it's hard to get through *The American Spectator.*" "And *The New Republic*?" Tom asks. Dan responds, "With his voice brightening." "I enjoy reading *New Republic* articles." Tom observed that *The New Republic*'s articles "have been very critical of Mr. Quayle, incidentally."[19] Why would Dan diminish three perfectly sensible conservative magazines while building up one of ritualistic liberalism's house organs?

At the time of the interview, Dan had at least three *Spectator* writers on his staff. In an interview with another publication, Dan told Fred Barnes that he had hired Carnes Lord as an advisor on strategic matters after reading him in *The American Spectator.*[20] Now he was being interviewed by the *Spectator*'s Washington correspondent. I said a few chapters back that conservatives have presented me with more problems than liberals. Here is a prime example of the kind of trouble I have been alluding to. Needless to say, *The New Republic*'s businesspeople had hurriedly sent Dan's quote around to our mutual advertisers.

Yet Wlady and I took Dan at his word. Maybe his admission of his inability to read the magazine was an admission born of humility, and so we planned for our June issue to produce "A Danny Quayle Reader," featuring large type and simplified vocabulary. Something that a grammar school boy would find easy to read and not too long. But whom could we get to do the writing? Somewhat to my surprise, Vic Gold volunteered. After all, Vic was very close to Danny's boss, President George Bush, and what if the press got hold of Vic's involvement? But Vic, too, was irate with Danny's insulting answers, and an angry Vic was not to be taken lightly. Yet he was perfect for the job of "A Danny Quayle Reader." He could mimic anyone. I would trust him with Shakespeare. Surely a semiliterate schoolboy would present no problem for this gifted farceur. "A Danny Quayle Reader" would be a snap for Vic. Naturally, Vic did not want his name attached to the finished product, and so Vic's authorship has remained a secret until now.

Here is the first paragraph as it appeared in "A Danny Quayle Reader" in our June 1989 issue:

> Holy Cow! Why didn't you tell us sooner? Like, you know, it's not as if we would do this for just anybody, but for an old Indiana chum we will gladly go the extra mile to help you "get through" our magazine.
>
> Here then, just for you, Danny, an eminently (EM-I-NENT-LY) readable page—brought down to Quayle-speed—of subjects we've covered in recent months.

Yet, as I read Vic's ridiculous pastiche, I suspected that there was a method to his madness. Wlady and I agreed that Vic would not write such a spoof on Danny if his pal, the president, did not approve. Anyone who looked into the relations between the president and the vice president realized that ever since the president nominated Danny, and Danny practically leaped into his arms, the president recognized that he had made a mistake in choosing his giddy running mate. Danny's artless handling of questions about the conservative press was still more evidence that Danny had to be roped in by his boss. The president succeeded. Late in the summer of 1989, when things had settled down and I could ask Vic if the president had seen his work on Danny, an impishness came into Vic's eyes. He would not say.

As the 1980s gave way to the early 1990s, Wlady and I noticed a growing accumulation of news stories, many of which had long-term negative effects on Republicans and conservatives and few of which ever brightened one of their target's haloes. We called these stories Black Cat News Stories, and they all shared the pessimistic tone of stories written about George Bush's election, for instance, that November 10 story in the *New York Times* right after his election. Bush had won the 1988 election, but the media were full of foreboding about what came next for poor George. He was now putting the final touches on our Cold War victory. He continued to work with Gorbachev and Boris Yeltsin on nuclear disarmament. He was securing peace with Russia. Yet this was no cause for celebration. With the media, he was on thin ice.

A Black Cat News Story is a bizarre phenomenon known chiefly to national news reporting, usually in Washington, DC, and New York City. It is an ominous, catastrophic story that, like a black cat, leaps across a public figure's path. Suddenly that public figure's luck turns sour. Usually, the public figure is on the right. He is abandoned by friends and often has trouble at night securing a designated driver. On his way to a photo op, say with the United Nations Secretary-General, the zipper on his pants breaks. During a reception in the White House Rose Garden, an overhead bird evacuates on his new tie, the brilliant red one that was a gift from his mother. The telephone rings, and it is Arianna Huffington announcing that she will be his weekend houseguest; and she is bringing her new boyfriend, the one with the ponytail, who does not wear shoes.

You think I am kidding? These Black Cat News Stories can cause a lot of grief. There was one years back that Vice President Dan Quayle had a girlfriend, a girlfriend in common with half the Republicans on Capitol Hill. There was another one that President George Bush had two girlfriends. These Black Cat News Stories cause little damage in the long run, but in the short run, they can really hurt, especially if one's wife is already on edge. I recall one about Reagan's attorney general, Ed Meese, being caught jaywalking across Pennsylvania Avenue by an alert journalist. Then there was one about a Republican senator taking a second helping of dessert at a public reception. He might even have taken it before everyone else had finished theirs.

These last two Black Cat News Stories were probably the work of Michael Kinsley, the neoliberal journalist we have already encountered in these pages. Michael could always raise official Washington's moral indignation about some indiscretion that was actually quite petty. There was the time when he spilled thousands of sanctimonious words upon a page of the *Wall Street Journal* over what he viewed as the wanton use of frequent-flier mileage by business executives, presumably white males. He chided: "[I]t's a minor but ugly moral blot on the landscape of bourgeois life, as well as a healthy reminder that there's at least as much waste, fraud and abuse in the private sector as there is in the government." And he added: "What we are witnessing is a massive, open and wildly successful campaign to corrupt the morals of the corporate class."[21] This is the same Michael Kinsley who while editor of *The New Republic* ran an article about conserving water by recycling it through one's toilet. He later defended himself saying he was in jest, but few people believed him. As with his frequent-flier campaign, Kinsley's toilets went nowhere. For at least a year, possibly more, my friend Peter Apple, using the nom de guerre Pedro Manzano, attempted to employ Michael as a masseur for Apple's fictional massage parlor, "Marble Hands." His slogan for the fictional massage parlor was "Reaching for the Stars." Michael never bit. Probably it was not his first encounter with a snide fellow like Pedro.

In the spring of 1990, I like to think I was in my Bernard Baruch mode with the forty-first president of the United States. Baruch was the New York investor who in the last century gained a reputation for counseling presidents, though he only counseled two, Woodrow Wilson and Franklin Delano Roosevelt. I have counseled six, about which more later. That spring, President Bush invited me to the Rose Garden for a luncheon with two of his aides, John Sununu, his very bright chief of staff, and Charlie Black, a shrewd political advisor. Both were longtime conservatives. It was only the three of us sitting with the president outside the Oval Office, though there was one other participant at the luncheon, Millie, the president's springer spaniel who was flicking in and out of the shrubbery that walls off the garden's dining area and provided a bounding squirrel cover from the relentless Millie. The president called this "the Great Squirrel Hunt." And I am duty bound to report that the squirrel won. The president carried on two conversations, alternately talking with Black about campaigns all over the country and with me about the *Kultursmog*. This is the second president with whom I have raised the issue of the *Kultursmog*. I had yet to give up. The *Kultursmog* was killing him in the press, and he knew it. No matter what he did to finish off the Cold War peacefully, there would be a Black Cat News Story just around the corner.

Toward the end of our luncheon, the president asked us what he should do about taxes. As I recall, I replied first. I said he promised no new taxes in 1988, saying, "Read my lips." The president should stick to his statement. If he were to raise taxes, the Democrats would merely raise their spending. Sununu and Black agreed. I left the White House, confident that we had saved his presidency. On June 26, 1990, in a written statement released to the press, the president reneged on his promise of "no new taxes." Hoping to solve the deficit problem, he increased taxes on November 5, and he lost the presidency in 1992. His polling tumbled from a Gallup approval rating of 89 percent to an approval rating of 29 percent. My message to Ronald Reagan and George H. W. Bush was always to ignore the voices of official Washington and remain resolute. President Reagan did so most of the time. President Bush did so less frequently, and he lost the presidency in 1992.

The result was the near extinction of the "Reagan Revolution" and the renewal of the 1970s turmoil. Never again did we have the initiative that we had during the Reagan-Bush years. Bush was a gent, but he and his son Bush II never realized how dangerous the spendthrift Democrats led by the Clintons could be. The Clintons were going to be a dominant force in our politics for three decades. I lost some close friends because of my insistence on this, and I wonder what my ex-friends think of me now.

Was I really, in the words of P. J. O'Rourke, "suffering fits of credulity" over the Clintons in the 1990s?[22] After all these years, I still cannot discern what "fits of credulity" might be. The Clintons have provided me and *The American Spectator*'s audience with a lot of laughs, but they have been poison for America. The same poison that they and their like-minded "reformers" brought to the universities in the late 1960s and have spread throughout the country, first with Bill in the White House, then throughout the Democratic Party, and right up to Hillary's idiotic Russian dossier in the election of 2016. They and their servitors have ruined the Democratic Party. We shall be lucky if their legacy does not ruin America. I think that is an important news story and an enduring one. It is the enduring news story of the past decade of the twentieth century and the first two decades of the twenty-first century. I am glad that *The American Spectator* ran with it. I have no regrets.

In raising taxes, President Bush was listening to the *Kultursmog* as represented by our old friend from the Reagan White House, Dick Darman. Remember him, the diligent reader of *The American Spectator*, the guy that wanted to have a cup of coffee with me in the afternoon after my lunch with the president? Darman was a casualty of the *Kultursmog*; from it, he got the idea that the Reagan tax cuts did not work. The tax cuts, according to the smog, increased rather than decreased the deficit, and they did not create the prosperity that Reagan and the Reaganites said they had. Darman was a Bush carryover from the Reagan administration who was never a true Reaganite. He, Dave Gergen, and Jim Baker were all carryovers who were typical of the assistant presidents then bedeviling the president. The true Reaganites were the likes of Ed Meese, Bill Clark, Jeane Kirkpatrick, and Cap Weinberger, all of whom were frequently opposed by the likes of Darman and Gergen and Baker. Darman reeked of *Kultursmog*. Thus, it was no surprise that Darman would breathe in and exhale the Capital Beltway *Kultursmog* that demanded that President Bush reverse himself on his signature 1988 pledge of "no new taxes." It was indeed Darman, as Bush's OMB director, who paved the way for Bush to reverse himself. In so doing, Bush cost himself reelection in 1992 with a little help from H. Ross Perot running on a third-party ticket.

The deficits throughout the 1980s were caused by spending increases, not by tax cuts. By the end of the 1980s, deficits were coming down. Total revenue from taxes climbed from $600 billion in 1982 to $1 trillion by 1989.

I have joked about my long-standing desire to visit behind the Iron Curtain only if I were accompanied by an armored column and perhaps with a complement of jet fighters overhead. In truth, I never made it to Eastern Europe until the fall of the Berlin Wall, and then only with the help of Andrew Whist, whose philanthropic work with the foundation Libertad, helped many libertarian groups to advance freedom in the former Communist countries.

In 1991, I visited Prague, Budapest, and Warsaw, and I witnessed many hallmarks of communism's noble achievements. There was the used toilet paper blowing across the verdant fields of Gellért Hill park in Budapest because, I was told, the commissars could not provide public comfort stations. Cars that had not moved in years clogged the streets of Prague. Warsaw was still a gray, dingy ruin. Everywhere there were broken old men and women who had participated in the exuberant life of the "Soviet Experiment." Upon my inquiries, they told me that they were about my age and that healthcare, food distribution, and other amenities of the West were not readily available where they lived. The truth was that their lives were almost over, whereas my public life was in its early stages.

I returned from Eastern Europe more convinced than ever that communism (and, in fact, socialism) wherever practiced has been a failure, at least for ordinary people. So why do a sizable number of ordinary people vote for it and parade about town talking it up? Why is it not as dead as Nazism? I have come to the realization that virtue flaunting—or virtue signaling, as others call it—is a reward in itself, a powerful reward despite the impoverishment it brings. If you want to feel good about yourself, claim to be for communism despite all the evidence against it, most notably the mountains of corpses it leaves in its wake. There are other motivations, for instance, the timeless, though often ignored, motivation of boredom. Communism and socialism are two ways to liven things up, at least for a while. Also, there is the promise of getting something for nothing, a promise that is usually left unfulfilled. Finally, there are some people who derive great satisfaction from expropriating the property of others. They are commonly recognized as thieves.

Yet, to return to the spring of 1992. It ought to be remembered by me as my presidential spring. I have counseled with presidents before, but not with so many in a single season, and one was not even an American. That would be Boris Yeltsin and we met in the White House, no less. In the spring of 1992, I met with former president Reagan, former president Nixon, and President Bush, all of whom were very cordial. My presidential spring ended with President Boris Yeltsin, the Russian president, visiting the White House with President George Bush. Boris had recently stepped down from a tank—a red tank!

My presidential spring began with President Bush (President Number One), and it did not begin in a genial atmosphere. Vic Gold had called me to his home a month earlier to show me a hand-typed letter from Camp David that had been typed by President Bush complaining about my recent criticism of his "character" in our March issue. Vic said something about testing the limits of the First Amendment on a friend. He suggested I "propitiate" the president with a letter of apology as he probably was going to be reelected—alas, a lot of White House insiders still thought so. I wrote the necessary letter and gave it to Vic to hand deliver to the president. A few days later—and before Vic had handed the president my letter—I was at a dinner that former president Richard Nixon (President Number Two) was having in Washington. He seated me at the table next to his, and to my surprise, President Bush and Mrs. Bush were at Nixon's table. Former president Nixon introduced me to the Bushes, and I noted the troubled look in the president's eyes. I told him I had given Vic my letter of apology, which admitted that I had gone a bit "over the top" when I questioned his character. We had a brief but very amiable chat.

The next day, I got a call from Vic announcing that at 7:15 a.m. that morning the president called him to tell him that "Tyrrell made

239

my day." The president had admitted the night before that he was a bit "wobbly" in recent campaign appearances, but he planned to tighten up his campaign as he had in 1988. Vic decided there was no need to deliver the letter to the White House. Yet a week later he got another call from the president asking for "Tyrrell's letter." After getting it, he wanted to take me to the Kennedy Center restaurant for dinner. Vic told him I was abroad, whereupon he sent me a handwritten letter assuring me that another invitation would be forthcoming, and he welcomed "my advice." Yes, "my advice," and did Bernard Baruch, counselor to FDR and Woodrow Wilson, ever counsel four presidents in one springtime? As I have said, George Bush was a gent, and his invitation came a few weeks later. It was for a state dinner with President Boris Yeltsin (President Number Three).

On May 30, 1992, I was in Los Angeles for coffee with former president Ronald Reagan (President #4). I have in my possession two letters dated April 19, 1991, and May 10, 1991, that are handwritten by the fortieth president of the United States—and, let me add, hand-addressed. They have some striking similarities both in phrasing and in choice of words. Frankly, they betray signs of some mental disorder, perhaps dementia. Yet here I am with the former president a year later. I spend a half hour at least with him. He is fit and tan and looks like he can still bench press his weight as he told me he could four years before when he dined at my dinner table. He is now eighty-one, and at the outset of our interview, he complains that he is having trouble with his memory. Though he has not one memory lapse in all the time I am with him. When I tell him that President Bush has invited me to the Yeltsin dinner on June 16, he tells me that President Bush "served me well." I expected the same anecdotes he used to share with me back in Washington, but he had some new ones. He talked about how he waited until the end of the primaries to endorse George Bush and adds that if Ross Perot were to win in the fall election, he would "think he bought America." He says that with a twinkle in his eye.

When I mention a physical attack on him by an ignorant peacenik back in April that left a crystal trophy smashed (along with the thug) he has his aide, Fred Ryan, show me its replacement. I mention Lady Thatcher's testimonial to him about winning the Cold War, and he interrupts, saying, "And remember we won it without firing a shot." He seems especially proud of that achievement. In our half hour together over coffee, the former president is jovial, quick-witted, alert, and I can recall no loss of memory or hesitancy of thought. He ends the conversation as he began it by thanking me for what I said about him in *The Conservative Crack-Up* and for sending him the book. A couple of years after our meeting, on November 5, 1994, he made public his letter about the onset of Alzheimer's disease. My guess is that he had been fighting it on and off at least since those 1991 letters were sent to me. I have no doubt that he fought it gallantly. As he said at the end of his letter to his fellow Americans, "When the Lord calls me home, whenever that may be, I will leave with the greatest love for this country of ours and eternal optimism for its future." He was a great man.

I was back in Washington by June 5 to lunch with Bob Gates, Bill Casey's successor as head of the CIA. Bill had told me early in his stewardship of the agency that Bob, Bill's understudy, was going to be a prodigy and to keep in touch with Bob, which I did. Besides, Bob had attended IU where he received his master's degree in Russian studies around the same time I received my master's degree there in American diplomatic history. Now, since Bill's death, I was meeting with Bob fairly regularly, exchanging off-the-record thoughts. Bob was walking evidence that Bill was right when he would boast that he worked "at the best shop in Washington." Having watched John Brennan's dithering at the agency in recent years, I am reminded that Bob Gates has been replaced at the CIA by his intellectual and moral inferiors several times over. An emotional wreck, Brennan voted for the Communist Gus Hall in 1976. I have no idea how James Comey at the FBI has voted, but he is cut from the same cloth as Brennan. What is more, in a matter of days, I would be having dinner with President

Number Three, Boris Yeltsin. Who could better prep me for my dinner with Yeltsin than Bob Gates? According to my diary, we met for a two-hour lunch.

Bob was very worried about the Russians. He feared that the political reforms there, which were then extensive, would be endangered by the failure of the economic reformers. Bob had read Hélène Carrère d'Encausse's *The Russian Syndrome: One Thousand Years of Political Murder*, wherein she wrote that no nation escapes its history, and that Russian history is one of vast carnage and political murder. Bob feared that the Russian reformers were not going to have enough time. They needed short-term aid to improve their position with the Russian citizenry, and they needed long-term aid—particularly technical assistance—that would be relatively inexpensive. Bob said that 1992's intelligence problem was not the problem of earlier times. Now the problem was not too little intelligence as in the past but "too much." Moreover, he bewailed the low quality of intellect on Capitol Hill. He said that the Russians were desperate to join Western civilization even as such universities as Stanford strived to de-emphasize Western civilization. "Russia," Bob said, "wants to be accepted and admired for its level of intellect and artistic achievements." And he made another point: "George Bush made all the big calls in the Gulf War with superb timing."[23] Now that is a news story that I never read.

I took detailed notes at this lunch. I am uncertain whether I told Bob that I was going to be at the Yeltsin dinner. As I leave, Bob tells me that he and the president admire me because, though I attack stupidity with ardor, I never attack a person's motives or divine his intent—ah, so that explains George's recent pique with me. Bob closes by saying that Bush's foreign policy people are first-rate and understand domestic policy, but that his domestic political people have hurt him. I take this as more evidence of the president's looming problems on Election Day.

On June 16, 1992, a few days after my lunch with Bob Gates, I tripped across the threshold of the White House for a state dinner with

Boris Yeltsin (President Number Three). President Bush had not forgotten me. Two reporters stopped me as I entered the White House to ask my view of Independent Counsel Lawrence Walsh's indictment of Cap Weinberger. I responded that Walsh was no independent counsel but rather an archeologist who "deals in antiquities." Hearty laughter from the press! My point was that Walsh's corpus delicti was old news, and, of course, President Bush eventually pardoned the former secretary of defense before leaving office. Then a rather chic woman came up to me and said, "Oh, I know who you are. You're R. Emmett Tyrrell Jr. Congratulations." Somewhat startled, I replied "What?" She responded, "Congratulations on being R. Emmett Tyrrell Jr. You do it so well." Despite the lack of a proper introduction, I was not the least bit offended, though I did check to see if I still had my wallet.

President Bush was very friendly in introducing me to President Yeltsin. He told the Russian president that I was the editor in chief of *The American Spectator* and one of his favorite writers. President Yeltsin gave me a broad smile, and I recalled Bob Gates's advice that the Russians wanted very much to be seen as a part of Western civilization. They were particularly proud of their cultural and intellectual achievements. I told President Yeltsin that Russia is a great civilization and that I had recently read *The Brothers Karamazov* in preparation for this evening. Moreover, I had listened to Prokofiev's Fifth Symphony. He smiled again. Off I went to chat with Secretary of Housing and Urban Development Jack Kemp and with some young Russians who, like Yeltsin, were not wearing black tie, perhaps in deference to their recent anti-bourgeois past, possibly because they could not afford black tie. They did not look particularly well-heeled.

I was seated with Secretary of Defense Dick Cheney and Paul Volcker, the former chairman of the Federal Reserve Board, along with a Russian or two, one of whom judged that "change" was going to take time. There was something about the evening that seemed unreal. Here we were in the White House with people, some of whom only a few years ago were our mortal enemies. Now they were our friends.

The world as we knew it was changing, but where was it going? President Yeltsin was a large man, well-tanned, and sporting a mane of astonishingly silver hair. He danced up a storm that night, and as I drove home, I thought of his courage months earlier when he faced down hostile armor in Moscow. How long could this new bonhomie last? For almost my entire life, the Russians had been my enemies.

As we approached the fall election, George Bush, a World War II hero and a successful vice president, was facing an obvious draft dodger, a hayseed playboy whom the press had heard on tape instructing one of his lovers on how to lie to the press. He was also a marijuana user who insisted he did not smoke cannabis. He did something else with it. Possibly, he merely savored it. How could President Bush lose to this creature from Arkansas via Yale Law School?

Bill Clinton was probably the most flawed candidate for president in American history, but he represented a portion of the 1960s generation that shared his flaws. They did not care if he was America's first draft dodger to win the presidency. He was also America's first candidate who was a coat-and-tie radical, as was his wife and thousands, perhaps millions, more baby boomers. The other half of the generation, the young conservatives, whom I called the penny-loafer conservatives, had enjoyed their first decade in power. They thought they were going to enjoy more decades of increasing power. That was not to be. For one thing, their candidate in 1992 was not completely convinced of the wonders of limited government. Moreover, he was not in his prime, having suffered a curious thyroid condition (later diagnosed as Graves' disease) five months before the election. As some of us longtime veterans of the conservative movement noticed, the energy behind the conservative movement had been evanescing. There was not the energetic coherence of the early years when we would travel across the country to meet, speak, and hold conferences with our fellows. I called it the conservative crack-up and chose those words for the title of a book about it.

In 1992, America elected its first draft dodger to the White House, and along with him a gaggle of coat-and-tie radicals. Dramatic change had come to America, and I, at the helm of *The American Spectator*, experienced my third miracle. Along with the smoldering IRS document atop our Indiana garbage dump and the discovery of Wlady Pleszczynski amongst our proofreaders, I was about to send the magazine from a circulation of around one hundred thousand to a circulation approaching three hundred fifty thousand. We accomplished that feat in only two years. The drinks were on me—though Wlady remained a teetotaler.

Yet first, we had to celebrate the twenty-fifth anniversary of *The American Spectator* on December 2, 1992. We held it at Washington's Capital Hilton, and more than four hundred people were there, among them two future candidates for president, Jack Kemp and Arizona's Senator John McCain. We also had George Gilder, Andy Ferguson, Bill Kristol, John Podhoretz, and three board members—General William Westmoreland, Bob Novak, and Jeane Kirkpatrick, the last being a valiant defender of *The American Spectator* in the years to come. The news of the evening was that our circulation had surpassed one hundred fourteen thousand. That would be seven thousand more than *The New Republic*'s, and our keynoter for the evening, P. J. O'Rourke, was exultant. "What a joy to be able to turn to the helmsman of our good ship *Spectator*," P. J. sang out, "and say, 'Captain Bob, bring the guns down to deck level and load with grapeshot.'" P. J. could not be suppressed: "So stand warned, Boy Clinton… Mr. Bill… Wet Willie… You and your 'Presidential Partner'…. President Clinton and First Person Hillary… Pudge and Ruffles…. Anyway, stand warned the pair of you. We're going to laugh you out of office. We did it to the Carters and we'll do it to you."[24]

Almost precisely five years later, as our circulation was climbing ever higher, the very man who at our twenty-fifth anniversary was urging me to mayhem and grapeshot, sounded a very different note. Then he told Howard Kurtz of *The Washington Post* that "The tendency of the magazine [*The American Spectator*] to do this Clinton-obsessive stuff, I don't get… It seems strange and somewhat embarrassing. Some of these articles over the last few years seem to undercut the credibility of *The American Spectator*."[25] What had happened to the man urging me on with such relish in 1992? Indeed, what happened to all of them? Was it the *Kultursmog* or just simple cowardice? Turn the page.

Chapter IX

"HIS CHEATIN' HEART"

On the morning of December 13, 1993, I called Kenneth Lynn of the Johns Hopkins University Department of History to come to my house and render his scholarly estimate of an article that was about to be published in *The American Spectator*. As you might recall, I mentioned two men from the older generation that I would often call for their wise counsel, Vic Gold and Kenneth Lynn. On this occasion, the judgment of a historian was preferable to the judgment of a political sage, for, if I was right, the article in question was going to be groundbreaking. I had been educated as a historian and I judged it "the most devastating piece ever written about a sitting president." But Kenneth had decades on me and a long list of scholarly publications to boot. What did he think? After almost spilling his matutinal coffee on one of my Oriental rugs, he agreed. It was "the most devastating piece ever written about a sitting president." Or, as Kenneth quipped, "A president sitting, standing, or lying."

Written by David Brock, we called the piece "His Cheatin' Heart," and it did indeed make history. It set in motion a train of events that is still going on. Before "His Cheatin' Heart" was published, there were things that happened to women that they would be reluctant to admit to, much less to admit to voluntarily. Now, in the aftermath of "His Cheatin' Heart," women stepped forward with their personal revelations. Paula Corbin Jones was reluctant and weighed filing a lawsuit against *The American Spectator* before she filed her sexual harassment lawsuit against Bill Clinton and made history. Eventually, more women, following Paula's lead, became more talkative, and by the time it was Monica Lewinsky's turn, she was positively loquacious. She astonished the independent counsel's team of prosecutors with her detailed answers to their questions about what went on between her and the president; but, of course, she was then still—I would say—head over heels in love with Bill. After Monica, there came a seemingly endless line of abused women followed by their deflated abusers: Bill Cosby, Harvey Weinstein, Matt Lauer, Charlie Rose, Senator Al Franken. The list goes on. Who knows when it will end, but one thing has become clear: The sexual revolution of the 1960s has juddered to a halt. Sex may be a "beautiful thing," as the sexual utopians used to say in the 1960s, but nowadays it would be best for a prospective Romeo to sign a contract with his inamorata, and that is no joke. I believe such formalities have been proposed in California. Can New York be far behind?

The American Spectator's pursuit of the Clintons began in earnest with Bill's underwear, and Chelsea's too, for that matter. In a well-researched piece by Lisa Schiffren published in our August 1993 issue, Lisa essayed Hillary's "stunningly aggressive tax deductions," that began back in her Little Rock days when Bill and Hillary's joint income put them in the top 3 percent of American families.[1] Nonetheless, every year Hillary—or some trusted aide in the governor's mansion—took the time to tout up their deductions from charitable giving: Bill's underwear, one dollar a pair; Chelsea's, one dollar a pair; and his undershirts, three dollars a shirt. Before we ventured into the Clintons' underwear, we tapped Danny Wattenberg to excavate Hillary's past. He found her to be far to the left of Bill. As Danny wrote in our August 1992 issue, she was

> standing well to the left of her husband and enjoying an independent power base within his coalition. Hillary is best thought of as the Winnie Mandela of American politics. She has likened the American family to slavery, thinks kids should be able to sue their parents to resolve family arguments, and during her tenure as a foundation officer gave away millions (much of it in no-strings-attached grants) to the left—including sizable sums to hard-left organizers.[2]

Bill and Hillary proved to be the first coat-and-tie radicals to achieve the White House and possibly the last. They were from a stratum of the 1960s generation that for some six decades has been profoundly separated from the rest of America. They were the eager young things that usually could be characterized as teacher's pets, particularly if the teacher was a left-winger. They were reliably left of center, though rarely full-blooded radicals. By being full-blooded radicals, they might endanger their possibilities for law school, graduate school, or divinity school, and there was always the possibility of blowing up your parents' basement while fashioning a bomb for which you almost certainly would land in jail assuming you survived. What a setback that would be! The coat-and-tie radicals were always enormously ambitious. They were colossal megalomaniacs. More specifically, they were stupendous narcissists, often solipsists, who—despite all the bosh about their idealism—were coolly amoral in their aspirations and their goatish pursuits. Nor did this amorality in any way put a damper on their self-righteousness.

During Ronald Reagan's 1980s, I thought the coat-and-tie radicals had disappeared or possibly grown up. Yet having lived through the 1990s, I know better. Some died of pathetic drug overdoses or ghastly sexually transmitted diseases, but the majority just laid low and watched reruns of *The Big Chill*, that poignant depiction of a group of coat-and-tie radicals who came together in the early 1980s to commemorate the death by suicide of a college pal who in his youth had been among the group's most idealistic and promising revolutionaries. They wanted to confront the stark question: "Have we sold out?" I have always wondered how their sad dialogue might compare with what was said among the Clintonistas who gathered in Arkansas in July 1993 to bury Vince Foster.

In the early 1990s, they had a comeback, and they turned out in force at the 1992 Democratic Convention. Which, despite its triumphalism—Bill was rapidly catching up with President Bush—was perhaps the saddest Democratic Convention thus far on record. Things were going to become more lachrymose for national Democratic Conventions in the years ahead, but for now, 1992 was a real tearjerker. The Germans have a word for people who take pleasure in the troubles of other people: Schadenfreude. Well, after watching the 1992 Democratic National Convention and hearing about all the grief and catastrophe that Democrats were suffering, I came up with a word for this unhappy condition: "Schadenfarming." With plow and oxen, the Clintons and Gores of this world walk the furrows of human suffering. For whole seasons, these Schadenfarmers water and fertilize every gripe, calamity, and paranoia. Ultimately, they harvest misery and take it to market, where there are apparently many buyers.

Frankly, I do not find America so full of pain, and even if I did, I think I would be loath to exploit the suffering of others. Not Al Gore and not Al's presidential running mate in 1992 whom I was beginning to call Boy Clinton and whom I would soon be calling Mr. President. Al began the convention, which was held in New York City—and which I attended—by rebuking the rich and the powerful. He blubbered about the penury of the middle class and then he made one of Schadenfarming's most colossal and tasteless efforts, asserting that "I know what it's like to lose a sister and almost lose a son."[3] About his sister's loss, we are told no more, but about his son's accident, we are given gruesome details. The sheer ignominy of his revelations captivated the audience. Gore really had a heart.

Then it was Boy Clinton's turn to deliver his acceptance speech, a speech that proved to be the convention's saddest, and according to the journalists, Jack Germond and Jules Witcover, was "longer than might have been prudent"[4]—but what the hell. Bill talked about his future. He talked about his past. He talked about his faith. He discoursed upon his father. The one he never knew. Then came his mother, then his grandmother, finally his grandfather. "Grandfather had a grade-school education.... He taught me more...than all my professors at Georgetown...than all the philosophers at Oxford...than all the jurists at Yale Law School."[5] In his youth, it appears that Billy Clinton never saw sunshine or happiness, and then he started in on Hillary, but I had to take a bathroom break, and by the time I got back he had returned to his grandfather. Let me be candid. On the way back to the auditorium, I took a nip, possibly two nips. But I dutifully recorded in my reporter's notepad: "Tragedy after tragedy! Tough times! Grandpa, the barefoot sage!"

I jotted it all down:

> Listen folks. The winters were cold. The summers were hot. We all had bad breath, no money for mouthwash.... There was body odor. Grandpa had plantar warts and bunions. Mother got yeast infections. For six months ah lived in a garbage can. But ah never et the garbage. Granpa wouldn't let me. He distributed it to the really poor, to people who couldn't afford the rent on the garbage can. There were people in Hope [Hope, Arkansas, Bill's hometown] who considered my garbage can a mansion. Of course, ah'm not really sure ah had legal title to that garbage. Ah've asked Hillary about it. Some day we plan to do a scholarly

paper on who owned the garbage and its nutritional value. At Yale we called this sort of research paper a cross-disciplinary study.[6]

What a speech!

The Democratic field in 1992 was spectacularly weak, made up mainly of has-beens and never-wases. There was the former governor of California, Jerry Brown, a has-been, and Senator Tom Harkin of Iowa, a never-was, and there were others. As for the most likely Democratic candidates for 1992, they had taken a look at President George Bush's huge popularity in the polls and decided to pass on 1992. So, we were left with Bill and Jerry and what's-his-name from Iowa. When I heard in early 1991 that a political wunderkind was stirring in Arkansas, I assumed it was my old classmate, Jim Guy Tucker, from the 1978 class of the Ten Outstanding Young Men of America. Jim Guy, the effervescent Arkansas congressman, had left his mark wherever he went with his broad smile no matter how rainy the day might be and a ready hand to greet anyone, even an inhabitant of the state penitentiary to which he was eventually sentenced on Whitewater-related charges. But no, Jim Guy was not the presidential candidate from Arkansas in 1992. That honor was reserved for the state's young governor, Bill Clinton, who despite suffering far more run-ins with the law than Jim Guy, has yet to spend a night in the hoosegow, though his run-ins kept accumulating with the years.

In fact, so riotous did Bill's campaign for the White House become in 1992 that it is unthinkable that any seasoned political observer still believed him to be the Goody Two-shoes he presented himself to be by the time of the Democratic Convention. Bill, his wife, and their fellow coat-and-tie radicals represented a new breed in American politics, the Chronic Campaigner. The Chronic Campaigner was, by the way, thoroughly corrupt. My colleagues at *The American Spectator*, such as P. J. O'Rourke and Andy Ferguson, can be forgiven for not recognizing the phenomenon, but other seasoned observers are not so innocent.

Word was seeping out about the Clintons even before the Democratic Convention began, and the words were not favorable.

By mid-January, the *Star*, a supermarket tabloid that was to become an early authoritative source on the Clinton family, printed a story that the young governor had used state funds to pursue five adulterous affairs, one with Gennifer Flowers, an ex-television personality who was to become a major figure in the 1992 election and throughout the early years of his presidency. For now, the New York tabloids were booming the story, with such flavorous headlines as the *New York Post*'s: "Wild Bill" and the New York *Daily News*': "I'm No Gary Hart." Then on January 23—one week later—the *Star* struck again with an interview of Gennifer in which she vividly spoke of a twelve-year affair with the governor. The *Star* raved, "They Made Love All Over Her Apartment," and the paper reported that it had tapes of their conversations, one of which featured Flowers telephoning the governor seeking his advice on how to respond to reporters' mounting inquiries into the couple's intimacies. "If they ever hit you with it," came the avuncular reply, "just say no and go on. There's nothing they can do." In other words, Bill was caught on tape coaching his paramour to lie to the press, but—not for the last time—the press did not mind being lied to by Bill.

On and on, the questions came. The Clintons appeared on *60 Minutes* after Super Bowl XXVI, which attracted 34 million viewers, and denied that he had had an affair with Gennifer. The next day, she countered with a press conference at New York's Waldorf-Astoria, which went well enough until a fun-loving reporter asked, "Did the governor use a condom?" Gennifer was noncommittal, and so the off-color questioning continued until late in 1992 when Gennifer was interviewed by *Penthouse* magazine and included Bill in one of the few athletic references ever associated with his name. She said, "He ate pussy like a champ." That was the end of Gennifer Flowers, at least for a while.

How much damage the questioning caused is disputable, but on February 6, the most dangerous scandal of Bill's campaign was begun by *The Wall Street Journal* when it broke the news that presidential hopeful Clinton had arranged a Vietnam deferment from an ROTC program that he never joined. Thus began a back-and-forth between him and his 1969 ROTC recruiter, Colonel Eugene Holmes. It ended when Bill's heretofore unpublished letter to Colonel Holmes appeared in the press with Bill's disingenuous admission to Holmes, thanking the veteran cheekily for "saving me from the draft."[7] Bill also admitted to the Colonel—a survivor of the World War II Bataan Death March who had languished in Japanese POW camps for over three years—his "loathing [of] the military."[8]

So now you had Bill recognized *by* the press as a serial adulterer, recognized *in* the press as an anti-military war protestor, and soon to be identified for his involvement in the Whitewater affair. That came in the *New York Times'* stories appearing in March. In all these scandals, he was shown to be a liar. Some said he was shown to be an "unusually good liar," but I have to point out that he was exposed almost every time he lied. His problem was that he told a lie when he did not have to, and he told a gigantic whopper when a little white lie would be perfectly adequate. What was becoming apparent was that in the culture of the 1990s, the press increasingly shared Bill's culture, which is to say the culture of the coat-and-tie radical. At *The American Spectator*, we took note.

So far as I have been able to ascertain, I was probably the first journalist on the national scene to allude to Bill's errancies, and I did so on October 29, 1992. That was when *The Phil Donahue Show* invited, me and, as I recall, Chris Matthews and Dave Gergen (Wlady's Mr. Potato Head), to discuss the Arkansas wonderkid, and I pretty much shut off debate when I said, "Bill has more skeletons in his closet than a grave robber." Four years later, the show's stars were still scratching their heads over what I meant. They, like most members of the media, followed a course of expecting great things from Bill. Then, when he let them down, say with an intern under his desk or with a donation from an obscure Indonesian bicycle shop, they were thrown into despair. Yet gradually their hopes for him were revived. They followed this cycle for years. They still follow it. Call them repeat offenders. Bill went on to win the election with 43 percent of the vote to 37 percent for George H. W. Bush. The spoiler here was Ross Perot, who won no electoral votes, though he took 19 percent of the popular vote, mostly from the president. Arguably, had he not been in the race, George would have won and America would have been spared the Episodic Chaos of the Clinton years, and much of the Chaos thereafter.

The Episodic Chaos that made its appearance in the scandals of Bill Clinton's 1992 campaign abated somewhat during his Glorification Rites that highlighted his amazing inaugural events, transforming Washington, DC, into Mardi Gras time. Then came the Clintons' second period of Episodic Chaos, surprising even me. After all, the Clintons had spent their entire adolescence preparing for public life. Remember the stories about Bill bragging to his Georgetown class-mates that someday he would be president? Actually, there were many such braggarts in those days, but Bill made it part of his political leg-end. One can imagine no wonkier pair ever entering the White House than Bill and Hillary.

Yet something went wrong. Maybe the Chaos was owing to the coat-and-tie radicalism that they brought to 1600 Pennsylvania Avenue, but every time the Clintons nominated someone for a high government position, they had to be prepared to duck. Looking back on 1993 and 1994, and even reaching into 1995 and 1996, the nomi-nating process rarely went without a hitch. Distinguished Democrats were often casualties. As our Lisa Schiffren noted in the August 1993 issue, Democrats such as Kimba Wood, Zoe Baird, and Charles Ruff "lost jobs over the issue of household help."[9] The press called it the "Nannygate Crisis," wherein the nominees had failed to pay his or her taxes or to fulfill some other legal obligations. Moreover, the delin-quencies spread out over other matters. So much so that in 1996, the

Los Angeles Times reported that "Federal law enforcement officials maintained Wednesday that more than three dozen White House employees had used cocaine, crack and other illegal hallucinogenic drugs before they were hired and were given security clearances despite concerns about safety at the presidential mansion."[10] As Byron York recalled in our pages, "It's no secret that the White House was a chaotic place in the early days of the Clinton administration. Jobs went undone, policy veered all over the map, even the phone system nearly melted down."[11]

The Clintons' problems began early. That eleven-thousand-word manuscript that I showed to Kenneth Lynn late in 1993 was indeed groundbreaking. It turned out that I was correct in describing it as "the most devastating piece ever written about a sitting president." The Clintons were headed for high seas in the years ahead, and the rough water originated basically from one piece, "His Cheatin' Heart," though we had help from CNN and from the *Los Angeles Times*. Moreover, the Clinton White House would soon get the hang of how to deal with a small intellectual review whose resources were limited. The White House would try to bankrupt it.

No man is a hero to his valet, and if in Arkansas valets are scarce, the state has its elected officials, one of whom has served as fair game for his state troopers, that being Boy Clinton. At least four Arkansas state troopers became famous for their low opinion of Bill and even lower opinion of Hillary. Bill was a source of ribald humor for them, and they dismissed Hillary as a bitch. By 2016, the country concurred. She was a bitch.

We got the four troopers to tell us what they observed in the governor's mansion, and two, Larry Patterson and Roger Perry, talked to us on the record. Later, we got another, L. D. Brown—Bill's "fair-haired boy"—to talk on the record, where he shared with us evidence of L. D.'s intention to commit murder. When members of the press read the troopers' revelations, they claimed to be appalled by the piece's salacious language and other crudities. But, bear in mind, the troopers were working-class guys, not clinical sexologists or marriage counselors. Furthermore, all they were doing was quoting Bill and Hillary's language. As our writer, David Brock, concluded, "Bill and Hillary Clinton's loose sexual morals and their habitual foul language" might be considered "irrelevant" by some readers, but most readers agreed it was essential to the story.[12] I shall let my readers judge for themselves from the following abridgement of "His Cheatin' Heart":

> According to Trooper Patterson, Bill had an affair with Gennifer Flowers that lasted years, though he strenuously denied it during his 1992 campaign. At the same time, he maintained a virtual harem down in Arkansas, to say nothing of his many one-night stands. The harem included, as Brock chronicled in his piece, "a staffer in Clinton's office; an Arkansas lawyer Clinton appointed to a judgeship; the wife of a prominent judge; a local reporter; an employee at Arkansas Power and Light, a state-regulated public utility; and a cosmetics sales clerk at a Little Rock department store."[13] Troopers Patterson and Perry told us, "Clinton visited one of these women, either in the early morning or the late evening, or one of them came to the residence to see him, at least two or three times a week."[14]
> No wonder he developed heart trouble!

Then there were instances when the governor, as Brock put it, "inexplicably permitted himself to be caught in flagrante delicto." There were times when "Larry Patterson said, he stood guard and witnessed the department store clerk performing oral sex on Bill in a parked car, including in the parking lot of Chelsea's elementary school, and on the grounds of the governor's mansion."[15] On another occasion,

> Clinton suggested a detour to Chelsea's school, Booker Elementary. When they arrived, Clinton told Patterson the sales clerk was sitting in her car, which was parked

in the otherwise deserted front parking lot. "I parked across from the entrance and stood outside the car looking around, about 120 feet from where they were parked in a lot that was pretty well lit. I could see Clinton get into the front seat and then the lady's head go into his lap. They stayed in the car for 30 or 40 minutes," Patterson said.[16]

And so it goes in "His Cheatin' Heart."

Then there was Hillary as seen by the troopers. One day, Patterson came into the mansion and found Hillary "standing at the bottom [of a staircase] screaming. She has a garbage mouth on her, and she was calling him motherf—ker, c—sucker, and everything else. I went into the kitchen, and the cook, Miss Emma, turned to me and said, 'The devil's in that woman.'"[17] Hillary could be importunate. Trooper Perry claimed she would "order troopers to fetch feminine napkins from her bathroom and deliver them to her at the firm."[18]

Yet then there was this revelation. It was rendered among all the foul language, among Bill's carnal adventures, and in the general chaos of these 1960s brats running amuck in the governor's mansion. When Kenneth Lynn read it at my home in 1993, the venerable historian thought it would hog all the headlines, for it involved the suicide of the highest government official since Secretary of Defense James Forrestal in the Truman administration. All the troopers told Brock that "Hillary herself was intimately involved with the late Vincent Foster, a partner at the Rose Law Firm and later deputy White House counsel. Foster killed himself in July [1993] under circumstances that remain murky."[19] Brock went on:

> According to all of the troopers, whenever Clinton left town, no sooner would he be out of the mansion gates than Foster would appear, often staying in the residence with Hillary into the wee hours of the morning. One of the off-the-record troopers drove Hillary and

Foster to a mountain cabin in Heber Springs, maintained by the Rose firm as an out-of-town retreat for its lawyers, where the two spent significant amounts of time alone.[20]

Only one of *The American Spectator*'s critics ever mentioned Hillary's affair with Vince Foster in print. Our critics quoted the vile language of which they claimed to disapprove. They cited the boorish behavior, which they labored to blame on us. Yet only one of our critics, Joe Klein of *Newsweek*, even alluded to Hillary's involvement with Foster. The rest have remained silent to this day.

The reaction to David Brock's first Troopergate piece was decidedly negative even before it was published. By late summer, word had gotten out that a group of troopers were talking about the Clintons with us and with reporters from the *Los Angeles Times*. I had agreed to let the *Times* publish its piece first, figuring that its piece would legitimize ours. My staff was already anxious about publishing another piece critical of the Clintons. Our New York apartment and our Arlington offices had already been broken into three times in a matter of months. There was evidence that our telephone lines had been tapped. Betsey Wright, Clinton's fix-it woman from Little Rock, had employed a shadowy investigator to quiet "bimbo eruptions," and he was not unfamiliar with break-ins or telephone tapping. The investigator, Jack Palladino, was eventually murdered on a San Francisco street. Not only was there skittishness growing in our office, but the troopers were becoming restless, as was the man who had lined them up for us down in Little Rock, Cliff Jackson. Finally, the *Los Angeles Times* was becoming dilatory. It had held up anti-Clinton pieces in the past, and I feared its editors might try it again. Our piece had been ready to go since September.

Thus, I decided to consult one of the finest legal minds of the twentieth century, my own. It seemed to me that the dilatory tactics of the *Times* and of others we had worked with on the deal had so disfigured the original agreement that the agreement was now defunct.

Despite the disquiet it caused in our office, I announced that I was going ahead and printing it if I had to put the piece on the press myself. December was fast approaching, and I wanted it out by the end of the month, December 20, to be exact, in time for Christmas. So, our piece appeared as the *Times* was gathering its courage. The newspaper published its piece the following day.

Curiously, whenever our Troopergate piece has been written about—still, after all these years laden with disapproval—the *Los Angeles Times* is never mentioned. That is how *Kultursmog* works. The result was multiple explosions at the White House (spoiling the Clintons' Christmas party we were told), in New York City, in Washington, DC, and across the globe—most notably in London where the press relishes a good story. Yet I have always been of the opinion that on the weekend before "His Cheatin' Heart" hit the streets, a still unidentified sleuth at CNN had laid hands on it and arranged the interview with Patterson and Perry, making our piece famous. Now the piece could not be ignored—and it was not. CNN's interview of the troopers was the fourth miracle in the history of the magazine. Along with our IRS letter beckoning me from our Indiana garbage pile decades ago and Wlady's appearance among our proofreaders and our circulation explosion, there came this mysterious presence in CNN's newsroom on the weekend of December 18–19, 1993.

A hush of silence greeted our next two groundbreaking pieces, Troopergate II and our Mena airport piece. Yet silence did not greet this first Troopergate piece. It was more like pandemonium. *The American Spectator* was described as a Clinton-hating magazine, which is a gross exaggeration. To describe us as a Clinton-ridiculing magazine would be more like it. Nonetheless, we were accused of inaccuracy and error, though never did the pro-Clinton media offer proof of any inaccuracy or error. Even David Brock, after his feckless tergiversations against us later, only found the piece guilty of bad taste. Never did he admit to an error.

Michael Kinsley accused us of "dishonesty" and "fundamental bad faith." "Who would believe anything this fellow wrote," or presumably anything in *The American Spectator*. "Not me," Kinsley quipped in pieces written for *The New Republic* and *The Washington Post*.[21] E. J. Dionne, Jr., joined the chorus along with Ellen Hume and Paul Duke, who—in wrapping up 1993 for *Washington Week in Review* called Brock a "loser"—"wrote that slimy magazine article that revived all those old charges about Bill Clinton's personal behavior."[22] Joe Klein in *Newsweek* accused Brock of being the "purveyor of uncorroborated and hyperbolic accusations by a handful of gold-digging Arkansas state troopers."[23] Though the testimony of Brock's four troopers was four more witnesses than Klein offered in his book about a randy hick governor from rural parts. Klein called his book *Primary Colors* and gave as the book's author, "Anonymous." His fainthearted contribution to the Clinton genre lasted about a month before he was exposed as the book's author, and he had to know that *The American Spectator*'s portrayal of the Clintons was accurate. Andrew Sullivan, at the time editor of *The New Republic*, lamented that the once intellectually distinguished *American Spectator* had been "reduced to pubic hair and women in hotel rooms."[24] Finally, *The Washington Post*'s David Maraniss wrote a biography of Bill in which he substantiated most of what we said in our piece without ever mentioning us. By the way, he, too, relied on only one source, Betsey Wright. So much for our critics' veracity.

Suffice it to say, Troopergate was not American journalism's finest hour. Of our aforementioned critics, only Sullivan paused to apologize. He did so in a breezy parenthetical, "(O.K., Tyrell, you were right.),"[25] spelling my name incorrectly with only one "r." As for the rest, they probably still believe in Bill's virginity.

A little over a year after our publication of the first Troopergate story, David Brooks, then an editor at the *Wall Street Journal*, having read Maraniss's thinly sourced book, was among the few people who considered me vindicated and he invited me into the *Journal*'s pages to "gloat." Well, a gentleman never gloats, but I did set the record straight, and, in passing, noted how far out on a very shaky limb such *American Spectator* critics as Sullivan, Kinsley, Dionne, Klein, and the wretched Duke had wandered. Oh yes, and Ellen Hume, a retired journalist now embalmed at something called the Annenberg Washington Program. She wrote: "You're not a journalist, David." I only wish I had included Frank Rich of the *New York Times* in my *Wall Street Journal* piece. He was, when he wrote it, the newspaper's leading champion of homosexuality, though he found our Troopergate piece the occasion for outing David Brock as a homosexual. Talk about a fair-weather friend. A few days after my piece appeared in the *Journal*, I was introduced to Klein at a reception where he accused me of "taking a cheap shot" at him in the *Journal*. I responded, "Joe, all I did was quote you." Around the office, we amusedly coined a new journalistic offense, "Tyrrellism, to defame a person by quoting him." It apparently worked with Klein. I never heard from Klein again.

The herd mentality is now rampant among American journalists who have no need of the protections of the First Amendment. They rarely say anything that would test its limits. There were hundreds of other bovine hacks joining in to attack us, but I did not expect the attacks from conservatives. Wlady was more suspicious, and sure enough, the conservative crack-up manifested itself once again, and it came not from the young upstarts on the right who were always such pests. It came from our erstwhile friends and mentors, from Bill Buckley, Pat Buchanan, and a few other veterans from the days when you could have put us all in a very small room. For instance, Jeffrey Hart of Dartmouth who accused me of hoping to bring "Clinton down" and of "financial extravagance" that "wrecked *The American Spectator*."[26] That was thirty years ago. He never came up with any evidence of my extravagance. The collegiality of the 1960s and 1970s had been abandoned long ago by conservatives. Actually, there was not much collegiality left on the right even then, but attacks from Bill and Pat were unexpected.

Bill wasted no time. Shortly after we published "His Cheatin' Heart," Bill wrote in his nationally syndicated column, "On the matter of sleaze: Some of the charges made by the Arkansas troopers to David Brock are inherently incredible," and he went on to question the plausibility of oral sex being delivered in an automobile within sight of a trooper.[27] Frankly, Bill should have consulted his son, Christopher, before disparaging us. Yet Bill was from an earlier generation. He was from a generation that was pre-sexual revolution and he can be forgiven for his naivete. Pat was a different case altogether. He was a child of a less innocent generation than Bill's. I was appalled when I read his assessment of "His Cheatin' Heart." He wrote, "I've never seen this kind of detail in a respectable magazine," and he went on, "This is the kind of stuff that used to be confined to the supermarket tabloids. It's very lurid and lewd, and I think it's degrading to the national debate on issues like Nafta and health care, which is where we ought to be putting our energies."[28]

Well, back in the early 1990s, as I have said, a cultural battle of enormous dimensions was shaping up in America. Some of us took it seriously, and some of us were plainly befuddled. I wonder what Pat made of the cultural changes that took us from 1993 to, let us say, the past few years when such Democratic presidential contenders as Beto O'Rourke incorporated the word "fuck" into his campaign as he addressed a CNN audience on a Sunday morning saying, "Yes, this is fucked up," and in his concession speech praising his supporters with "I'm so fucking proud of you guys." Or candidate Senator Kirsten Gillibrand who tried to stir up an audience with "If we are not helping people, we should go the fuck home."[29] She began her campaign with a *New York* magazine profile that included one "fuck," two instances of "fucking," one "bullshit," a "pissed off," a "they suck," and a mild concession to conventional standards with "what the hell is going on?"[30] Senator Bernie Sanders used the famous word in public also and John Kerry, too. While Democrat Representative Rashida Tlaib began 2019 with "We're gonna impeach the motherfucker,"[31] referring to Donald

Trump. And forget not Jill Biden's outburst during the campaign. Then, the soon-to-be first lady told soon-to-be Vice President Harris to "Go fuck yourself." [32] Unfortunately, Pat, at *The American Spectator*, we were fated to[33] apprehend the future better than you.

Some years after Pat passed along his judgment of our Troopergate piece, he offered this further judgment. "The great failing of conservatives," he said, "is that they do not retrieve their wounded." Pat was repeating the judgment of Whittaker Chambers, one of modern conservatism's founders, and Pat was apparently unaware that some of us would remember his earlier assessment of the *Spectator*'s Troopergate piece. It was about this time that Bob Bartley, the great editor of the *Wall Street Journal* and a longtime friend of mine, had made a decision about the attacks on *The American Spectator* and me. Bob was famous for saying he would never leave conservative victims of the growing culture war bleeding in the field, and unlike Pat, he never did. When Bob retired from the *Journal*, he asked our mutual friend, Seth Lipsky of *The New York Sun*, if Seth thought he should "throw in with the *Spectator*." Seth thought he should. Bob agreed, and in the October 2003 issue, he became senior editorial advisor to the magazine. From Troopergate until the day he died, we never had a better friend than Bob Bartley.

The magazine took a tremendous verbal beating from our enemies and, as I have said, from some of our longtime friends, too, but we endured. Truth be known, I rather enjoyed the obloquy of the mob and their misspellings of my name. Simply because I knew we were right, and as it has turned out, history has vindicated us. Yet, David Brock was not having a good time. He was a splendid writer and a fine investigative journalist. All he lacked for his role as one of the great investigative journalists of any era was courage. From time to time, David got a case of the nerves. I remember the time when David became terrified down in Little Rock and afraid to take his rental car to the airport. He feared some kind of encounter with the troopers' representative. Instead, he drove to his parents' home in Dallas. There was another time when he joined Dave Henderson, a shrewd investigator for me, Ted Olson, one of our country's top lawyers and eventually George W. Bush's solicitor general, and me in reading over raw FBI files on Governor Bill Clinton at my home in McLean. As I say, they were "raw" files and had yet to be vetted. We never used their reports of Bill being with underage girls (though we knew where the girls ended up, alas) or of his taking cocaine and other drugs with his brother, Roger, much less his telephone calls to the Southern Mafia. It was pretty lurid stuff. At the end of our readings, David blurted out, "I'm never going down to Little Rock again," and he never did. Eventually, we learned that he entered into talks with the White House.

People have long asked me, "What happened to David?" My answer is that fear and a love of money got the better of him. In politics, the left wing has always been where the money is, and it did not take David long to figure this out. He made a bundle, picking Bill and Hillary's pockets. What I never could figure out was why they let him do it. Hillary has a long history of using private investigators, such as Jack Palladino and Anthony Pellicano, to gather information for her. Surely, she could provide such thugs with a competent writer. Bill and Hillary's books have usually been competently written. Nonetheless, David, while working for the Clintons, destroyed his reputation as a writer and he suffered for it with bad health and even a heart attack. I would categorize him with such people as Webb Hubbell and Vince Foster, all victims of the "Clinton Curse."

About this time, Dave Gergen, who had with stupefying ease departed the Reagan White House in the 1980s for the Clinton White House in the 1990s, called me from his White House office. He had heard that we were about to run another Troopergate story, Troopergate II. Dave was cordial. He politely asked how I was doing. "Better than you, Dave," was my reply. He tried an alternative tack. Could he get an advance copy of Danny Wattenberg's piece prior to our publishing it? Apparently, the White House had let its subscription run out. Mike Wallace of 60 Minutes also asked for prepublication rights. Mike apparently thought I would be naive enough to enter into some sort of clandestine arrangement with him. I delayed my response for a few tantalizing days before saying no. With Dave, I was more forthright. I told him I would send him a subscription card through the mail. We were, by now, receiving a great deal of attention. The *New York Times Magazine* planned a piece on me, as did *Esquire* and *Vanity Fair*. Television and radio were after us, and *New York* magazine listed *The American Spectator* as one of America's "Nine Most Powerful Opinion Factories." Yes, nine, not ten.

On Monday, April 11, 1994, Dave Henderson manned the telephones for me as we expected a blizzard of calls resulting from Danny's piece. It came out that morning and thunderously corroborated David Brock's Troopergate I. Henderson sat at his post all day. No one called. We got the piece initially thanks to an Arkansan by the name of Joyce Miller, who said that an Arkansas state trooper by the name of L. D. Brown had tried to "hustle" her for Clinton at a dance. She had kept his card and presented it to us. When Danny showed L. D. a reproduction of his card, he could not place her. He said he had solicited sexual partners for the governor often. "My God, it was so many times," he said, "I mean, good grief."

Brown had accompanied Clinton on innumerable trips back in the early 1980s as a member of Clinton's security detail. Clinton even shared some of the women who were called "residuals." As their relationship became closer, Bill shared books with L. D. In one, Bill had underlined "adultery is not a crime" twice. In another book, his underlinings were more earnest; the book was titled, *The Handbook of the Conscientious Objector*. Sally Perdue, one of his mistresses who was also a former Miss Arkansas, smoked marijuana with him and was dumbfounded when he insisted on the campaign trail that he "never inhaled." She told Danny that Bill claimed that "it enhanced his sexual pleasure." As for Hillary, she confided to Brown that she had had an affair with Vince Foster, backing up Brock's troopers.

Yet little of this made it into the mainstream media. The Clinton White House had learned how to minimize our Troopergate pieces. They would issue a terse denial and move on. It seemed to work. Danny was never demonized as David had been. On the other hand, Troopergate II never made the headlines as sensationally as Troopergate I, though its content was not much different.

Hence, by the spring of 1994, we had finished our adventures with Troopergate but not our adventures with L. D. Brown. There was an undercurrent with the Troopergate stories to the effect that if *The American Spectator* ever published an exposé of Clinton that was *serious* or *adult*, the mainstream media would pay attention. As though the mainstream media had not paid plenty of attention to Paula and her fellow victims when they appeared in our pages. Well, I happened to have leads on a story involving Mena airport, a regional airport in Arkansas and on our fifth trooper, L. D. Brown, who was rumored to be at the center of the Mena story. Furthermore, by May 6, Paula Corbin Jones had become a major figure in what was fast becoming a major theme of the Clintons' presidency: scandal, all kinds of scandal, sexual, financial, electoral, you name it. May 6 was the day Paula filed a civil suit accusing Bill of "willful, outrageous and malicious conduct" at Little Rock's Excelsior Hotel involving Bill's pants.

We will turn to Paula later, but first, let me take up the Mena airport story. I broke the story in the pages of *The American Spectator* back in 1995. It assuredly was an *adult* story involving drug running and illicit arms shipments to the Contras. The story has never been refuted, though it troubled even some of my colleagues at the *Spectator*, one of whom disparaged it in the pages of *The Atlantic* as "the Mena debacle."[34] Yet nothing in the story has ever been shown to be wrong, and, to the contrary, the story has been shown to withstand the test of time for almost four decades. As recently as July 20, 2020, the Associated Press paraphrased me without mentioning my name under the headline "FBI memo reveals drug smuggling at Mena airport in 1980."[35] How the Mena story got mangled in the media still amazes me.

I spent the better part of my time in 1994 and 1995 trying to crack the story. L. D. Brown was the key. He had been Danny's chief source in Troopergate II. Now he would tell me what he knew about Mena, though it was apparent that he was mysteriously frightened to talk about Mena. It took a lot of booze and a lot of very late nights, but he began to open up in February 1995, and by the summer, we had enough information from him to feature the Mena story on our August cover. Later, we got more information.

L. D. Brown, under the impression that he had been hired as a contract worker for the CIA, flew off in what he described as a "cavernous" C-123K military transport from Mena airport in October 1984. I have filed all the correspondence between the agency and Brown, along with much more regarding Mena, in the appendices of my bestselling book, *Boy Clinton: The Political Biography*. On the airplane were two pilots and two "kickers." When the airplane reached its target—presumably over Nicaragua—after a hair-raising flight variously at low altitude and high altitude, the kickers kicked palettes loaded down with M16 rifles out of the airplane to the Contras below. Then the airplane flew on to Tegucigalpa in Honduras where the lead pilot, Barry Seal, and his kickers picked up duffel bags and cash, $2,500 of which was to go to Brown. Brown never talked to the kickers or the other pilot, though he did converse with the pilot in charge of the flight, Seal, who turned out to be a renowned drug trafficker.

Another flight was planned for late December 1984, and after this flight, Seal gave Brown another $2,500. Then Seal tried to tempt Brown with a kilo of cocaine to join what had obviously become a drug operation—whether the CIA was aware of it or not is still unknown. Brown, who was still on Bill Clinton's security detail and earlier had served as a narcotics investigator, exploded at Seal. When he got home, he exploded again. This time at the governor. Clinton tried to calm him down, saying, "That's Lasater's deal. That's Lasater's deal." Perhaps Clinton remembered that L. D. had attended parties with him and Dan Lasater, a Clinton financial supporter. At those parties, cocaine was served. Though L. D. never saw him snort the stuff, Clinton often appeared "stoned" at the parties and his bodyguard hurried him to safety. Clinton's efforts at mollifying Brown on this occasion only made Brown angrier, and he eventually left the governor's detail. When I reported on this story back in 1995, I assumed that Clinton was telling the truth about Lasater. I have since come to the conclusion that Clinton was quite possibly exaggerating his knowledge of Lasater's involvement with Seal, hoping to burnish his reputation as the omniscient wizard, aware of everything going on in the governor's office. In so doing he only dug himself in deeper with L. D. Brown and with other aficionados of the Mena story.

That is, the Mena story that we printed in our August issue. We left out a few details. As I said, some of my colleagues at the magazine were growing timorous about our investigations, and the entire L. D. Brown story might have been too much for them. I published the rest of the story in *Boy Clinton: The Political Biography*, complete with appendices that should leave no doubt as to how much danger L. D. was in or as to how much evidence I had for Mena. After L. D. broke with Seal, a man named Felix Rodriguez, whom L. D. thought was his CIA contact man, called him and asked him to fly to Puerto Vallarta, Mexico. Rodriguez claimed that his employer had identified Seal's copilot and wanted L. D. to kill him. Of course, L. D. had an added motivation. The pilot was the only other man—the only other English-speaking man—who had witnessed L. D.'s Central American flights. Seal had already died in a hail of bullets on February 19, 1986.

Rodriguez supplied L. D. with a gun, plane tickets for a flight on June 18, 1986, a map of the hotel's floor plan—the hotel being the Playa Conchas Chinas—and money. Rodriguez also included instructions on how to carry out his mission. When L. D. arrived in Puerto Vallarta, a guard standing by the guardhouse of the port's naval installation had the gun ready for him. It was disassembled and hidden in a straw bag, which explains why Rodriguez had sent L. D. the gun's manual before he flew to Mexico. I have seen the manual. When he got to the hotel, he had been instructed to identify himself to the hotel clerk, who gave him fifty dollars and then directed him to his target. All went according to plan until the clerk pointed out L. D.'s prospective victim.

The man did not look at all like Seal's copilot. L. D. left the hotel, ditched the gun, and flew back to the US on American Airlines flights 292 and 512. It is all on display in the appendices of *Boy Clinton*. The man whom L. D. had been set up to kill was, according to Rodriguez, Terry Reed, a man who had helped Seal train Contra pilots in Nella, Arkansas. From here the story descends into speculation. How much knowledge did the CIA have of the operation? How involved was Clinton? Who wanted Reed killed? The story moves from solid reporting to murky conspiracies. Who *was* Rodriguez working for? According to rumors he had a hand in killing the Cuban revolutionary Che Guevara. So, Rodriguez cannot be all bad.[36]

As with our Troopergate II, the Mena story never made many headlines, though when *Boy Clinton* came out, it became a bestseller in large part because of its Mena prologue. Mena did continue to reverberate throughout the decades as our critics, one by one, fell silent. In 1995, there was a hullabaloo in our office over it, and I wondered at times if I would keep my job. Yet our board of directors remained stalwart, and two figures on our masthead never flinched, John Corry and Vic Gold, the two most senior journalists at the magazine. John volunteered to edit the Mena piece after Chris Caldwell, our senior editor, gave himself over to hysteria. Vic, my quotidian source of sound advice and occasional protests, pronounced the piece sound, and he was astounded that the staff was so timid. But my soundest endorsement came from the man who would increasingly be coming to my support, Bob Bartley. In a lengthy editorial for *The Wall Street Journal* on July 10, 1995, he wrote: "Mena cries out for investigation." Most other editorial voices maintained their silence. I wonder what they would bleat today.

By September 1995, it became clear to me that another conservative crack-up had arrived. That was when Bill Kristol, my friend since he was a sixteen-year-old schoolboy, came out with *The Weekly Standard*, a weekly magazine employing almost a dozen *American Spectator* writers and competing with us for a conservative audience. For years, Bill and I had stayed in touch with frequent weekly telephone conversations. He never told me what he was planning. His coconspirator was Rupert Murdoch. Rupert and I went back to the mid-1980s when I defended him against Harold Evans, once the editor at the London *Times* whom Rupert had let go after one disagreement too many. As I recall, Evans was a very nice man, and we debated several times on television, but he was a bit tame for Rupert.

Rupert was what I would call a ruffian, and that is why I liked him. He was a civilized ruffian who will be responsible, in part, for turning America into a two-cultured society if he and his son Lachlan have their way. His influence has been felt in newspapers, book publishing, Hollywood, and—in a big way—television. With Roger Ailes, he had terrified the creatures of the *Kultursmog*, and I never held it against him that he might nibble away at our audience. The danger to *The American Spectator* was the federal government, not Rupert.

Actually, there were plenty of conservatives out there to cultivate and many of them were happy to subscribe to both magazines. I had it from a member of Rupert's board of directors that he was considering me before he chose Bill to be his editor. His fear was that he could not control me. Well, I am not sure he could control Bill after hearing about Bill's budgets at the *Standard*. They seemed awfully extravagant, and Bill's sense of national politics always seemed odd. For that matter, his treatment of me was odd. How long did he think I would remain oblivious to his planned career change? Moreover, he had a reputation for picking the wrong presidential candidate every time. Bill seemed destined for the classroom and maybe that is where he will end up.

Chapter X

THE BAIT SHOP JUNTA

When L. D. Brown's story about Mena airport was published in the August 1995 issue of *The American Spectator*, I was unable to get an official White House response. That was not terribly surprising. I had not heard from the White House since I snubbed Dave Gergen's request for a gratis subscription back in 1994. Since then, I would say that our relations with the White House had only grown more strained. More surprising was the silence of all major news organizations, with the exceptions of the *Washington Times*, the *Wall Street Journal*, and the *Arkansas Democrat-Gazette*. As mentioned, after Troopergate I and Troopergate II the major news organizations were still claiming an interest in our stories if only we would deal with adult material. Not Bill's lewd peccancies, but grown-up news stories, for instance, stories of drug trafficking, gunrunning, and desperados, such as Barry Seal the drug trafficker. Of course, those were actually the constituent elements of Brown's Mena story, but the news organizations ignored Mena. Hollywood did make a stab at it with a potboiler film called *American Made*, dealing with drug trafficking, gunrunning, and Seal's supposedly ambiguous relationship with the CIA; but there was little about an Arkansas governor or his state troopers. *American Made* was mostly hogwash, but hogwash that left America looking a little shabbier and the Clintons untouched. As I have said, Hollywood always disfigures the truth.

Thus, you can imagine my delight on the evening of July 17, 1995, a week after the publication of the August *Spectator*, when the president and his immensely self-satisfied wife, Hillary, paraded into the dining room of Washington's Jockey Club. He was with a dozen or so friends, and they were all seated across the room from me, my fourteen-year-old daughter Annie, and her young friend Zaina Arafat. Finally, I would get the official White House response to our Mena airport piece and from the White House's preeminent spokesman, the president himself. Tell me there is no God in heaven. The president proceeded to his table where his friends greeted him, while I consulted my conscience and the principia of good manners—at the time, the invaluable Miss Manners. I called for the maître d', whose name was, as I recall, Agnès, and asked her to tell the president that "Mr. Tyrrell of *The American Spectator* would like to send him over a bottle of champagne."

The Secret Service, of course, had to be consulted, but apparently, the president was pleased. A beaming Agnès returned to tell me that "President Clinton" would like to thank me personally after my meal, but, she advised, there were fifteen people in the president's party. "Two bottles," I insisted. My generosity is the stuff of legends.

Frankly, I was somewhat surprised by the president's response. Since late in 1993 when *The American Spectator*'s Troopergate stories began detailing the scortatory side of Clinton's social life, I had overseen an investigative team of journalists that both in Arkansas and Washington had turned up reports, as you may recall, of the Clintons' conflicts of interest, abuses of power, and campaign irregularities, such as using "walking around money" to buy votes and filing false financial papers. We had reported real estate shenanigans, banking scams, and sharp tax filings that revealed the Clintons taking deductions on such triflings as Bill's underwear. At the Jockey Club that night, Bill should have given me a wide berth. Yet on second thought, I should not have been surprised. For the past two years, I had been doing research on the Clintons for my book *Boy Clinton*. I learned that Clinton was a very reckless man, and he has many quirks. One of which is his weird trait of schmoozing. Down in Arkansas, it was known that if there was one person at a party who, he felt, disliked him, he would spend the entire party heaving himself at the skeptic. The evening of July 17, 1995, was my turn.

As we were almost finished with our meal, I sent over the champagne, notifying Agnès that I was ready to accept the president's gratitude. Past a wall of security personnel and through a corridor of flunkies, we were led. The Clintons were seated at one long table with their guests and fifteen tiny servings of champagne. Large and amiable, the president rose from his chair to greet us. He was all smiles; Mrs. Clinton, seated across from him, was less joyous.

Awash in a sense of the ceremony, I exulted: "And so we meet." He somewhat hesitantly joked, shook my hand—it was large, but it was weak—and immediately turned his practiced charm on my daughter and Zaina. He asked the girls for their ages. He spoke of Chelsea's summer camp. Out of the corner of my eye, I espied an increasingly perturbed Hillary. Time might be running out. Her eyes put me in mind of a snake about to strike. Quickly, I made my move for the White House's official response to the L. D. Brown-Mena story. Reminding the president of my respect for the Clintons' characteristically 1960s trait of "talking and talking" or "rapping and rapping," and always debating every issue with the utmost rigor, I briskly addressed the issue of the moment. "So, what did you think of the L. D. Brown story?" I asked. He reddened. He ignited.

He denied that he had read the piece. He said I should be "ashamed" of publishing the piece that he had not read. "Lies, lies," he intoned indignantly. The flunkies stiffened. The president's next charges were curiously familiar. He called Brown a "pathological liar" who had tried to destroy his own family. Those were precisely the lines that the White House's operatives had employed months before against Brown to kill a planned ABC interview with him. Actually, their use by the White House operatives was one of the reasons that L. D. Brown gave me for giving me his story rather than a major network. He did not trust them.

I replied that the president's hometown paper, the *Arkansas Democrat-Gazette*, had just described Brown as a very credible witness who had never yet been caught in a lie. The president began reiterating his charges word for word. I mentioned that it seemed to me he *had* read our piece. He continued with his charges and showed no sign of breaking off with what was becoming an increasingly uncomfortable conversation. Surely, I thought, he will wheel on me and, as the socialites say, "cut" me. But, no, he continued to sputter and whine. This, too, was what Arkansans had told me to expect. There stood this large man surrounded by friends and accompanied by Secret Service bodyguards. His anger, however, was completely without force. The president was angry. His voice was labored. Yet this was anger without strength. What came to mind was not the anger of a grown man but rather Tinker Bell in a snit.

The next day, when *The Washington Post* called me asking about my confrontation with the president, I admitted that "I had to break the conversation off; he was getting worked up."[1] I told President Clinton to go back to his table and enjoy his champagne. Breezily I told him: "We can take this matter up on another occasion." Alas, the occasion did not present itself again during his presidency. Life became hectic for him in his last years in office with his impeachment and everything. Again, it was our proofreader's fault that Bill's last years in office were so hectic. Yet we did meet again in Toronto, eleven years later for his sixtieth birthday as you will see.

There was one more amusing story about my presidential summit at the Jockey Club that long-ago August evening. When the press began pestering me about the event, I pooh-poohed their questions. Tim Watters, at the time the leading impersonator of Bill Clinton, was a friend of mine. I insisted that it was Watters whom I had encountered the night before. Surely the real president of the United States does not accept champagne in a restaurant from someone he does not know. Nor does the leader of the free world go meekly over and sit down when he is told to do so. Tim Watters was up to his old tricks again. I had encountered an imposter, but a pretty good one.

Yet, let me now turn to the case of Paula Corbin Jones as she is known to history, and to the Bait Shop Junta, which history might otherwise overlook. Though between Paula and the Bait Shop Junta, we shall pause to explain the Arkansas Project, which has been much maligned in the media and deserves a more serene judgment from history.

Paula is the woman whom Bill Clinton invited to a room in Little Rock's Excelsior Hotel for a tryst. At least, he was contemplating a tryst. I am not sure she was. The details of the event are subject to dispute, as it seems so many things are with the Clintons. In Troopergate I, we included Paula's name by mistake. Another way of putting it is that all the grief that Bill incurred resulted from his unruly libido and *The American Spectator*'s shoddy proofreaders. To be specific, the inclusion of Paula's name was a typographical error, though it became the most significant typographical error in American history. We did not mean to name any of the women mentioned in the piece, but we slipped up with Paula and included her first name. When she read it in our monthly issue, she claimed to be mortified. Why she picked up the *Spectator* that month, I have no idea. There was nothing in the issue about fashion trends or Mediterranean cuisine or interior decorating. Possibly she has always been a literary type, but I have my doubts. At any rate, she seemed to think every Arkansan would now recognize her as the Paula who caused Bill to lower his pants in broad daylight at the Excelsior Hotel. So, on May 6, 1994, she sued him for sexual harassment.

Thus, began a yearslong legal battle that eventually ended badly for Bill. As Bob Bartley summed it up in the *Wall Street Journal*, by

> his [Bill's] signing an "Agreed Order of Discipline" on his last day in office as president. It stipulated that he "knowingly gave evasive and misleading answers" about his relationship with Monica Lewinsky, violating Arkansas legal ethics. He agreed to accept suspension of his law license for five years and to pay a fine of $25,000. Earlier the Arkansas judge found him in contempt for the same testimony, and he paid more than $90,000, not to mention the $850,000 settlement in the Paula Jones suit.[2]

As for his impeachment trial, the House found him guilty. The Senate let him off the hook. So much for Bill's claims that he never did anything wrong.

Through most of these years, we were sidelined because of a government investigation of us that began in the spring of 1998. Our finances suffered thanks to legal bills and a reduction in donations. We moved from having a million-dollar cushion to living practically from hand to mouth. Many donors stuck by us, but a significant number did not, and we were in no financial shape to turn out blockbuster stories, even though I already had evidence that more blockbusters were out there. The donors who deserted us apparently thought that the good times were to last forever, while, by reducing our revenue, they helped the Clintons to survive. Still, we continued to publish, and the readership stuck with us. Yet our business operation was in a state of near collapse.

The problem began in the fall of 1997. Our publisher, Ron Burr, got into a row with the Scaife people. He had become increasingly difficult to work with, apparently taking credit for the product that the editorial department was putting out. On one occasion, he threat-ened to send a menacing letter to Dick Larry at Scaife. I implored him not to. We all traipsed down to board member Ted Olson's office—the Baron Von Kannon, Wlady Pleszczynski, Burr, and myself—and argued with Ron for some two hours, pleading with him not to send the letter. In the end, Ron said we were too late. He had already sent it.

Ironically, Burr was made out to be a hero. Of him, P. J. O'Rourke lamented erroneously that he "has given his whole life to this thing [that being *The American Spectator*]."[3] He had not. In the same *Washington Post* article, Andy Ferguson re-enforced P. J., saying Burr "was treated reprehensibly." Those that had to deal with Ron during these days often saw a different side of him, apparently, than O'Rourke and Ferguson did. There was no arguing with a person as stubbornly insubordinate as Ron. Paul Charnetzki, a member of our board and a partner at the Arthur Andersen accounting firm, was a longtime friend of Burr. Burr called him in to investigate our books covering the Arkansas Project. Paul told him that the books revealed that no crimes had been committed. Burr persisted. The FBI was called in. Its agents even paid Paul a visit. Alas, they agreed with Paul. No crimes had been found. Reluctantly, I let Burr go and then endured the attacks of those who thought my separation agreement with Ron was too generous. I have always said that leading *The American Spectator* has been a lot of fun, but some seasons have been more entertaining than others.

Any discussion of the Bait Shop Junta must begin with the Arkansas Project, which predates the emergence of Paula, though only by a few months. As a noted environmentalist, I have always spent as much time as possible in the forest and on the glistening waters of the Atlantic coast. In the forest, amidst the butterflies and the flowers, I accounted for a three-hundred-pound black bear back in the 1990s, and on the water, I have accounted for a plenitude of fish. Often, I have mixed hunting and fishing with work, usually with the likes of Dick Larry, my great friend from the Scaife Foundation and an environmen-talist in his own right. On one such outing, we apparently made our mark on history, at least on leftist history. On that outing, we dreamed up the Arkansas Project, which in leftist lore was but one more dirty trick perpetrated by us on the virtuous Clinton family. Hillary called it the "vast right-wing conspiracy."

The Scaife Foundation kicked in some $2 million to the Arkansas Project, and it was money well spent. We officially called it the "The Editorial Improvement Project" in our budget, though to the wags around our office, it quickly became known as the Arkansas Project. That was a joke, but the Left recognized it as a threat to democracy, ignoring similar endeavors, such as National Public Radio's "Collaborative Journalism Network," the *Huffington Post*'s "Investigative Fund," *Politico*'s "investigations team," and so forth. Enunciating the words "Arkansas Project" in a slightly menacing tone is, incidentally, another way the *Kultursmog* is created. By contrast, NPR's Collaborative Journalism Network is intoned with hints of solemnity on the airwaves.

By the way, Arkansas Project money was spent on projects well beyond the Clintons' errancies. Today, scholars who study the Clintons understand why much of the money we spent was in Arkansas. Arkansas was where the crooked stuff went on: from crooked fund-raising in Arkansas, to Indonesia and China, to crooked real estate dealings back home, to crooked cover-ups resulting from Bill's amorous seizures. There was an ongoing dispute in the office over how successful the Arkansas Project was. When asked about the quality of the research that the Arkansas Project came up with, James Ring Adams, a veteran of *The Wall Street Journal*, assessed it as "excellent." Danny Wattenberg claimed it was "totally useless."[4] I sided with Adams, who was a far more seasoned journalist than Danny. All the veteran journalists in our office—Adams, Corry, and Gold—were less excitable than the younger ones. As the years pile up, I believe that their views on the Arkansas Project have prevailed.

Another untruth about the Arkansas Project is that it was a secretive scheme designed by Dick Scaife to scandalize the Clintons. There was nothing secretive about it. It appeared in our public documents with the funds all properly accounted for. Furthermore, the Clintons themselves provided ample scandal to work with. As for any doubts about the Project's objectivity, consider this: Eventually, Dick Scaife quit funding us entirely after Corry unfavorably reviewed a book by Dick's friend, Chris Ruddy. It was the only time in some forty years that Dick ever pressured us for anything, though I knew we disagreed on some major issues, for instance, abortion. I withstood his pressure and stood by Corry. I lost Dick's support, though we remained friends. In fact, I always stood by my writers. I only wish they, particularly the young ones, had stood by me. Yet their disloyalty has served as even more evidence for one of Seth Lipsky's favorite rules, to wit: Writers are au fond, children—with rare exceptions.

Dick Scaife can even be absolved of Troopergate I and II. When he, working with his aide Dick Larry, was laying out the details for the Arkansas Project, Troopergate I was on its way to the printer, and Troopergate II was well underway. The Scaife organization is completely innocent of any damage that Troopergate I or II might have inflicted on the Clintons. I claim full credit for the two Troopergate stories, both of which were fully funded by *The American Spectator* before we undertook the Arkansas Project. Though we were all quite amazed by the stir created by the Arkansas Project in the media. All it was was an attempt to improve our investigative capacity. In this, we succeeded. Our board of directors was happy, even if our enemies were not. I am not sure that NPR and *Politico* succeeded, but then I am not an avid member of either group's audience.

If the Arkansas Project *became* a joke around the *Spectator* office, the Bait Shop Junta was nothing but a joke from beginning to end. We claimed that it was our response to the Clintons' attempts at prosecuting us (about which more shortly), and it did take the edge off the Justice Department's claim that we had engaged in witness tampering, a felony, opening up for me the prospect of jail. The Bait Shop itself was somewhere in the Ouachita Mountains, and it was run by

Parker Dozhier, a multifaceted Arkansan, who had worked in television and public relations but was most comfortable as a trapper and fisherman—another right-wing environmentalist. He claimed to be the magazine's "eyes and ears" in Arkansas, though we only kept him on a retainer. He kept in touch with the locals, the most important of whom was the independent counsel's key witness, David Hale. The Justice Department wanted to charge us with getting Hale to change his testimony, and though its investigation went on for more than a year, it never got much traction because of a fundamental problem with the charge. Hale never did change his testimony. Even much of the media recognized this.

I never put much trust in either Hale's or Dozhier's probity. Moreover, they did not seem to like each other. They had countless spats. For instance, when Hale was asked by the *New York Times* about the source of Dozhier's income, Hale's only response was, "He sells worms for a living."[5] Surely Hale could offer some colorful details. What about the pelts and the fish? Dozhier did live with a weird New Age girlfriend, Caryn Mann. Just the kind of reader that the *New York Times* now attracts. She had served as a delegate for Bill Clinton at the 1992 Florida State Democratic Convention. She told Dozhier that she knew where Jimmy Hoffa was buried, and she boasted that she had the power to turn the rain on and off. She was full of New Age hocus-pocus and "had given psychic readings and taught astrology at a Hot Springs bookstore."[6] In another report, Tony Snow wrote that "She says she telepathically manipulated troop movements during the Gulf War."[7] At this writing, we are still looking for evidence.

Meanwhile, Paula was pursuing her case, claiming that Bill Clinton sexually harassed her. On May 27, 1997, the Supreme Court agreed that she could proceed, and on January 17, 1998, all hell broke loose when the Drudge Report broke the story that *Newsweek* had been sitting on a story that Bill had been having an affair in the White House with a twenty-two-year-old intern: pretty, perky, albeit also porky, Monica Lewinsky. Bill, of course, proceeded to lie about it. In his deposition on Monica, given the same day as the Drudge Report story, Bill said he never had sex with her. Nine days later, he famously said, "I did not have sexual relations with that woman, Miss Lewinsky." Now he had lied under oath and was in big trouble. He was headed for impeachment, and all because of a sleepy proofreader in our office. Yet, his lie about sex helped to vindicate *The American Spectator*.

In Troopergate, Trooper Larry Patterson explained in amazement Bill's biblical exegesis of oral sex. "He told me," Patterson said, "that he had researched the subject in the Bible and oral sex isn't considered adultery."[8] That was precisely the sophistication that he used with Monica more than a decade later and God knows how many women in between. Bill was obsessed with oral sex. He had nine sexual encounters with Monica in the Oval Office and nearby without ever having intercourse with her. On September 9, 1998, the *Starr Report* was given to Congress, and whatever began with Bill and Paula in the Excelsior Hotel culminated in the House of Representatives on December 19, 1998. Bill was impeached. On February 12, 1999, the Senate voted to acquit him.

From the publication of our first Troopergate exposé to our eventual exoneration for witness tampering in July 1999, we had our eerie moments. There were nights spent with hired bodyguards in the Arkansas countryside. Even worse, there were nights spent without bodyguards. As mentioned earlier, our offices in Northern Virginia were broken into twice, our New York apartment once. Thieves stole the manuscript to *Boy Clinton* while it was being sent across town to Bob Novak for a blurb. Then there was that anonymous package I received a few weeks after Hillary Clinton's January 27 challenge to the press to look into that "vast right-wing conspiracy," which we called the "vast white-ring conspiracy." It was a Priority Mail package from the White House postmarked February 26, 1998. Was I supposed to be frightened? I still have it, and it has yet to explode. All it contained was an autographed copy of the forty-second president's collection of sermons, *Between Hope and History*—no cover letter, no lock of hair. Like Prince Metternich, when confronted by the death in 1838 of Talleyrand, I thought, "I wonder what he meant by that."

By 1998, enough financial backers had withdrawn from the fray for our finances to demand fresh resources. My friend George Gilder came to the rescue and saved an embattled conservative institution single-handedly by purchasing it. He handed it back to me in the middle of 2002 for $0.00 in an act of colossal generosity. At the time, George could have used the proceeds of a sale for himself. I talk increasingly throughout this memoir of how the conservative movement was cracking up. George's act of selflessness demonstrates that there were still those in the movement who remembered the old days. George and Bob Bartley were two such conservatives. Bob invited Seth Lipsky, George, and me to an absurdly posh restaurant to plan the magazine's future. As for Bob, he did not have much future left. He was dying of cancer, but he wanted to do one more favor for the magazine. When George offered to give the magazine back to me despite having buyers in the wings, I said, "I'll take it." As Lipsky said at the time, "you did not have enough money to pay for the dinner." He was right. Bartley picked up the tab.

It was about this time that our former board member and occasional writer, Ted Olson, was nominated by President George W. Bush to be his solicitor general. Vermont's Senator Patrick Leahy, a Clinton loyalist on the Senate Judiciary Committee and an early and ardent propounder of the "vast right-wing conspiracy," wrote to me demanding access to the records of The American Spectator's board meetings. He hoped to prove that Olson was a party to that burning Clinton bugaboo, the Arkansas Project. Again, I had to defend the interests of the organization against government intrusion. Again, the integrity of the First Amendment was threatened. And again, our documents made their mysterious appearance in the Clinton press. For one more time, almost no one in the press joined me in defense of the First Amendment, except for Bill Safire of the New York Times, Wes Pruden of the *Washington Times*, and the inevitable Bob Bartley with his big gun, the *Wall Street Journal*.

Bob even called the self-appointed keeper of the First Amendment, Floyd Abrams, telling him I would be calling him for advice. I called and called. Abrams never called back. One day, years later, I heard he was giving a talk on the First Amendment. I stopped by, hoping to hear something inspirational. When he was finished doling out his pablum, I introduced myself and asked him why he never returned my calls after Bob Bartley had asked me to call. He answered, "Because Tyrrell, you never listen." I thought it an odd reply. I had never before met him.

Ah well, by late July 1999, after spending a million dollars in legal defense and staring down charges of witness tampering and threatening to murder a young man, we were given a clean bill of health from government investigator Michael Shaheen. The time had now come to close down the Bait Shop Junta. The Clintons had turned up the heat in the kitchen. They thought that by prosecuting us, they would put pressure on Ken Starr's key witness, David Hale. Yet after reviewing what the government accomplished, I think we can say with confidence that it was *The American Spectator* that cooked the Clintons' goose. As Grover Norquist and Tom Wolfe were to affirm in the years ahead, the investigative journalism of *The American Spectator* in the 1990s assured Hillary's defeat in 2016. With Hillary's defeat in 2016, the Clintons were finished as a force in American politics.

I recall walking back from my only appearance before a government inquiry with my immensely competent and quite beefy lawyer, Dick Leon, who is now a respected judge but at the time looked like a figure out of *The Godfather*. I asked him how I handled the FBI agents, the Department of Justice lawyers, and others who attended the proceedings. Dick replied with amazement that I handled them with the utmost professionalism. Not one of their inquiries did I flub, not even the question asked of me about how I wrote a bestseller. Dick had at the time interjected that if the agent had literary ambitions, he would have to ask "Mr. Tyrrell" for advice "on his dime not on Tyrrell's." Then Dick asked how I knew how to reveal so little under examination. "Dick," I told him, "some months ago, we published a piece on Bill Clinton's appearance at his grand jury hearing." He was querulous, sanctimonious, condescending, and verbose. "I think his unctuousness and verbosity sank him. I sought to do just the opposite, and so I did."

The American Spectator was exonerated, a word that the Clintons have rarely heard directed at them. Stephen Glover in the London *Spectator* handed down the judgment that most American news organs still cannot say out loud:

> These journalists, whether of Right or Left, stood outside the charmed circle, never receiving invitations to attend White House parties and enduring the vituperation of the Clintonites. One of them is Bob Tyrrell, editor of *The American Spectator*. Another is Ambrose Evans-Pritchard, latterly of the *Sunday Telegraph*...[9]

I remember Ambrose with great affection. He was one relentless journalist.

I wrote up how we at the magazine felt about our exoneration in the September 1999 issue under "The Continuing Crisis":

> July has passed and with it *The American Spectator*'s long national nightmare. For over a year this magazine has been the only magazine in American history pursued by its own Independent Counsel. In the Spring of 1998 Good Government Democrats, led by Sen. Robert Torricelli, Rep. John Conyers, and Mrs. Hillary Milhous Clinton, prevailed on the Justice Department to demand the investigation of *The American Spectator* and its secret agents who were then perpetrating a "vast right-wing conspiracy" against Mrs. Clinton's husband and all of his girlfriends, even those who freely consented. The demand was based on charges made by Miss Caryn Mann, one

of Arkansas' most respected tarot-card readers and a patriot who admits to having used her psychic wizardry to direct American troops to victory in the Gulf War. (She also uses the little elves in her cranium to turn rain on and off over Arkansas' parched fields.) Reporting to former Arkansas Senator David Pryor and to one of Mrs. Clinton's favorite journalists, a UFO watcher for the soft-porn Internet magazine *Salon*, Miss Mann attested to seeing vast sums of monies pass hands from *Spectator* agents to a Whitewater witness, Mr. David Hale. The alleged transactions took place in a rural Arkansas bait shop, Dozhier's Bait Shop at Rainbow Landing. Thus was born what generations of American school children will learn to call the Bait Shop Junta. In the Clinton legacy it will rank with the works of John Wilkes Booth and Benedict Arnold. Forgotten will be the names of Monica Lewinsky and Paula Corbin Jones. That was mere sex.

According to Miss Mann, there in that historic bait shop—whilst thousands of minnows and night crawlers turned a blind eye—she saw thousands of dollars change hands. Then it was only hundreds of dollars. Then it was her 13-year-old son who witnessed the evil transaction, the one who does math with his fingers. On CNN Miss Susan McDougal's lawyer mentioned $2.3 million! Though the Clinton administration likes to keep the cost of government investigations to a minimum and feels very badly about Independent Counsel Ken Starr's exorbitance, Attorney General Janet Reno persuaded Mr. Starr to commence a special investigation of the Bait Shop Junta, hauling the alleged conspirators before a specially convened Arkansas grand jury and gathering documents. The investigation was conducted by Mr. Michael E. Shaheen, a former head of the Justice Department's Office of Professional Responsibility known for his exhaustive quests. Boiling with anticipation, *Salon*'s UFO watchers temporarily put aside their celestial examinations to boom his work (part of which would include contacting over 160 persons) as the most important government inquiry since perhaps the 1950's Army McCarthy hearings. Alas, all was for naught, aside from the no doubt considerable sum Miss Mann's allegations cost taxpayers and the lesser amount inflicted upon *The American Spectator*. On July 28 the Office of the Independent Counsel released Mr. Shaheen's finding: "Many of the allegations, suggestions and insinuations" that were not simply "unsubstantiated" were "in some cases, untrue." Mr. Shaheen's office further concluded that "no prosecution be brought in this matter as there is insufficient credible evidence to support criminal charges." [10]

Or, for those skeptics who think I am making light of a serious legal matter, allow me to quote Mr. Shaheen's press release on his two most devastating judgments:

> After conducting an independent investigation into allegations the [sic] David Hale may have received payments to influence his testimony in matters within the jurisdiction of the Office of the Independent Counsel (OIC), the Office of Special Review has concluded that many of the allegations, suggestions and insinuations regarding the tendering and receipt of things of value were shown to be unsubstantiated or, in some cases, untrue.

And the Office of Special Review concluded that:

> In some instances, there is little if any credible evidence establishing that a particular thing of value was demanded, offered or received. In other instances, there is insufficient credible evidence to show that a thing of value was provided or received with criminal intent defined by any of the applicable statutes.[11]

In other words, we members of the Bait Shop Junta had done no wrong.

Sprinkled through what remained of the late 1990s were a few more memorable events. One was the emergence in early 1997 of a 332-page report drawn up in the Clinton White House chronicling the "conspiracy commerce." I am afraid that the White House viewed me—a country boy from the cornfields of Indiana—as a party to conspiracy. As the White House's press secretary, Mike McCurry, explained it, the 332-page report was "an effort [by the Clintonites]…to really help journalists understand that they shouldn't be used by those who are really concocting their own conspiracies and their own theories and then peddling them" to the credulous mainstream media.[12] News sources such as the *Washington Post* and the *New York Times* were finding stories that were appearing in *The American Spectator* and the *Daily Telegraph* of London irresistible. Working with the crafty journalists at the *Telegraph*, we had devised what the White House termed a "media food chain" of wild stories about Bill Clinton and women, extravagant fundraising schemes, and vast corruption. The major news sources gave our work a big play. There was only one problem with the 332-page report. Most of our allegations we now know were true. As Fred Barnes of *The Weekly Standard* appraised it, "This is paranoia at the highest level of government." He continued, "This is a remarkable role reversal. It used to be that the wild conspiracy theories were on the right."[13] C. Boyden Gray, who served as George H.W. Bush's White House counsel, called it "kind of goofy."[14] Yet it was very amusing, reminding us that Hillary still had a role to play at the White House.

Another memorable event took place on October 1, 1997, the publication date for *The Impeachment of William Jefferson Clinton: A Political Docu-Drama*. It was a book that was written as though the impeachment had already taken place, and I coauthored it with "Anonymous," causing somewhat of a controversy in our nation's capital. Speculation immediately and inaccurately centered on Ted Olson as Anonymous. Ted was my close friend and a legendary Washington lawyer who had appeared before the Supreme Court by 1997 eleven times. He also served on the *Spectator*'s board and was suspected of writing anonymously in our February 1994 issue under the Hobbesian pen name Solitary, Poor, Nasty, Brutish, and Short. In that piece, he speculated that Bill Clinton was potentially subject to 178 years in prison for crimes he had already committed as president and to $2.5 million in fines. Hillary got off easy. She had, since coming to Washington, run up potential penalties of forty-seven years in the penitentiary and $1.2 million in fines.

We chose Bob Bork, President Ronald Reagan's defeated Supreme Court nominee, to review the book for our December issue, triggering rumors that Bob was Anonymous. All the rumors were false, though Ted did have a hand in writing the Solitary, Poor, Nasty, Brutish, and Short piece. I had decided to haul Vic Gold, our incognito author of *The Danny Quayle Reader*, out of retirement for one more shot at namelessness fame. For some twenty-five years, no one guessed Vic's role in *The Impeachment of William Jefferson Clinton*, not even Wlady. He admitted this as this memoir was going into galleys. There should have been a place for me at the CIA. I can really keep a secret.

Bob Bork's review was sublime. He wrote in his review that "Bill Clinton came to office promising the most ethical administration in our history and has instead given us the sleaziest." When Vic and I were writing *Impeachment*, we did not have the delightful Monica to deal with. She was then unknown, but we did manage Bill's impeachment based on Whitewater, Travelgate, Hillary's missing papers, the Riady family's China connection, and the suppression of the Resolution Trust Corporation investigation. As Bob summed up, "Clinton has worked overtime to justify Mark Helprin's judgment that he may be 'the most corrupt, fraudulent and dishonest president we have ever known.'" A fair assessment that, by a fine judge of character, but still Bob should have been raised to the Supreme Court back in 1997 rather than having to serve as the opening target for what was to become the vicious partisanship of the following decades.

As we closed out the twentieth century, I personally felt the chill winds of what would be called within twenty years the "cancel culture." For me cancel culture was not so painful. As Lally Weymouth said to me in the 1990s, "You've got yours. There is nothing people in Washington can do for you."[15] She was right, but I noticed how what we now call cancel culture particularly affected people who appeared on television. They were desperate for the tube's attention. For years, I did a couple of versions of a show called *The Editors* out of Montreal. The Canadian, Larry Shapiro, produced and directed the shows. He was one of the few people involved in television whom I considered fair-minded and interested in ideas, but then he had coached wrestling before his stint in television. A lot of the big names who established themselves in television got their start with Larry. We would come up to Montreal on Friday nights, tape as many as a half dozen shows, and Larry would be set for weeks. Generally, we would end a taping session with a lively dinner.

I remember aspiring politicians, such as Stephen Harper, who would become prime minister of Canada, and old-timers, such as the Canadian novelist Mordecai Richler, a certified curmudgeon. There were the rising Americans, such as Juan Williams and Chris Matthews. They could not be stopped in their pursuit of television glory. If one of these guys found a door open at a major studio, he would be in in a flash. Getting him out of the studio would present difficulties. I will admit I relished crossing swords with the likes of

Governor Howard Dean of Vermont, who was a regular. The gov and I had no-holds-barred, mano-a-mano combat on numerous occasions. I vaguely recall taunting him into making a rude reference to Iowa's caucus system. It was to cost him his front-runner role in the next season's primaries. I liked the relaxed way of the Canadians, though there was always pressure on them. The show accepted money from the Corporation for Public Broadcasting, and on at least one occasion the CEO of WETA in Washington, Sharon Rockefeller, told Larry that his show would have a better time slot on Saturday night if he arranged my retirement. Larry saved me from that episode of cancel culture, but not the next time.

In the late 1990s, I disappeared from CNN. By then, Larry's show had ended owing to his poor health. I did not disappear as dramatically from CNN as my colleague at the *Spectator*, Jeff Lord, did twenty years later. He got a rude telephone call from the studio protesting his charges of anti-Semitism from one of the usual left-wing sources. As for me, I just stopped getting calls. Finally, I telephoned a reliable spy at CNN. He had told me years before that a CNN executive named Ed Turner liked my style. Now he told me I would not be invited back: "Because of what you did to the Clintons." I did not ask for further elaboration. An explanation could be too gruesome. But truth be known, I had tired of television by then.

Some of those people who are featured on the tube have been around for years—no, make that, for decades. Back in 1984, when I appeared on *Summer Sunday, U.S.A.*, the host of the show was Andrea Mitchell. Thirty-seven years later, she was still going. She and TV personalities like her spend so much time in the greenroom that they seem to develop a green pallor. I have held the same job for more than fifty years, but it has allowed me to do different things. All that poor Andrea and others like her do is to slowly decay on the screen. They read the *New York Times* by day and regurgitate it in the evening. The television audience has become increasingly impatient with television's obvious bias. It has taken on the character of propaganda,

Kultursmog's propaganda. Viewers think it is a sign of ingrained prejudice. I have an alternative explanation. It is a sign of how many years they have been hanging around the station. After thirty or so years, they sink into a state of arrested middle age.

One day, toward the end of the 1990s, I got a surprising telephone call. An unfamiliar but friendly enough voice said to me something to the effect of, "This is going to surprise you, Mr. Tyrrell." He was calling me from *George* magazine, John F. Kennedy Jr.'s monthly magazine of political gossip, and he wanted to send over a photographer to take my picture. I had been chosen by the editors of *George* as one of the best-dressed men in Washington. I would be featured with such luminaries as Pat Moynihan, Rahm Emanuel, and Vernon Jordan. Well, what the hell? They were all liberals, but my tailor in London would be happy. So, I sat with the photographer for an hour or so and got on with a busy week. It was toward the end of 1997, and I soon forgot all about sartorial stardom. That was until the November issue of *George* made its appearance. Wlady broke the news. Pat was in it, and Vernon and Rahm too, but no one in the office could find me. They even checked the back of the book and the help wanted ads. In those days, we did not call it "cancel culture." We called it bad manners, and within four years, *George* was no more.

I ended the 1990s, and all the Episodic Chaos that went with it, in the company of two very tough ladies, Jeane Kirkpatrick and Jeanne Marie Hauch—two Jeanes or Jeannes. When the Clintons began attacking us, and the summertime soldiers began deserting us, Jeane Kirkpatrick stood by us. She would repeat the words of the Eric Clapton song, "Nobody Loves You When You're Down and Out," but she certainly stuck by us. At a climactic board of directors meeting at the Cosmos Club toward the end of 1998, I reiterated Conrad Black's offer to us. He was the second-largest owner of English-language newspapers in the world, and he offered to take *The American Spectator* off my hands for $100,000, take control of the board, and he would install David Frum as editor. I said no. Bob Novak objected. In his famous made-for-television growl, he challenged me, saying, "Who do you think you are, Tyrrell?" Before I could properly identify myself, Jeane stood up. She cleared her throat much as she had before defending the United States and Israel at the United Nations in the 1980s and said, "I'll tell you who he is. He is the founder and editor in chief of this magazine, and if he says he's not giving it up, he's not giving it up." Several years later, Conrad—whom I still admired, though with care—was on his way to jail, and Jeane and her fellow board member, former secretary of the Treasury William Simon, who could not attend the meeting in question, presided in tranquility on the generally peaceful board. As for Bob Novak, as I explained in Chapter IV, he apologized over dinner at the Cosmos Club.

This brings me to Jeanne Hauch. The night after Barbara Olson arranged my impromptu meeting with her, I invited Jeanne to dinner à deux in Washington, and on that wintry night, I decided I never wanted to be apart from her again. She was as tough as Jeane Kirkpatrick and as devoted to our principles. My children loved her, and she loved them. She had a great sense of elegance and was very funny. A former prosecutor, she carried from time to time a .45 caliber Smith & Wesson. She purchased it after being accosted in her apartment by a would-be assailant who somehow left the apartment in one piece. Jeanne is excitable. Oh yes, she is a blonde. Gentlemen prefer blondes who attended Princeton University and Yale Law School, was a Fulbright Scholar, clerked for a Supreme Court justice, and can cook.

Our wedding was held at Holy Rosary Church, the Italian national church in downtown Washington—though neither of us is Italian. Ted Olson was best man, and his wife, Barbara, was numbered among the bridesmaids. Jeanne and I were well aware that we owed her everything. She was the cause of my failed playboy status. What is more, she was a rising star in the conservative intellectual world. When she died as American Airlines Flight 77 hit the Pentagon, our loss was incalculable. A great source of laughter and wisdom was no more.

As the proceedings against *The American Spectator* had yet to be wrapped up, I always figured that the FBI was in attendance at our nuptials, along with some lawyers from the Justice Department. Jeanne married me anyway, and she brought her cat named Sheena. I am allergic to cats, and Sheena lived to be twenty years of age. It was what the shrinks call a testing period. We never got a replacement for Sheena. We settled on Labrador retrievers.

We honeymooned in Positano along Italy's Amalfi coast. A couple of miles down the mountainous coast was Ravello, where my longtime adversary, Gore Vidal, maintained a lavish home amidst a block of elegant villas overlooking the glistening Tyrrhenian Sea some twelve hundred feet below. The home next to Gore's was for sale. I immediately put in a bid on the place. Jeanne and I never heard from Gore, though I sent a ceramics dealer—a local character—who lived at the bottom of the road leading up to Gore's residence with a bottle of cheap wine and a note to my prospective neighbor. Actually, I was remiss. I should have delivered the wine myself.

Chapter XI

THE INFANTILIZATION OF AMERICA

At the very end of the 1990s, as the Clintons were preparing for Hillary's Senate race, she granted the inaugural issue of *Talk* magazine an interview, which I would very much like to have attended, accompanied, of course, by a psychiatrist. In her interview, Hillary was intent on clearing up some questions about her husband's sex life that the Monica Lewinsky affair made unavoidable. She told *Talk* magazine that her husband's sexual misbehavior might have arisen from a troubled childhood, and she was trying to help him with his "weakness," though she must have known that the recidivism rate for sex offenders is very high. Yet Hillary is a trouper and so she was, once again, a good sport.

She had initially blamed Bill's behavior on the "vast right-wing conspiracy," but even her usual apologists in the media were not convinced. So, she tried a different tack. She traced his problem with sex as going all the way back to when he was four years old. According to

Hillary, he "was so young, barely four, when he was scarred by abuse that he can't even take it out and look at it."[1] Where did he keep "it"? Hillary does not say. Who fed "it" when "it" was hungry? Again, she is evasive. Did "it" ever make noise, perhaps late at night when others were trying to get some sleep? The question is left unanswered. This is where the psychiatrist would be helpful. Hillary does say: "There was terrible conflict between his mother and grandmother."[2] Can you imagine the wife of any other American president talking in this way about her husband? It is as though some part of Bill is still four years old and some part of Hillary is not much more mature. Scholars who study cultural decline tell us a country can never escape its history. The Clintons have, for over a generation, played an inordinate role in American history. It is time to end it.

I can imagine millions of Americans sounding like Hillary in her *Talk* magazine interview. It began with her fellow coat-and-tie radicals in the 1960s, but it has steadily spread throughout the Infantilized sectors of America and now professors study it at the great universities. Perhaps someday, along with Episodic Chaos and Episodic Calm, the professoriate will devote whole departments to the Infantilization of America. It is of a piece with the Dumbing Down of America. How long can it last?

I suppose the leading countries of the world are often depicted by the history they have made. Great Britain has a history of colonizing and civilizing that has been, for the most part, an improvement over the way it found its erstwhile colonies. France, too, has a similar history, though on a lesser scale. Germany, after a late start, was headed in a promising direction until the Germans encountered Nazism and simply could not resist it. The historian Hélène Carrère d'Encausse has painted a much darker history of Russia. In her magisterial work, *The Russian Syndrome: One Thousand Years of Political Murder*, she writes that "the history of Russia is first and foremost a *continuous history of political murder*."[3] What literate soul can doubt her? America comes off much better, perhaps even better than Great Britain and France.

Though only some 250 years old, America has remade the world along republican lines or, at least, tried to remake the world along republican lines. America saved the civilized world in two world wars, and ushered in modern times, rendering a massive frontier, one of the most modern landscapes on earth though time may be running out for us.

Now its civilization is disappearing before the onslaught of Americans who do not feel comfortable being adults. They have discovered that they can flourish as "kids," and they are flourishing as "kids" for now. Some cash their Social Security checks every month and still live like "kids." The scholar who has written most extensively on the subject of the Infantilization of America is Professor Simon Gottschalk who teaches at the University of Nevada in Las Vegas, where he apparently watches a lot of television and takes notes in the course of this scholarly work. He has come up with an insightful, if alarming, thesis. According to the prof, television assists in spreading the "Infantilization of the West."[4] In fact, television is essential for the Infantilization of the West, though for my purposes I shall just stick with the "Infantilization of America." I do not want to take on more Infantilization than I can handle.

For instance, if you have seen a grown man wearing short pants despite the approach of winter, pay attention. To be sure, Professor Gottschalk does. Probably the man in short pants is carrying a bottle of water and has his baseball cap on backward. Perhaps he is wearing a T-shirt with an infantile declaration across his chest. If this spectacle troubles you, you are probably in Professor Gottschalk's camp. You certainly are in my camp.

I live in the Washington, DC, area and I see spectacles such as the above all the time. Since the Biden administration settled in, I have even seen an influx of this sort of dress around the White House. In fact, I would not be surprised to see a fellow dressed like this on the very steps of the Old Executive Office Building. He probably checks his water bottle at the front door and submits his attaché case for the Secret Service's inspection. Protocols have declined in our dress code, but I assume everyone still observes security regulations. By the way, I would not be surprised to see women in the Biden White House attired in this way, too, particularly wearing their baseball caps backward as they skip into the Oval Office. For a certitude, Professor Gottschalk would be troubled, even if he is a Bidenite. He comes across as a man who observes standards, even when he is in a majority that is on the decline.

He also seems to find it troubling for television to feature "a cartoon bear pitching…toilet paper" to his television audience. Equally troubling to the prof is, he says, "a gecko with a British accent selling you auto insurance and a bunny in sunglasses promoting batteries." I do not mean to be picky, but I have seen the same advertisements and I am certain that the gecko is Australian. Yet I have no problem with the professor's conclusion when he says that "This has always struck me as a bit odd. Sure, it makes sense to use cartoon characters to sell products to kids—a phenomenon that's been well-documented. But why are advertisers using the same techniques on adults? To me, it's just one symptom of a broader trend of infantilization in Western culture"[5]—or at least in American culture.

Professor Gottschalk proceeds to demonstrate how we "routinely infantilize large swaths of the population." We do it when we refer to grown women as "girls." We do it when we treat the aged as children when they live in adult care centers, and I love this: The prof trains his focus on higher education. He accuses administrators at higher education asylums of infantilizing their students by promoting "safe spaces," and such nonsense as "trigger warnings" about an indelicacy that might lie ahead for them when they are reading a book or entering a museum. Then he goes off the rails a bit when he talks about the treatment of teenagers. He thinks we demean them much as we demean the aged. Nonetheless, Professor Gottschalk is on to something when he warns against cartoon bears or "safe spaces" or "trigger warnings;" but he has already made his point. Our culture is in trouble.[6]

Along with Episodic Chaos and Episodic Calm, we now live with an Infantilized America that can make an appearance at any moment. All three have been a major theme of the late twentieth century, extending on into the twenty-first century. The stylish culture that America shipped abroad in the first half of the twentieth century has disappeared, to be replaced by the work of angry children. Some really are children. Others are hanging onto their childhood well into middle age. The Clintons did not begin the Infantilization of America, but they certainly helped it along. What might be the outcome if the last fifty years of Infantilized America encounters an angry Russia full of what Hélène Carrère d'Encausse calls a thousand years of "political murder"? Will there be large enough "safe spaces" for the little darlings to withdraw to in America? I know that America saved the world from the last completed edition of Russian political murder—before Russia's attempted rape of Ukraine—but that was when America was ruled by Ronald Reagan and George H. W. Bush. Now, if Professor Gottschalk is right, we are headed for serious trouble.

The American generation that fought World War II is called, at the risk of exaggeration, the Greatest Generation. I would have thought the barefooted generation that shivered through the winter at Valley Forge had a superior claim to the title, but I shall let it pass. The Greatest Generation gave birth to the 1960s generation, which certainly was the most overrated generation in our history while being probably the most political generation in our history. The 1960s generation divided itself between the coat-and-tie radicals, whom we have already met, and the penny-loafer conservatives, who helped Ronald Reagan and George H. W. Bush with the conservative revolution. We at *The American Spectator* would be numbered among the latter.

The coat-and-tie radicals were the most ballyhooed, but the penny-loafer conservatives governed America longer, from 1980 until 2008, with a two-year hiatus from 1992 to 1994. After which, Newt Gingrich and his Republican majority came in to finish the conservatives' renewal. That is the way we at *The American Spectator* saw things. In 1994, the Republicans captured both houses for the first time in four decades. A dazed President Clinton was forced to declare, "The era of big government is over," a declaration as famous as his line "I did not have sexual relations with that woman, Miss Lewinsky." The stage was set for the election of 2000.

It pitted Vice President Al Gore against Texas Governor George W. Bush, and Gore was expected to win, which should come as no surprise. In the *Kultursmog*, the Democrats are always expected to win. Moreover, in 2000, Gore was running on President Clinton's record of peace and prosperity, and his opponent, Governor Bush, was relatively unknown. Nonetheless, in my syndicated column, I stuck my neck out and chose Bush, but the race was, in fact, very close. On Election Day, Wlady joined Bob Novak at Bob's traditional reception at The Palm restaurant and reported back that the assembled, mostly Republicans, were gloomy. Both the exit polls and Bob's sources reported that the race was going to be very close.

Yet the vice president had broken with his boss's centrism. In the course of the race, he had veered far to the left, too far, thank God. Possibly he was still smarting from the reaction he had provoked a year before when Bill was impeached. Then, standing at Bill's side, Gore declaimed him as "one of our greatest presidents." A year later, sensible independents still had not gotten over that howler. George W. lost the popular vote, but he won the Electoral College. Gore called Bush late in the night and conceded. But wait! After conferring with his staff, Al called back and retracted his concession. Bush expressed his amazement, provoking Al to respond, "You don't have to be snippy about it."[7] Thus began the historic wrangling that was settled only when the Supreme Court stepped in and issued a controversial five to four decision that effectively awarded the presidency to Bush. Bush officially won by 271 to 266, one more than the required 270 votes. At *The American Spectator*, we were exultant. After all, Bush's lawyer was Ted Olson who only recently had left our board of directors.

The Democrats have always played hardball, but the Republicans whom George W. had recruited showed that they, in 2000, could play hardball too. The year 2000 was a turning point in American politics. Now both sides would play hardball, and our man Olson was right in the thick of it. I do not know how many times Al Gore's lawyers had appeared before the Supreme Court, but I know that Ted had by now appeared fourteen times before the Court. On December 11, he appeared again, and he won. From December 11, 2000, on, America experienced one of its longest periods of Episodic Chaos, with very little Calm to relieve the Chaos. Charles Krauthammer, the Pulitzer Prize–winning columnist, was also a certified psychiatrist, who twenty-five years earlier had discovered the psychiatric syndrome known as "Secondary Mania."* After observing the Democrats' frenzy over Bush, Charles confected another syndrome. He called it the "Bush Derangement Syndrome" and described it as "the acute onset of paranoia in otherwise normal people in reaction to the policies, the presidency—nay—the very existence of George W. Bush."[8] Years later, the symptoms were spotted again during the presidency of Donald Trump, and the syndrome was renamed the Trump derangement syndrome. More on this later.

After the Episodic Chaos of the 2000 election, America experienced six months of Episodic Calm before being confronted by contemporary America's own modern-day Pearl Harbor attack, known generally as 9/11. Americans rose to the challenge and performed admirably, most notable was the president from the penny-loafer-conservative wing of the 1960s generation, George W. While his predecessor from the narcissistic coat-and-tie-radical wing of the generation lived up to expectations. Bill pouted. No less a source than the *New York Times* reported that Bill fretted that he was no longer president

---

* Interested readers will find Dr. Krauthammer's entry in the Archives of General Psychiatry, November 1978.

and could not partake in the glory he assumed would be George W. Bush's.[9] Alas and forsooth!

The darkest day that many of us can remember in Washington was actually bright and sunny—a beautifully clear September day.

I was driving my car north out of Alexandria's Old Town district to get a haircut when my wife called from her office in Washington to tell me that an airplane had just crashed into one of the World Trade Center's twin towers. "An idiot in a Piper Cub," I exclaimed. A few minutes later, Jeanne called again. Another plane had struck the second tower. That had to be an act of terror, I thought. Proceeding north on George Washington Memorial Parkway, I encountered clouds of smoke off to my left from the Pentagon. I am not sure that I put the two events together. My barbershop was about two miles from the Pentagon, and the stench of burning fuel was in the air. More ominous still was the piece of mangled equipment in the street as I approached the barbershop. When I left the shop, Wlady called and explained the day's events. Shortly thereafter, he called again with the news that Barbara Olson was rumored to have been on one of the fated flights. Soon Jeanne confirmed the rumor and told me that we should all drift out to Ted and Barbara's home. Jeanne was preparing provisions. So were others. That night it seemed like all of Ted and Barbara's friends were at Ted's home offering consolation to him. He held up like the man he has always been. In two weeks, he had to appear before the Supreme Court in his role as solicitor general. He would be ready.

As I remember the evening of September 11, people kept stopping in with food and refreshments, as many as a half dozen at a time. If the Olsons had been liberals, Hollywood would have made a movie about that night. I remember Bob Bork and his wife Mary Ellen were there, and Kellyanne Conway, and Barbara Ledeen and her husband Michael. Judge Ray Randolph and his wife Lee O'Connor were constant fixtures as well as Ken Starr and his wife Alice and, of course, Justice Clarence Thomas and his wife Ginni. There were many more. Barbara Ledeen and Barbara Comstock completed the Herculean task of putting together a film of Barbara's life for viewing that evening. Michael delivered the chilling judgment that the atrocity could not have been accomplished without state support. Later, we discovered that Michael was right. The state was America. All the pilots of the highjacked airplanes were trained in America.

I remember that the mood that night was sad. Highlights? Well, at one point, I believe Ted found a note from Barbara on the home telephone. The sadness was made all the more poignant by what seemed to be an endless parade of delivery trucks coming up the driveway with gifts purchased by Barbara while on a recent buying spree made during happier times, now gone forever. Yet the saddest story of all was the story about how she got on flight 77 to Los Angeles. She was supposed to leave the day before, on September 10. Instead, she stayed to be with Ted on the morning of his sixty-first birthday, September 11. It was the last time they were together.

Yet our lives at *The American Spectator* were never without amusement for long. At about this time, an amusing fellow began to make his mark on the national scene. He had written for us before and he wrote quite well on public policy, albeit he was egregiously fussy. So much so that Wlady, who had by now become our editorial director, was given to calling him David Frump, though he was more widely known as David Frum. We shall encounter him later in this chapter under less amusing circumstances. At any rate, he became a speechwriter in the early Bush administration, though his career as a speechwriter for the president became a cropper when he was caught encouraging the false claim that he had authored the administration's phrase, "axis of evil," which the president used in his State of the Union address. Upon being exposed, he settled for being identified as a writer who had *assisted* in creating the phrase, which does not ring true, either. After all, even in a government bureaucracy, how many writers are needed to create a three-word phrase? Well, he soon left the Bush White House. Some said he was pushed out. He rapidly turned out *The Right Man: The Surprise Presidency of George W. Bush*, in which he proclaimed that the forty-third president was "nothing short of superb."[10] Frump was not done growing. Brief years later, he wrote another preachy book titled *Comeback: Conservatism That Can Win Again*, wherein he wrote that President Bush "led his party to the brink of disaster."[11] Frump's growth continued. He wrote a roman à clef about me among others that depicted the conservative movement as dominated by cynics devoted to a vacuous cause. Onward his growth proceeded. Perhaps today he is writing about Mongolian cuisine. So much for David.

There has not been a hard drinker in the Oval Office since Harding, though I am told that George W. came close in the 1980s. As a matter of fact, I believe I glimpsed him in a, shall we say, "hilarious state" back in the 1980s when he was with a somewhat raucous group entering the White House as I was exiting it. By 2000, those happy days were long gone. In fact, they ended on July 28, 1986, in celebration of George W.'s fortieth birthday. But that does not mean that the Bush White House was dour. George W. always seemed to be in a pleasant state of mind and at times even festive, especially at Christmastime. I attended his annual Christmas reception with Jeanne every year that he was in the White House, and the president often stopped me in the reception line to chat. On one occasion, he took indulgent pleasure in talking up fitness with me. I suspect he wanted to remind the assembled journalists of how flabby they had become, or, if a journalist was a health enthusiast, how gaunt.

"Hey Bob, how you stayin' so fit?" he began. Startled, I responded that I was "tryin' to keep up with you on the bench." His workout then was rumored to involve bench pressing, dumbbell lifting, and biking with the sorely pressed Secret Service lagging behind. In fact, an agent told me that his detail dreaded a recent visit from Lance Armstrong, the celebrated Tour de France rider who had informed the president how to arrange his knees for increased speed. The Service Secret was equipped for something other than keeping up with a fitness fanatic on his long rides. The president then asked me, "What about your cardio?" Somewhat flummoxed, I lied and mentioned jogging. "I can't do it," he said wistfully. "My knees," he said, tapping one knee. He would delight, it seemed to me, in discussing fitness and leaving the journalists stranded in line. As the years passed, his relations with the press continued to deteriorate, as did mine.

I would wander through the crowd of journalists at every Christmas reception, and at each, the crowd seemed to grow frostier. These were not the lively days of Meg Greenfield from the *Washington Post* or of Abe Rosenthal from the *New York Times*, much less the days of Bob Bartley's *Wall Street Journal*. We were slipping into the era of the activist journalists. I would occasionally encounter E. J. Dionne from the *Washington Post*. I had known him years before when he was stationed in Paris with the great John Vinocur of the *New York Times*. Still, we kept in touch, and when I got to Washington, I invited him to our monthly meeting of the Saturday Evening Club. I remembered Bill Buckley's regular meetings with Rosenthal and others in New York. I attempted to invite liberals such as Dionne, Sam Tanenhaus, and the historian Sean Wilentz to our meetings. It was hopeless. Such liberals were forever claiming they longed for an ongoing conversation with conservatives, but they could never quite make the connection with a real breathing conservative. Possibly, they were waiting for Edmund Burke to appear, a conservative of their intellectual heft. I could not even get them to come as my special guest. I think I spent two years on Wilentz before giving up. I once had Sam Tanenhaus as a special guest. He ingratiated himself with everyone by calling them racists. It was a memorable occasion.

As for the war in the Middle East, it did not take long for the pacifist streak in the Vietnam-bred Democrats to manifest itself. Typical of their leanings was their infantile slogan "Bush Lied, People Died." The way we got into a war with Saddam Hussein did not involve a Bush-orchestrated conspiracy. Pursuant to gaining support for taking action against Saddam, President Bush on September 4, 2002, addressed Congress identifying Saddam as a "serious threat" and alluding to "regime change." Then on March 19, 2003, he addressed the nation, informing Americans that the United States had declared war on Iraq. The war did not last long. On May 1, the president standing on the deck of the USS *Abraham Lincoln* announced, "Mission Accomplished." Yet up there in the *Kultursmog*, the hunt for weapons of mass destruction was on, and no weapons were found. So, Bush must have lied. On October 2, 2003, our chief weapons inspector, David Kay, reported that his fourteen-hundred-member team, the Iraq Survey Group, had come up empty-handed, though he admitted that his team had found some evidence that Iraq still had the capacity to create weapons of mass destruction in the future.

As for the *Kultursmog*'s repeated falsehood that Bush lied in telling Congress and the American people that Saddam had weapons of mass destruction, it was clearly not a lie created by the president. It was a falsehood created by Saddam, and it did him in. On the part of George W., it was a mistaken belief that he shared with intelligence agencies throughout the world. If Bush was lying, he would have to be about as stupid as Saddam, for his lie would be exposed soon after the US Army subdued Iraq and found no weapons of mass destruction. We were eventually to discover that even Saddam's military commanders believed his boasts about possessing these weapons. Since Saddam's fall, scores of articles and books have proved that Bush was operating on mistaken intelligence, not in the hope of deceiving the public. Perhaps the most persuasive book covering the matter is Charles A. Duelfer's *Hide and Seek: The Search for Truth in Iraq*. In it, Duelfer, a respected UN weapons inspector in the 1990s and later head of the Iraq Survey Group, reports that Saddam admitted to his American captors that he had lied to the world about having weapons of mass destruction so as to intimidate neighboring countries. Once again, the *Kultursmog* is polluted by an untruth.

I suppose it was to be expected that the conservative *American Spectator*, founded in 1967 by young men, would acquire some sort of connection with the conservative London *Spectator*, founded in 1828, even if the connection was only informal. It began early with the London *Spectator*'s political editor, Patrick Cosgrave, contributing to our November 1973 issue and later contributing to our 1977 book, *The Future That Doesn't Work: Social Democracy's Failures in Britain*. Both magazines share an atmosphere of sophisticated commentary, an irreverent point of view, and erudition, mixing scholarship with journalism. Thus, it did not take us long to start publishing the likes of Paul Johnson, Professor Maurice Cranston, and Taki along with our own Milton Friedman, Professor Hugh Kenner (whose research into the plagiarism of C. David Heymann ended his career as a scholar), and our aspiring youth movement. Of course, over the years, we naturally mixed journalism with socializing, and after more than fifty years of drawing sustenance from similar wellsprings—both political and intellectual—there have been some embarrassments, though many more shared conclusions. The pursuit of Bill and Hillary comes to mind. *The American Spectator* and the Telegraph Media Group, the owner of the London *Spectator*, were the only news sources that steadily pursued the Clintons through the years, the *Sunday Telegraph* pursuing them from almost four thousand miles away.

A particularly convivial and constructive period extended from the 1990s to 2019, when Boris Johnson was making his transition from editorship of the *Spectator* to the House of Commons, the office of the mayor of London, and finally Number 10 Downing Street. During this gaudy period, I visited with him fairly frequently. I saw him at the *Spectator*'s summer parties, and I remember a hilarious evening spent with his sister Rachel and her husband, Ivo Dawnay, at my home in McLean. She was even more outré than Boris as she orchestrated a ribald conversation. The topic was recent revelations about Bill Clinton's private parts, which of course had not been private for a long time. On another occasion, I attended the *Spectator*'s summer party with Jeanne, and we went away wearing Boris wigs, which the magazine's publisher, Kimberly Fortier, distributed. During the Republican National Convention in 2004, Boris was my guest for dinner at the New York Athletic Club, where I found him seated in the Club's Tap

Room wearing blue jeans and, if I recall correctly, gym shoes, both being strictly proscribed by the Club's dress code in those days. In today's more relaxed atmosphere, I would not be surprised if beach attire is allowed. At the time, Boris said he had informed the maître d' that his blue jeans were actually considered the latest in smart trousers in London. Somehow, Boris got away with it.

By 2005, Boris was engaged in the hurly-burly of Parliament, and if I saw him at all, it was only at the *Spectator*'s summer party, but by then there was another festive occasion to look forward to, dinner with the Prince of Wales. President George W. and the first lady invited Jeanne and me along with 130 other notables to dine at the White House with the prince and his wife, the Duchess of Cornwall. *The Washington Times* called it the "A-list." Jeanne sat with Vice President Cheney. I sat at the table of Secretary of State Condoleezza Rice. Laura Bush introduced me to the prince as one of the Bush family's favorite writers. Then she raised me to being one of the Bushes' favorite editors. Yet she was not finished. She called me a "philosopher," and I was on my way to becoming a metaphysician or possibly America's next poet laureate when I lowered the heat in the State Dining Room by telling the prince that I also edited *The American Spectator*. The prince was suitably dignified but not a lot of laughs. Possibly it was his German blood. I believe it was Billy Wilder who said, "German humor is no laughing matter."

Some chapters back, I raised the question of why I was never considered for a position at the CIA despite my many connections with the agency, including a friendship with three of its directors. As I look back on my life, the evidence of my clandestine acumen cannot be ignored. From my encounter with Bob Kennedy on the stage at IU back in 1968 to my surreptitious celebration of Bill Clinton's sixtieth birthday in 2006, I had a lot of practice. On September 9, 2006, Clinton celebrated his sixtieth birthday in Toronto at the Fairmont Royal York hotel. It was the latest stop in what was becoming a world tour to celebrate a fabulous life and throw in a little fundraising. His tour began at a friend's home out on Martha's Vineyard on August 19, the historic date of Bill's birth, and it continued for months. Now he is in Toronto, for a night with "the stars." One of the stars is Kevin Spacey who will emcee. Another is Billy Crystal to joke it up, and James Taylor is there to sniffle his way through another of his lugubrious songs. Also, there is Carly Simon who is to sing "Happy Birthday" to Bill. She will be fully dressed.

Bill arrived in Toronto under heavy security from both the United States Secret Service and the Royal Canadian Mounted Police, but I outfoxed them all. I arrived with an Israeli beauty on my arm, and I even had my picture taken with Bill during the evening. You can see it on the internet. Later, Bill and I entered the men's room together. Throughout the evening, I kept worrying that he was going to recognize me. My Israeli companion and I entered the hotel unnoticed, though we used unconventional means that at least Israeli intelligence would admire. We were brought into a very select reception for Bill's most generous donors. That was where I expected to be unmasked. We were taken to the head of the line, which surprised me. I feared the jig was up when I was directed to proceed behind Bill's back and stand on his left. My companion took up her position on his right. Surely after chatting with her, he would turn to me and *whammo*: explode. Yet he accorded me only a wan smile. My guess is that he was feeling unwell. Then *click*, *click*, our pictures were taken, and Bill turned to his next prospect. He had to be wondering who that brunette beauty was and where his Arkansas state troopers were when he needed them— but those days are long gone.

Frankly, I was relieved and now we moved to the dining room and found ourselves seated practically at the head table. To my right was seated Amed Khan, an aide to Bill. I presumed he was Bill's bagman. Next to him was Doug Band, whose card bore the title "Counselor to President Clinton." Doug was the only member of Bill's entourage to ask where I came from. I told him the Washington area. His curiosity was limited. The president's counselor liked Washington, and he gabbled on concerning something about his travels with the boss, plans for a fundraiser here, a fundraiser there. He made no further inquiries. Whew, I was relieved, though the lady next to me wanted to know more details. "What do you do in Washington" she enquired. I answered, "I am a writer." Then she asked the trigger question: "What have you written that I might have heard of?" Well, I had heard enough rodomontade for one evening and I could restrain myself no longer. She was an Irish lady from Dublin. I said, "I wrote *Finnegans Wake.*" Her reaction was electrical. "Oh," she enthused to the entire table, "He wrote *Finnegans Wake.*" Doug Band was impressed. Amed Khan was, too. Do you remember when the Democrats were the intellectuals of American politics? I never asked the Irish lady if she really thought I might be James Joyce and had, by 2006, reached the advanced age of 124 years old. Perhaps she thought I had obtained a really good face-lift, even better than Hillary's.

Later in the evening, my companion and I repaired to the lobby, and who came up to us but Bill? He started to chat with the brunette, not with me. I told him that I admired what his foundation was doing in Africa. He nodded tentatively. Then I headed for the restroom. He did, too. Once finished in the bathroom, we went our separate ways. Bill was careful to wash his hands.

There were a few more memorable events in Washington before the curtain came down on George W. and went up for the Obama years. In the spring of 2002, *The American Spectator*'s great friend Tom Wolfe received the National Humanities Medal, and Wlady and I were at the Daughters of the American Revolution Constitution Hall to applaud him. The coverage of it reminded me yet again of how the *Kultursmog* spreads its pollution. On this occasion, and some years later, when Tom passed away neither Wlady nor I were asked to comment on Tom's achievements. This despite Tom's public statements on at least two occasions that *The American Spectator* "did a more thorough job with Bill Clinton than Woodward and Bernstein did with Nixon." He called our first Troopergate piece "the most important article of the 20th Century."[12] If you agree with me that that piece sounded the death knell for the sexual revolution, I think you will agree with Tom's assessment of Troopergate.

Then there was, on December 15, 2006, the Medal of Freedom ceremony that I attended with Wlady honoring Paul Johnson, *The American Spectator*'s British writer, and there was a White House luncheon for my friend Andrew Roberts. You will remember him from Chapter VIII where he was complaining about plaster in his hair and the body bags in the streets of Mostar. I had a hand in orchestrating the luncheon for him. Early in the year 2007, I learned that Andrew was going to be in Washington, and I asked Tim Goeglein, a presidential aide, if the president would be interested in meeting Andrew, who was then doing research for his Churchill biography. Tim got back to me and said the president would like to host a luncheon for Andrew at the White House. He asked me to put together a guest list, which I did, including Norman Podhoretz and his wife Midge Decter; Gertrude Himmelfarb, the Victorian scholar, and her husband Irving Kristol (not to be confused with my dog of long ago); and several others. The president included his own list of attendees, including his speechwriter Michael Gerson and his political advisor Karl Rove.

We met on February 28, 2007, in the family dining room on the state floor of the White House after Andrew and the president conferred for a half hour in the Oval Office about Winston Churchill, who had fascinated the president for years, and the war in Iraq, which was very much on his mind. When we all sat down to lunch, the conversation continued. At the time, there was a rising movement in Congress to remove our troops from Iraq, but as I noted in my diary "the President showed no sense that such a setback was even on his mind." He "brought up the question of right and wrong and said he was proceeding as it was the right...and [the] just course."[13] Andrew said in an internet communique to me later that the president was responding to Andrew's remarks. He emphasized, "[T]hat is the correct impression."[14] Andrew added in a subsequent communiqué that

"I did indeed say that he could nor [not] leave a nuclearized Middle East as his legacy, which he acknowledged."[15] There were no doves in the family dining room that cold December day. We concluded with a general appreciation that Winston Churchill was right about World War II, and the British upper class was otiose.

As I wrote back in Chapter III, during the early life of the magazine, "I was unaware of how having a magazine under one's name is like having a beautiful woman on one's arm. It drives some bystanders wild." I was to survive six, possibly seven, takeover attempts. Some were friendly; for instance, George Gilder, who, if I have anything to say about it, will receive the Medal of Freedom for returning the magazine to me back in 2002. Among the other takeover attempts, at least one was decidedly unfriendly and could have ended with my incarceration. I have in mind the Clinton Justice Department's pursuit of the Bait Shop Junta and the evil Arkansas Project. Yet I like to think that my endangerment was cushioned by the Tyrrell Curse. We saw how it brought Representative John Conyers to grief back in 1998. Doubtless, its diabolical workings have played a role in the miraculous disappearance from the world stage of pests such as Al Gore in 2000 and John Edwards in 2004 and finally in 2008. At the magazine, we called Edwards the "Breck Boy," that being a play on Edwards's soft and lovely head of hair. Whatever happened to him?

In Chapter IX, I mentioned Rupert Murdoch's interest in our magazine. I had a friendly spy planted on his board of directors who kept watch over his doings. I do not think Rupert ever meant us any harm. At least, that was my conclusion. Perhaps there was a time when he represented a threat, but it quickly dissipated, especially when he settled on Bill Kristol as his editor. Bill had the last name of a distinguished editor—his father's—but not the record. If Rupert had hired Bill's father, Irving Kristol, I would have been worried. As he settled on Bill, I was willing to wait and see. Some of my staff panicked. Still, I waited. Bill was an editor with no record of achievement. Eventually, Rupert lost interest in *The Weekly Standard* and sold it off. The new

proprietor looked at the magazine's books and Bill's choice of candidates over the years and closed the magazine down—just weeks before
Christmas in 2018.

A more dangerous threat to my leadership of the magazine came
from our publisher, Ron Burr. When I learned that he was creating
dissension in our office, I ordered my secretary, the ever-loyal Lonnie,
to remove from my office a trophy that had been given to me by a
baseball fan. If it fell into the wrong hands, it could be dangerous. It
was a Louisville slugger, a baseball bat. There obviously were loyalty
issues emerging in our office. Perhaps it was only an unfortunate coin-
cidence, but our publisher had the same last name as Aaron Burr, the
famous traitor. With Ron, however, I was taking no chances. He was
excitable. When he became agitated by the Arkansas Project, I asked
him to take a leave of absence and recover his composure. He refused,
and I let him go. By the way, it was Ron who humorously confected the
name "Arkansas Project." Ron could be impatient, and he did have a
vindictive streak, but he also had a wonderful sense of humor. I missed
him when he left.

He left in the fall of 1997, along with the gifted writer, but hopeless coward, David Brock. It turned out that Burr, working with Bud
Lemley—my family's and the magazine's investment advisor—was
feeding our documents to Sidney Blumenthal in the White House from
which they were passed on to the media—the *unbiased* media. Burr
could have lost his severance agreement with *The American Spectator*
and Lemley could have been disciplined by his professional regulatory
association—you would not want to take investment advice from such
a man. Yet I made the decision to ignore this brazen breach of loyalty
because Burr had a young family to raise and the Lemley proceedings
would have distracted me from my always amusing and usually fruitful pursuit of the Clintons. However, anyone who doubts my claims
against Burr and Lemley can read all about them in Blumenthal's mendacious book, *The Clinton Wars*. Lemley gave our papers (which, presumably, he obtained from Burr) to Blumenthal in the White House,

and Blumenthal was sufficiently dishonorable to betray Lemley and Burr in his pages. As I say, it is a mendacious book filled with propaganda, but enough of the narrative is true to validate my claims.

By the way, Burr's career as a liar began with his claiming that he "cofounded" the magazine with a person naturally left unnamed, presumably me. Burr did eventually turn up at our Bloomington office, but Steve Davis and I had founded the magazine before we ever met Burr. Burr continued by exaggerating his role as publisher. Truth be told, he was not the publisher until the April 1980 issue. The curious reader can consult our early mastheads in looking for Ron Burr. As for Blumenthal, here is how he describes the author of this memoir: "Tyrell [sic] had been a passive player [at *The American Spectator*], more interested in leisure than editing, and he had been paid off as a front man—half of his mortgage on a house in Virginia, an apartment in New York, club fees, credit cards, posh vacations."[16] Of course, decades later, Tyrrell is still the editor in chief. In fact, I am often referred to as the "Editor in Chief for Life."

The most unfortunate victim of the Tyrrell Curse was Conrad Black, who was only trying to help *The American Spectator* when he answered affirmatively to my late-1999 request that he join our board of directors and kick in some $200,000. On February 18, 2000, he made an offer, saying that "as a longtime friend and admirer and contributor to *The American Spectator* I was advised some while ago about the company's financial difficulties." The difficulties came from our burning our way through a reserve fund of over a million dollars to ward off the government's assault on such endeavors as the Arkansas Project and the Bait Shop Junta. In so doing, we saved the magazine from the Clintons, but we were now bleeding and on the ropes.

There followed months of negotiations with Conrad from faraway places, such as London and Rome, and his base in Toronto. The upshot was that Conrad was coming in not with $200,000 but $400,000 from two additional foundations. That was the good news. Less welcome was the news that Conrad wanted control of our board and two senior editorial positions, one going to the Canadian David Frum, who would replace me as editor in chief, while I became editor-at-large. What is more, he wrote that "the magazine needs to be relaunched and a clear break made from the period of intensified hostility to the Clinton administration as exemplified by the 'Arkansas Project,' which, fairly or not, damaged the *Spectator*'s editorial reputation."[17]

Apparently, Conrad had fallen prey to the same hysterics that influenced Ron Burr and other Laodicean friends of *The American Spectator*. Moreover, the added financial support that Conrad was offering us would barely cover the cost of his two employees, one of whom, our prospective editor, David Frum, had already earned the enmity of my staff who called him "David Frump." The formidable Chuck Brunie, then the chairman of our board, answered Conrad with a thunderous "no." Jeane Kirkpatrick and Bill Simon, President Gerald Ford's secretary of the Treasury, reiterated their "no's." Most surprising of all—and very gratifying—was Henry Kissinger, who told his friend and business associate, Conrad, repeatedly that to remove Bob Tyrrell from the editorship would be "an injustice."[18] Most of the political practitioners who came to my defense recognized what those who wrote about politics but did not practice politics apparently could not grasp, to wit: Anything that would diminish me or discredit me would repristinate the Clintons who were then being bathed in scandals while I was not. In fact, I had just been vindicated by Inspector Michael Shaheen, and my vindication has increased with the years. I wonder what the hysterical people who condemned us for our steadfast campaign against the Clintons are thinking about the Clintons now.

Yet the Tyrrell Curse was still at work. This time it struck Conrad for matters unrelated to the governance of *The American Spectator*. Late in 2007, after a long legal battle, Conrad was sentenced to seventy-eight months in prison on three counts of fraud and one—a particularly contrived count—of obstruction of justice. I stood by my friend, attending some of his hearings, and even writing a letter to the judge on Conrad's behalf. The judge, Amy St. Eve, had been a prosecutor with

R. EMMETT TYRRELL JR.

Independent Counsel Kenneth Starr's team during the Whitewater business. She was rumored to admire my tenacity in pursuing Bill, but all was for naught. Though I got Conrad a brilliant lawyer, Miguel Estrada, who sprung him for a year, Conrad ended up doing most of his time. He did have the satisfaction, however, of seeing Miguel win in the Supreme Court the unanimous order vacating his convictions for fraud. It took a more compassionate friend of freedom than me to see that justice was done for Conrad Black. President Donald Trump pardoned him in 2019. I also visited Conrad in the minimum security prison where he was housed. His friends thought it was very big of me; however, I had an ulterior motive. The prison next door to Conrad's was a maximum security prison. I always suspected that Hillary had high hopes of sending me there if she became president, possibly in solitary confinement for life.

We were to endure two more takeover attempts whose cruel fates suggested that the Tyrrell Curse was still mobilized against my enemies. One involved Al Regnery, which was to be expected. Al had been playing with fire since shortly after I raised him to the position of publisher in 2003. His demise was only a matter of time. The other involved the *Spectator* of London, which I had not expected, but then neither had I expected the call I had received from London in late 2016 or early 2017.

In the case of Al, Wlady and I rather liked him, even if he did have a penchant for hiring people whom I had to fire or, as I recall, firing people I would have to rehire. What was odd was that Al never seemed to notice what was going on around him. Nor did he notice that our management model was that of the early *National Review*, where no one ever questioned that Bill Buckley was in charge and the publisher (Bill Rusher) was not in charge. At any rate, I came into the office one wintry morning in 2012 and met Al at his corner office. Such trappings of power mattered more to Al than taking a head count of our board of directors. As I recall, the first thing he said was something to the effect of, "You will be leaving by the weekend." Then he brought

Bill Buckley into his reasoning, saying that Bill became editor-at-large of *National Review* when he was my age. I do not know how old Bill was when he became editor-at-large, but whatever he did, he did it by choice, and, by the way, Al was older than me. Furthermore, I always had the board's head count in mind. Al had but one vote on the board.

As I recall, I nodded and walked down the hallway to my modest office, where I called Chuck Brunie, still the chairman of the board, and briefly told him of Al's plan for me. He responded the way most normal persons would respond to such abnormal conditions. He called board members Al Somers and Tom Tarzian, my lifelong friends, and told them that we would have an executive meeting on the morrow in our Washington office to deal with the unpleasantness. They flew out the next morning, examined some books and records kept under Al's watch, and conveyed the bad news to Al that afternoon. Chuck delivered the coup de grâce. He said he had never encountered such incompetence in all his years on Wall Street. Later, I heard that Al was accusing me of stacking the board against him. I had not heard of that charge since the fall of 1997.

Over the years, the *Spectator* of London had launched at least three attempts to take over *The American Spectator*. The first two were friendly, reasonable, and to say nothing of flattering—such attention paid by the world's oldest magazine to a mere stripling of a magazine is always good for one's ego. The third takeover attempt cost the *Spectator* of London dearly. The chairman of the *Spectator*, an anurous braggart with orange hair, had not taken into account that we now had a chairman of our board who was a serious businessman and not in the habit of losing money. The first takeover attempt in 2000 led to an exchange of manuscripts for a short while but little else. The second takeover attempt failed to get very far also, but it did get me invited to join Conrad Black and Taki in debating three leftist advocates for Hillary in 2016. It also apparently emboldened the *Spectator*'s chairman, Andrew Neil, the moderator of our debate, to call me some weeks later and propose what he called a "crazy" idea. He had in mind some sort of "arrangement" between our magazines. I told him I was open to it, though I remembered, if he did not, that some years before he had monopolized my booth in a London nightclub with his insufferable gasconade. Then he tried to take off into the night with my blonde of the moment. His chances with the blonde were about on a par with his chances with *The American Spectator*.

The American Spectator was in a far stronger position than when Neil first became interested in it. We now had a new chairman, Bob Luddy, who ran a network of free-market schools in North Carolina and the largest commercial ventilation manufacturing firm in the United States. Bob put together a formidable defense of our copyright against the *Spectator*'s encroachments on it. Eventually, the *Spectator* folded its case and paid our legal bills. As for Andrew Neil, on September 24, 2021, he started "to cry and confesses to me [a *Daily Mail* interviewer] how he nearly succumbed to mental collapse..."[19] The Tyrrell Curse takes another victim.

He was seventy-two years old.

Chapter XII

THE PRESIDENT WHO LEFT NO SHADOW

*T*he laudations expended on Barack Obama in his brief but efficient pursuit of public life has extended from historian Michael Beschloss's straightforward sycophancy, "[Obama] is a guy whose IQ is off the charts" and "He's probably the smartest guy ever to become president," to the frankly embarrassing.[1] Said the *New York Times*' David Brooks during an interview with *The New Republic*: "I don't want to sound like I'm bragging, but usually when I talk to senators, while they may know a policy area better than me, they generally don't know political philosophy better than me. I got the sense he [Barack Obama] knew *both* better than me." It gets worse: "I remember distinctly an image of—we were sitting on his couches, and I was looking at his pant leg and his perfectly creased pant, and I'm thinking, (a) he's going to be president and (b) he'll be a very good president."[2] What would this precious Washington insider have reported if he had known Senator Obama was wearing pantyhose?

Barack Obama's election in 2008 perhaps never surprised the historian Beschloss, but it surprised us at *The American Spectator*. John McCain, whom Obama beat, was a legitimate war hero, not a community organizer. After serving four years in the House, he had served in the Senate for nearly twenty-two years; Obama had not even served four years in the Senate. I knew John McCain well. I flew with him on his campaign plane. I attended some of his campaign events. I entertained him in my McLean, Virginia, home, and he hired my daughter, Katy, as an intern. He was among my favorite senators, though he departed from the conservative camp now and then. The way he handled himself as a POW—always resisting the North Vietnamese's offers of medical care and pledges of leniency when they learned that his father was commander in chief of all US forces in the Pacific—made him a hero by my lights. Nonetheless, he lost to a cipher just as George H. W. Bush—another war hero—lost to a draft dodger. Such is the trajectory in modern America.

In 2007, *Vanity Fair* neatly conveyed a sense of the five-and-a-half years of hell John went through upon bailing out of his plane over North Vietnam. He broke a knee upon ejecting from the cockpit and both arms upon landing in a lake. His suffering had just begun. When the Vietnamese captured him, they bayoneted him in the ankle and beat him senseless. His arms were never set, but the Communists did coerce his taped confession. When they offered to release him, he refused to take a place before longer-serving POWs in the queue, and for this act of nobility he was beaten again and survived with cracked ribs, teeth broken to the gumline, and tortured with ropes tightened behind him so that for the rest of his days he could not raise his hands above his shoulders to comb his hair. John was a regular guy in all respects except one. He was as brave as they come.

We used to joke about how I served as a tail gunner on his plane, which, in truth, was impossible given the configuration of the plane. As jokes go it was not particularly amusing, and it became less amusing when the likes of Senator Richard Blumenthal, a Democrat from

Connecticut, turned out to have faked his experiences in the Vietnam War by the 1990s. The Democrats in Connecticut seem not to mind being represented in the Senate by a liar and a fraud, but I cannot see them giving me and John a pass on my little joke.

If we could salvage anything from John's defeat it would be that Obama's election should have finished off using race as an issue in American elections. President Obama by virtue of his election could have put an end to playing the race card in American politics. He could simply assert that his election was about policy, not race. Well, the retirement of the race card lasted about seven months. Then, at a press conference on July 22, 2009, the president had an opportunity to soothe reporters and the nation with a generous and reassuring appraisal when he was asked about an unfortunate imbroglio that Harvard Professor Henry Louis Gates, a black man, had gotten into with the Cambridge police a few days before. What is more, President Obama continued to blow opportunities to put the race card behind him. As a matter of fact, by the time he left office, race was *more* of an issue in politics than it had been when he was elected. Shortly after his election, according to a *New York Times*/CBS poll, two-thirds of Americans polled regarded race relations favorably.[3] By 2016, that figure had declined to the point where 69 percent now viewed race relations as "generally bad."[4] In the years ahead, the trend continued.

The problem began when Cambridge police were called to Gates's home after he broke into it because he had misplaced his keys. The date was July 16. That was when Sergeant James Crowley, at the request of one of Gates's neighbors, entered his home and found Gates present. Sergeant Crowley asked Gates for his identification, whereupon Gates refused and called Crowley a racist, engauding his charge of racism with insults against Crowley's mother whom Gates did not know. Gates elaborated by yelling that "This is what happens to black men…" and "You don't know who you're messing with."[5] The row spilled out onto Gates's front porch where he continued his yelling. Eventually, after repeated warnings, Crowley clapped the cuffs on the professor.

The imbroglio continued as a local matter with Sergeant Crowley denying that he was a racist and Professor Gates charging him with racism and with racial profiling, but it got no further until the president's July 22 press conference. Then a reporter asked him about it and President Obama said that while he did not know much about the facts, "the Cambridge police acted stupidly in arresting somebody when there was already proof that they were in their own home."[6] A huge controversy followed that was not ameliorated by the president calling a "beer summit" between officer Crowley and Professor Gates at the White House. It was the first of many lost opportunities that Barack Obama could have used to end racism in multiracial America.

The worst and most infamous racial flare-up came on February 26, 2012. That was when two young men, Trayvon Martin, a teenager who was black, and George Zimmerman, a mixed-race Latino working a neighborhood patrol, came to blows. Trayvon was left lifeless on the ground. Once again President Obama's commentary made it a national event; in this case, a national tragedy. Responding to a reporter's inquiry the president replied: "[M]y main message is to the parents of Trayvon Martin. You know, if I had a son, he'd look like Trayvon."[7] Actually, that is not the case. President Obama is half white, and Martin was completely black. The president was raised by the white side of his family, attending toney schools in Hawaii and on the East Coast. As for his father, Obama Sr., he was a Kenyan national. He got Barack Jr.'s mother pregnant toward the end of 1960 when they were students at the University of Hawaii. She married Obama Sr. Then she took her baby to Seattle, Washington, while Obama Sr. stayed in Hawaii. Eventually, she and Obama Jr. returned to Hawaii, but by then, the father was off to Harvard on a scholarship. Young Barack met his father only once in 1971. Eventually, Obama Sr. returned to Kenya, where he died after having his third automobile accident. Barack was pretty much raised in Hawaii by his grandparents. We do not know very much about his relationship with his grandfather, but, apparently, his relationship with his grandmother could be tense. He once said that she "uttered racial or ethnic stereotypes that made me cringe."[8] On another occasion, he called her a "typical white person."[9]

Truth be known, Barack could lay claim to both his mother's heritage, whose parents he often lived with, and his father's heritage, though he spent almost no time with him. Barack, as a child of a mixed-race marriage, could have spoken with authority to the entire nation on matters of race, and he might have led America and the world into a truly multiracial era. But he chose to play the race card. He was not a great enough man to meet the challenges of history. He was no George Washington, who disavowed a kingship after leading the Continental Army to victory over the British, or Abraham Lincoln, who fought a bloody war to reunite his country—two matters the historian Beschloss overlooked in comparing Obama to prior presidents. Obama was—as I said in Chapter I—a soigné cipher, a well-tailored run-of-the-mill pol. By the time Trayvon Martin and George Zimmerman squared off, leaving Trayvon dead on the ground, I had had enough of Barack Obama's bogus melodrama. He was just another American politician devoid of substance.

Some years before I lost all patience with President Obama, I noticed a peculiarity about him that moved me to further inquiry. It seemed to me that he suffered a peculiar lack of substance. In fact, I dubbed him the one politician who, despite eight years in the highest office of the land, left no shadow. I drafted a couple of young writers on our staff to inspect Obama's bona fides. They studied pictures of him. They inquired of photographers and camera crews who employed both still and video cameras to cover his presidency. My investigators interviewed White House journalists, occasionally White House employees, and, of course, White House visitors, even tourists. All have been asked the same question: "Have you ever seen the president's shadow?"

Every interviewee who would answer the question has confirmed my suspicion. Barack Obama, no matter where he goes, leaves no shadow. The reason for this curious phenomenon is that he casts no shadow. Despite all the power at his command, he roams the world leaving no shadow—not even a smudge. The sun may shine down on him. A wall of floodlights may illuminate him. We all know about his neat and well-tailored physique; still, it betrays no shadow, no silhouette, nothing, zilch, as they say. He is that unsubstantial. He remains a community organizer. He is not a president.

Gertrude Stein, the famed 1920s phrasemaker, once said, "There is no there there." Well, with Mr. Obama, things got worse. There was not even a shadow there. Our forty-fourth president will go down in history as the first American president who departed the White House having left only a vast diapasonal sigh of relief across the nation. Even some of his supporters were relieved when he was gone.

Oh, there was wreckage all around. Our healthcare system, which had once been the finest in the world, was mired in even more bureaucratic dithering, and I am a hypochondriac who takes any tampering with healthcare as a matter of the utmost importance. Fragments of legislation cluttered the landscape, such as Dodd-Frank. You do not recall what Dodd-Frank stood for? Actually, I am a little hazy on it myself. The national debt that was dangerously high when President Obama entered office had nearly doubled by the time he retired from office. Yet nothing substantial or constructive had been achieved. A year after President Obama vacated the White House, he was replaced by a Republican real estate magnate from New York City who had never run for office. Donald Trump accomplished more in four years than Obama could manage had he been in office for forty years. Truth be known, when he left office in 2017, he had done very little except play golf. By my calculations, he golfed even more frequently than Presidents Warren Gamaliel Harding and Bill Clinton—though, unlike them, he did not cheat.

He could look back on winning the Nobel Peace Prize nine months after taking the oath of office, but no one on the Nobel Committee could offer a convincing reason for why he won it. It is a perfect example of his shadowless passage through life. In fact, the *New York*

Post reported that President Obama and his staff immediately tried "to wriggle out of accepting it" so preposterous was the honor.[10] "It is true," Geir Lundestad a member of the Nobel Committee explained, "Obama did not do much before winning. But he represented the ideals of the committee."[11] So maybe we can conclude that in 2009 the Nobel Committee gave the Peace Prize to itself in a supreme act of narcissism. That would be a first.

There is one more fact about President Barack Obama that is rarely noted by his adoring press. He is the only president to be reelected with fewer votes than he received initially. In 2008, he received just under 70 million votes. In 2012, he received just under 66 million votes. I say he never would have won a third term.

Chapter XIII

THE DONALD I KNEW

We have been having our *American Spectator* galas for decades but only a few will be adjudged historic. There was the time that Tucker Carlson poured a glass of champagne from a second-floor balcony onto the illustrious head of Grover Norquist, but Grover took it in stride. Then, there was the first year of the Obama administration when we conservatives began what we called our Wilderness Years. I put a huge order in for the L.L.Bean catalog, as many as a dozen per table, for I was told it gets chilly in the wilderness, and sometimes a nocturnal shot of Jack Daniel's is just not enough. I was hoping to get a tent near Sarah Palin's, but when she heard that I was calling her "the pulchritudinous Sarah Palin" in print, I am told she took offense. Our Wilderness Years were unceremoniously over.

I am afraid only one date will go down as truly historic in our long history of galas, and that is October 23, 2013. It was on that date that Donald Trump encountered a likely presidential candidate next to him at the podium. Donald concluded that he could beat him, and if the other candidates were no better, Donald could beat them, too. The likely candidate was our featured speaker for the evening, Senator Ted Cruz from Texas, eventually known—thanks to Donald—as "Lyin' Ted." Did it all begin that night? Some insist that it did. Donald had claimed an interest in the White House before, but after October 23 and the warm reception he got from some four hundred conservatives in attendance that night, he was a changed man.

It was on October 23 that Donald Trump appeared next to the senator, and he brought his personal bodyguard with him. Perhaps Donald had gotten wind of Tucker's "Champagne Tactics," as we called them. Trump was there to accept our T. Boone Pickens Award for Entrepreneurship. This was the Donald Trump I came to know. He was tremendously amusing. He was gracious. He had an abundance of energy—every great politician I have known has had enormous energy. He made a series of perceptive observations on public policy that turned out to form the foundation for his America First program. He even flirted with my wife. Telling me, as he swept down into the ballroom, that he greatly admired my journalistic achievements, but then he looked over at my wife and said: "But now that I've met your wife, I admire you all the more." After Donald accepted his award, he returned to his seat and insisted on staying with us for the evening. Other award winners have been known to leave early. Not Donald. He stayed the course and was particularly attentive to Senator Cruz. Wlady thought he took notes. At the time, Senator Cruz was the Republican front-runner for 2016 in the polls.

Some months later, I was in New York, staying at the New York Athletic Club, which is only a few blocks from Trump Tower. So, I arranged an appointment and once again he was friendly, gregarious, and full of questions about how a magazine such as *The American Spectator* had survived for almost fifty years. I told him his presence at our gala was one of the ways. We operate at a deficit as many magazines do, and I raise money in much the same way as the Metropolitan

Museum of New York or the New York Philharmonic, though not as much. He eventually wrote a check, but his real interest was politics that day. He had gotten to know my colleague, Jeff Lord, and they hit it off. I told him that I thought he had shown a unique "mastery" of politics the night of our dinner. I told him that the points he emphasized were the points that were on every conservative's mind that night. I said he should run for the presidency. He obviously agreed. Before I left his office that afternoon, he quietly confirmed that he "thought" he would make his run for the White House in 2016 against Hillary. I never doubted that he was going to run. Most other political observers thought he was a joke. They underrated him as they had underrated Ronald Reagan.

On June 16, 2015, he made his trip down the escalator at Trump Tower, and on June 23, I wrote admiringly that "I predict he is going to run a great race for president, and at the end of the day, when he has had the last laugh, some observers will say he made it a race. And one thing more: his children are his greatest monuments."[1] In the months ahead, I became more confident of his chances. I wrote six columns saying he would win, the last one being six days before the election. I did not want to leave anyone in doubt as to where I stood. The Donald Trump I met in 2013 was competent, friendly, and a man as good as his word. He eventually came through on all his major promises to the electorate—then he became enmeshed in battles with the upper reaches of the FBI, the CIA, and the Justice Department. I think one would have to be a psychiatrist of rare artistry to explain fully what their complaints were about Donald. No president has ever been exposed to such an assault in the history of the republic, and the assault was launched by his own intelligence community. John Brennan, the head of the CIA, spoke of the "treasonous" behavior of President Trump. He could have been talking about himself, about the behavior of his colleagues in the intelligence community, about people at the Justice Department, and, of course, about the incomparable Hillary Clinton.

Not since Vice President Spiro Agnew had I written a speech for a politician, but in the months ahead, my *American Spectator* colleague, Frank Buckley, who also was on the faculty of George Mason's Antonin Scalia Law School, talked me into joining him in writing speeches for Donald. George Will did such campaign work for Ronald Reagan. Why could I not lend a hand to Donald? Frank sent a list of conservative judges to Senator Jeff Sessions, who was collecting them for the Trump campaign, and Frank included a speech that he had written on the rule of law. He immediately heard back from Jared Kushner and Stephen Miller, Jeff's policy aide. Thus, began months of collaboration between me and a team made up of Frank and his wife Esther, who had written fiercely for *The American Spectator*. (Wikipedia claims her as a possible source for the first reference to Trump derangement syndrome.) Together we wrote a speech on "National Greatness" based on Frank's book, *The Way Back*. Jared was delighted. Then there were speeches on Virginia, on energy sources, and one that attracted considerable attention from the media and the political community on foreign policy. Delivered by Donald from the Mayflower Hotel in Washington on April 27, 2016, it broke with President George W. Bush and neoconservatism on the question of nation building. It sided with a man who had become an early supporter of Donald and was a close adviser to *The American Spectator*, Donald Rumsfeld. After Donald was elected president, he became the first president since President Eisenhower to resist sending American troops to fight in foreign wars. Once again, Donald was making good on a campaign promise.

My speech writing tenure was brief. Truth be known, Frank Buckley was better at it than I was (he wrote Donald Jr.'s convention speech), though I liked working with Jared Kushner, especially when he reported to me that Donald had told him to "ask Tyrrell about" some speech writing problem. "That's Tyrrell's department," he confirmed to Jared. Eventually, I flew on the campaign's Boeing 757 with Donald throughout the South and witnessed his astounding ability to reach out to an audience, no matter how diverse. Veterans gave him their decorations. I believe he picked up three Purple Hearts. Others gave him things that mattered to them. Who knows, possibly he collected a few toothbrushes and a hairpiece.

After the *Access Hollywood* tapes were made public, I was with Donald on the plane. The press reported that it was the campaign's "darkest hour." Over the weekend, Donald was being counted out. All the major polls had Hillary Clinton ahead. The tapes revealed Donald bragging, back in 2005, that a celebrity could "grab any woman by the p—y" and suffer no ill effect. That was how the *Washington Post* wrote up the story. I insisted in my syndicated column that "p—y" stood for "puppy." There was no reason to think "p—y" stood for anything other than puppy, to say nothing of a woman's private parts. I have forgotten if I shared my version of the news with Donald, though I did not notice that he was in the dumps, as the news reports claimed. In fact, he seemed pretty chipper. Perhaps I did share my explication of the word "puppy" with him. He was always upbeat at stop after stop. If he thought he was going to lose, he never betrayed it to me. Perhaps that is why I stuck to my prophecy, repeated regularly in my column, and uttered to his face: "Donald, you are going to win."

Back in July, Donald the neophyte politician, had committed one of the most reckless acts a politician can commit. It was to haunt his campaign for years. He told a joke. In my lifetime, only two presidential candidates have been able to joke with the press and get away with it: John F. Kennedy and Ronald Reagan. Donald at a press conference in Doral, Florida, on July 27, joked about the thirty thousand emails his opponent, Hillary Clinton, had deleted from a private server that she had set up while she was secretary of state. Smiling and cocking his head, Donald said, "Russia, if you're listening, I hope you're able to find the thirty thousand emails that are missing." He went on, "I think you will probably be rewarded mightily by our press."[2] When I heard Donald's joke, I laughed. I am sure most normal Americans laughed, too, except for the agelasts among us and they probably thought it was the beginning of World War III. The press naturally took it seriously, and over at the CIA, John Brennan took it very, very seriously.

Brennan thought that finally he had something to go on at "the interagency taskforce" that he had set up, probably back in April, to run down evidence of Russian-Trump collusion. The interagency task force, composed of FBI agents, Justice Department officials, and CIA sleuths, had not found any evidence for months, and those working on the Mueller report would not find any evidence in their years of investigating. It turned out that the Russian-Trump collusion did not exist. Not until the Mueller report was made public in the spring of 2019 did the Russian–Trump collusion's nonexistence become widely accepted. Then thoughtful Americans began looking into the Clinton campaign with much more promising results.

A few days after Donald made his joke about pleading for Russian help with the missing thirty thousand emails, the FBI proceeded formally to investigate Russian-Trump collusion, for which it still had no evidence. It was on July 31, 2016, and the investigation was called Crossfire Hurricane, which is a line lifted from The Rolling Stones' hit song "Jumpin' Jack Flash." Crossfire Hurricane grew out of Brennan's interagency task force and was spearheaded by the FBI's liaison to Brennan, Peter Strzok, a virulent Trump hater who was also very much in love with another employee working the case, a woman named Lisa Page. Whether he was responsible for bringing The Rolling Stones into the investigation of the Russians and Donald, I cannot say. Curious readers might check the Rock & Roll Hall of Fame in Cleveland, Ohio, for Peter Strzok's name.

How capable of objective judgment these two lovebirds, tasked with investigating the next president of the United States, might be is doubtful. Here they are, as captured by Andrew McCarthy in his book *Ball of Collusion*, discussing Trump's presidential prospects. Page asks Strzok for his assurance that Trump is "not ever going to become president, right?" The FBI's liaison to Brennan on the interagency task force replies "No. No he won't. We'll stop it." The "we"

Strzok is referring to, says McCarthy, is that legendary investigative organization known as the Federal Bureau of Investigation. At another point in McCarthy's authoritative book, he quotes Strzok, the Bureau's top counterespionage investigator, as he declares to Page—the legal adviser to Andrew McCabe, the deputy director of the FBI, who was then running a simultaneous investigation of Clinton and Trump—that "Trump is a disaster." Strzok continues, "I have no idea how destabilizing his Presidency would be." At another point, he says "I am riled up. Trump is a fucking idiot." And Page concludes a bit later, "I'm scared for our organization."[3]

Incidentally, there was another stooge working for the FBI on this operation, a Cambridge University professor, Stefan Halper, who played a minor role in comparison with the likes of Strzok and Page. McCarthy mentions Halper in passing and our erstwhile publisher, Al Regnery, got Halper to write for us on some foreign policy matter. I never heard Halper call anyone a "fucking idiot," but then we only talked about his manuscripts, not about potential candidates for the presidency. The professor befriended Carter Page and George Papadopoulos to pump them for information on collusion within the campaign but failed to collect anything incriminating. This failure did not give the FBI pause. Even after Halper came up empty-handed, the FBI increased the spying on Trump officials. It had Foreign Intelligence Surveillance Act (FISA) warrants on Page and Michael Flynn, the campaign's military advisor, which gave the FBI the power to intercept communications at Trump Tower, just as Trump would later complain. The FBI made use of the unverified Steele dossier—a collection of smears financed by Hillary Clinton's campaign—in its applications for those FISA warrants.

All of this made the partisan nature of the probe into the Trump campaign abundantly clear. But more proof of the partisan animus driving the investigation would emerge in the autumn of 2016. Hoping to hurt Trump before Election Day, Brennan met with Nevada Senator Harry Reid in October and briefed him on the probe. Brennan knew that the hyper-partisan Reid would leak the existence of this stigma-tizing investigation to the press. Reid would later confirm Brennan's gambit to authors David Corn and Michael Isikoff, telling them that Brennan had an "ulterior motive" for the briefing.

At any rate, why did the intelligence community hate Donald so? Why could its members not stop their investigation when they failed to come up with any incriminating evidence on Donald? What hap-pened to our constitutionally established system of checks and bal-ances? Finally, what happened to the agreeable, likable, gregarious fellow I met at our gala dinner on October 23, 2013? By May 2017, Trump was—well, let us say he had become *difficult*. In May, he fired Comey in a fashion designed to humiliate him. Let me tell you my theory of why he had become *difficult*. Throughout 2016, as it became ever more apparent to Donald that he was being investigated by the intelligence community and hassled mercilessly by the Democrats, he could not simply ignore these egregious enemies. Every time they took a shot at him, he took a shot back at them, or as they would say, he counterpunched. In fact, he reveled in counterpunching. It became a way of life for him, and it affected his performance as president.

He was doing a lot of things right. His deregulations sparked the economy, as did lower taxes and other inducements to commerce. He strengthened the courts with his splendid choices, and he built up the military. Moreover, he did sensible things with our southern border ("The Wall!"), and there are people in medical science who tell me that his management of the pandemic will be improving healthcare man-agement for years to come. He was amazingly solid on policy, though sloppy or perhaps careless when it came to personnel. One of my White House sources says, "only Trump could have pushed so much substantial regulatory reform," but he hired people like Steve Bannon who wore his trademark garbageman's coat, even in the White House. For some reason, Donald had an affinity for low-lifers whom he put in odd positions in our government, people such as Paul Manafort and Roger Stone and the odious Bannon. There is no explanation for this that I have been able to discern. The Donald Trump that I met in 2013 was a gent. The longer he remained in office, the less of a gent he turned out to be. As I say, going into combat against the likes of Comey and Brennan hurt him. He should have soared over them. His children and the staff that he left behind at Trump Tower were civilized and serious, but at some level, he took comfort in the Bannons, the Manaforts, and the Stones of this world. At least he never named any of them to the Supreme Court.

I think history will one day record that Comey, Brennan, and a self-selected body of high-level officers in the government wrecked a first-rate presidency run by a neophyte. A gifted neophyte, but a neophyte. Donald could not know everything about politics, and he did not know whom to ask about what he did not know. A key date to remember is recalled by my colleague Debra Saunders, who covered Washington politics for the *Las Vegas Review-Journal* and who also writes for us. She claims the date is January 6, 2017. That is the date when the then FBI director James Comey brought senior US intelligence officials to New York to brief Donald on Russian meddling in the election. In a private briefing later in the day, Comey told Trump about the unverified allegations being made against him in the scandalous Steele dossier. From that point on, Donald did not trust the intelligence community, and with good reason. Saunders points to his changed outlook. Donald moved from the sunny optimism of his victory celebration in which he spoke of it being "time for us to come together as one united people"[4] to the grim "American carnage" of his inaugural address.[5] It all began on January 6, 2017.

As for Frank Buckley's and my continued usefulness to Donald, Jared, and the campaign, the telephone stopped ringing sometime between election night and the inauguration. My wife and I did attend the inauguration, but it was our last invitation from Donald. I, who had helped Ronald Reagan and his campaign manager, Bill Casey, with staffing the Reagan administration, (Wlady and I counted some forty appointments suggested by us to the White House in the early 1980s), received only one more telephone call from the Trump White House. It was a curious invitation from Donald for drinks on November 5, 2019. That would be almost three years into his presidency. I brought along Wlady and Jeff Lord, and Donald was as jolly as he had been back at our gala in 2013. We met in the Oval Office, and Donald, somewhat theatrically, showed us the nearby premises: the room where President Obama watched basketball games and the room where Monica Lewinsky and Bill Clinton performed various presidential ceremonies.

What had intruded upon my special relationship with Donald? Well, my spies tell me that Bannon hated me, but that should have redounded to my credit once Bannon vacated the White House shrouded in scandal. Was Donald too busy to keep in touch with old friends? Did he not know about my past service to President Ronald Reagan? Was it a consequence of his unfamiliarity with Washington? Our defenestration without even a fond au revoir still makes no sense, particularly in light of Lally Weymouth's sound advice to me uttered over thirty years ago. Said Lally: "You've got yours. There is nothing people in Washington can do for you." Someone should have told Donald. I have always been content at *The American Spectator*, and, besides, being an ambassador to the Court of St. James's would really disrupt my handball schedule.

Besides, laughter is always more amusing than solemnity, and soon after Donald was inaugurated, I filed the following World Exclusive on our website. If I were off on government service, it never would have seen the light of day.

World Exclusive:

Curtains for Comey

By R. Emmett Tyrrell, Jr.

After an exhaustive inquiry by *The American Spectator*'s team of award-winning investigative journalists this magazine can now report that in February of this year former FBI Director James B. Comey was captured on surveillance cameras in the White House blowing his nose on White House curtains. The nose-blowing took place in the Oval Office after President Donald J. Trump excused himself for several minutes to take a call from his wife Melania. Mr. Comey was alone. A picture of President Andrew Jackson was clearly visible in the background.

Whether Mr. Comey's act involved the destruction of government property is at this point in time still unknown, though he has a powerful nose, and the curtains are fragile. As for now, the surveillance tapes have been handed over to Attorney General Jeff Sessions, who will make a determination as to possible criminality of Mr. Comey's actions. The destruction of government property is punishable by as much as three years in prison and a fine.

Among *The American Spectator*'s sources were three current and former U.S. officials who cannot be identified because of their prior commitments. Also there has been an additional problem with one of them, the former government official who has a drinking problem.

Mr. Comey could not be reached by *The American Spectator* for comment. The White House too was unavailable for comment. Yet *The Spectator* is continuing its investigation and will have more information as developments reveal themselves.

Spectator editorial director Wladyslaw Pleszczynski released this comment: "You get what you sow."

Well, I have had a lot of fun editing *The American Spectator* through the years. I have been invited into a lot of places where I might not otherwise have been welcome. I have had an opportunity to influence people and events mostly for the good. In more than fifty years of editing and writing, I did it my way. I extended freedom to writers and ideas to readers. I always wanted to be free to write, and no one ever had an opportunity to silence me. I like to think that along the way I allowed others freedom, too. To my board of directors and my supporters, my gratitude.

There is one more thing I would like to say, though on February 9, 2017, the editor in chief of BuzzFeed, Ben Smith, said most of it for me. It had to do with who saw Donald Trump coming first:

> It's easy enough to find editors these days who say they saw Donald Trump coming, hard to find ones who are telling the truth about that. By my estimation perhaps the only one who really did is R. Emmett Tyrrell, the venerable founder and editor of *The American Spectator*, and perhaps the only man to get marginalized in the right-wing journalism of the 1990s for being too hard on the Clintons.
>
> Tyrrell is a charismatic, spry, and unaccountably handsome 73-year-old whose mainstream political influence peaked during Ronald Reagan's first term. He's still got a pair of letters from Reagan hanging above the stairs, next to a photograph of his old friend and *Spectator* contributor Tom Wolfe. His roots in journalism are, he likes to say, "athletic"—he was inspired by the coach of his Indiana University swim team to found a conservative magazine, and moved it from Bloomington to Washington in 1985.[6]

Chapter XIV

LIFE IS SHORT, BUT ETERNITY IS FOREVER

When I was a young boy, I was often visited by a vision of the Virgin Mary standing by a stone well on a dusty road by her home, scooping up water in a jar to take back to her family, which of course included a rather illustrious child. In later years, the child appeared at the temple to the distress of his mother, and later still when he was a grown-up, he relieved his mother's anxieties on at least one occasion by changing water into wine, which Holy Scripture tells us was eminently potable. On and on, these visions flickered. Today I envision them again with increased frequency. They come unbidden. As if from nowhere.

I am not claiming some sort of supernatural experience, rather I believe that these images are probably the residue of holy cards I collected in school in my youth. I think they are a part of the memoirist's accumulated baggage. While writing this memoir, I have been reintroducing myself to my past and the more I think back over the years, the more images come forth. In some ways, I am now a different man than when I began disinterring my past. Sometimes the memories are painful. Most often, they are reassuring. I got through one adventure, for instance: the Clintons' attempt at putting me in jail. I proceeded on through another. You might recall my successful effort to crash Bill's sixtieth birthday party in Toronto, where I wowed the assembled Clinton brain trust when I told them that I was the author of *Finnegans Wake*. No one doubted.

Most of the adventures were a lot of fun, as you have doubtless noticed. Certainly, the images drawn from Biblical times on a dusty road in Nazareth were reassuring. In fact, every thought drawn from Biblical times is reassuring. Eventually, I came to the conclusion that God has been at the center of my life. As the Bible says, He is always with us whether we invite Him or not. He was with me through the raucous times and the more painful moments. Sometimes, I owe Him an apology. Other times, I thank Him for his consolation.

In my early years, I was troubled by very little, though some questions continued to nag at me. For instance, there is the question that I touched upon in Chapter I: "How do we get out of here?" Another is, "How did I get here?" Or, "Why am I here in the first place?" Finally, there is my objection, uttered evermore weakly through the years, "I never asked to be here," which left me with one more question: "So, what is it all about?" Fortunately, I came across the seventeenth-century French philosopher Blaise Pascal. Many young skeptics are never fortunate enough to find Pascal.

I was, and he supplied the initial answer to my question. The answer is God. I took Pascal's wager. According to Pascal's formulation of the wager, if one lives by what are commonly called God's laws and believes in God's existence, God will be satisfied. If God does not exist, it costs the fellow who took Pascal's wager nothing. He thereby avoided the hassle of living on the margins. On the other hand, if God does exist—and He is not playing the greatest practical joke of all time on us—He rewards the fellow who took the wager with eternal life and all the blessings that go with it. Intriguingly, the famed skeptic George Jean Nathan, Mencken's sidekick, and a founder of the first *American Spectator*, took Pascal's wager toward the end of his life. He became a Catholic. Allegedly, George—ever the pleasure-seeker—did it because he "wanted to go to Heaven." Or, as that mysterious woman said to Bob Novak at Syracuse University so many years ago: "Life is short, but eternity is forever."

Taking Pascal's wager was my first step. My second, which deepened my belief in God, was to consider the Thomistic proofs for his existence. They were formulated by St. Thomas Aquinas in the thirteenth century and deposited in his *Summa Theologica*. Aquinas argued that the existence of motion requires a first mover, that the existence of efficient causality requires a first cause, and that the design evident throughout the visible world requires a designer. St. Thomas marshaled other arguments for the existence of God, but by the time I had mulled those over, I was a believing Thomist. Anyone who takes the time to think about St. Thomas's five ways to prove God's existence will find them convincing. I knew Christopher Hitchens for years, first as an opponent, then as a friend. The Clintons could have that kind of seismic effect on rational minds. I am sorry I never took up the arguments of Blaise Pascal and St. Thomas Aquinas with Christopher. My guess is that he got to them eventually on his own.

But why did God create us? I would think that running the universe was pretty much a full-time job. We are told by people who ponder such questions that God is a loving God. He created humans to share His life with them. He made us rational and free—in His "image," as the Bible says. That makes sense. Otherwise, He created us for less generous reasons, to thwart and frustrate us, which makes no sense. Thus, I am putting my money on God, and if I am wrong, it costs me nothing.

Now, at the end of this memoir, I see Bob Kennedy standing before those massive black curtains of yesteryear. I wonder how he would have changed had he lived through the life I have lived through. Would he indeed be somewhat conservative, as Paul Corbin said he would? Or would he follow the path of the standard-issue liberal, leftward, leftward, ever leftward? Would he still pray the rosary at night? How about abortion? Where would he be on that vexed question? What about Sunday Mass? What would he think of me, the young guy who put a Reagan button in his outstretched hand before his driver drove him away from the IU auditorium? Would he still laugh? I like to think that he would, but given the contents of this book, I have my doubts.

Endnotes

Chapter I

1. Warren Weaver Jr., "Kennedy: Meet the Conservative," *New York Times*, April 28, 1968, E1.
2. "An Apology for Fascism," *New Republic*, vol. 49, no. 632, January 1927, 207–209.
3. George Washington's Farewell Address, September 19, 1796.
4. Robert F. Kennedy speech at Indiana University in Bloomington, Indiana, April 24, 1968.
5. Information conveyed to me in confidence by a member of the Kennedy family.
6. Thurston Clarke, *The Last Campaign: Robert F. Kennedy and 82 Days that Inspired America* (New York: Henry Holt and Company, 2008), 275.
7. Ibid., 178.
8. Paul Kengor, *The Crusader: Ronald Reagan and the Fall of Communism* (New York: Harper Collins, 2007), 37.
9. Ibid., 38.

Chapter II

1. George A. Panichas, ed., *The Essential Russell Kirk* (Wilmington, DE: ISI Books, 2007), 45.
2. Jacqueline Truscott and Victoria Dawson, "Reagan and The Gridiron's Good sports," *Washington Post*, March 30, 1987, B1.
3. R. Emmett Tyrrell, Jr., "Keepers of the Woodstock Myth," *Washington Post*, August 20, 1984, A17.

4   R. Emmett Tyrrell, Jr., "Woodstock, the Last Word," *Washington Times*, August 20, 2019.
5   William Kunstler, "A Woodstock 'Relic' Replies," *Washington Post*, September 15, 1984, A17.

Chapter III

1   Mentioned to RET in conversation.
2   Dinitia Smith, "No Regrets for a Love of Explosives," *New York Times*, September 11, 2001, E1.
3   Alfred S. Regnery, *Upstream: The Ascendance of American Conservatism* (New York: Simon & Schuster Threshold Editions, 2008), 202–203.
4   Vice President Spiro Agnew, speech on television news bias at a Midwest regional Republican Party conference in Des Moines, Iowa, November 13, 1969.

Chapter IV

1   Robert D. Novak, *The Prince of Darkness: 50 Years Reporting in Washington* (New York: Crown Forum, 2007), 224.
2   Ibid., 217.
3   Ibid., 228.
4   At a luncheon at the Four Seasons Hotel in Washington, D.C., in March 1991, Margaret Thatcher recalled the failures of Jimmy Carter's foreign policy.
5   R. W. Apple Jr., "Democratic Race Widens; Muskie Concedes Setback," *New York Times*, March 15, 1972, 1, 32.
6   In the spring of 1973, Jane Fonda went after the US POWs returning home who said they had been tortured in Vietnam prison camps. In an interview with KNBC-TV of Burbank, California, Fonda alleged that the POWs were "hypocrites and liars."
7   Pete Hamill, "Homecoming," *New York Post*, February 14, 1973, 37.
8   Steven V. Roberts, "The P.O.W.'s: Focus of Division," *New York Times*, March 3, 1973.
9   John W. Dean, *The Nixon Defense: What He Knew and When He Knew It* (New York: Penguin Books, 2015), footnote on 55–56.
10   US Congress, Senate, Select Committee to Study Governmental Operations with Respect to Intelligence Activities, Intelligence Activities and the Rights of Americans: Final Report of the Select Committee to Study Governmental Operations with Respect to Intelligence Activities, Book II, Report 94–755 (Washington, DC: U.S. Government Printing Office, April 26, 1976), VIII.
11   Alfred S. Regnery, *Upstream: The Ascendance of American Conservatism* (New York: Simon & Schuster Threshold Editions, 2008), 200–203.
12   Personal Diary Note.
13   Novak, 553.

14 Seth Lipsky, "How Spielberg's 'The Post' Misses What Really Happened in 'Nam,'" *New York Post*, December 27, 2017.

Chapter V

1   R. Emmett Tyrrell, Jr., ed., *The Future That Doesn't Work: Social Democracy's Failures in Britain* (Garden City, New York: Doubleday, 1977), 2.

2   "Margaret Thatcher: A Life in Quotes," *Guardian*, April 8, 2013.

3   Paul Johnson interview with C-SPAN, "A History of the American People," March 12, 1998.

4   "Periodical Halted by 'Tired' Editors; Nathan and Associates Drop The American Spectator to Retire to Their 'Estates,'" *New York Times*, February 28, 1935.

5   R. Emmett Tyrrell, Jr., "A Warning to Foreign Visitors," *Washington Post*, July 9, 1984, A13.

6   R. Emmett Tyrrell, Jr., "Gingrich Knows How to Whip 'Em," *Washington Post*, October 20, 1990, A23.

7   Personal Diary Note.

8   "God and Man in Bloomington," *Time*, March 7, 1977, 93–94.

9   Henry Mitchell, "The Great Gadfly," *Washington Post*, July 27, 1979, B1 & B3.

10 Linda Witt, "The Wales Are Safe, but Politicians Aren't from Bob Tyrrell's Editorial Harpoons," *People*, November 5, 1979.

11 "A Downer on the Way Up," *Washington Star*, June 5, 1979, A10.

12 *The New Yorker*, April 30, 1979, 139.

13 Aram Bakshian Jr., "Ragging the Conventional Unwisdom," *Wall Street Journal*, June 1, 1979, 20.

14 Elliott Abrams, "Poison Pen," *Commentary*, July 1, 1979, vol. 68, issue 1, 78–80.

15 Nina Hyde, "The List," *Washington Post*, December 31, 1980, D1.

Chapter VI

1   Peter Hannaford, *The Reagans: A Political Portrait* (New York: Coward-McCann, 1983), 9.

2   While in Paris, May 11, 1982, the Wonder Boy criticized President Reagan's policies on Latin American and the US economy.

3   Al Gore criticized President Donald Trump in Davos in January 2020. John Kerry criticized Trump in Davos on January 22, 2019. Hillary Clinton criticized the president in London at the London Literature Festival on October 15, 2017, saying Trump had "a psychological need to dominate and demean people" and warned that he could fire a nuclear bomb "in a moment of pique." What is more he is a narcissist: "I think he only thinks about himself. Anyone who challenges or contradicts him or raises questions about him becomes his adversary."

4   Rob Ferguson, "Troops Should Stay in Kandahar Past 2009 Deadline, Clinton Tells Summit," *Toronto Star*, November 14, 2007, A25.

　　　Katie Leach, "Obama: 'We Have a Temporary Absence of American leadership' on Climate Change," *Washington Examiner*, December 2, 2017.

5   October 28,1978, during a private conversation.

6   In a private conversation in 1979 in New York.

7   R. Emmett Tyrrell, Jr., "The Continuing Crisis," *The American Spectator*, May 1981, 2.

8   Ibid., 2.

9   Hendrik Hertzberg, "You're Wrong, You're Wrong, You're Definitely Wrong, And I'm Probably Wrong, Too," *New Republic*, November 24 & December 8, 2014, vol. 245, issue 19, 62–67.

10   Personal Correspondence.

11   Wlady Plesczcynski, "Father and Sons," *The American Spectator*, June 2009, 68–70.

12   Quoted in Everett Carll Ladd Jr.'s "The Unmaking of the Republican Party," *Fortune*, September 1977, 98.

13   David B. Frisk, *If Not Us, Who? William Rusher,* National Review, *and the Conservative Movement* (Wilmington, DE: ISI Books, 2012), 367.

14   James T. Patterson, *Restless Giant: The United States from Watergate to Bush v. Gore* (New York: Oxford University Press, 2005), 190.

15   Personal correspondence from Ronald Reagan to RET, April 12, 1983.

16   Michael K. Deaver, *Behind the Scenes* (New York: William Morrow and Co., 1987), 120.

Chapter VII

1   James T. Patterson, *Restless Giant: The United States from Watergate to Bush v. Gore* (New York: Oxford University Press, 2005),190.

2   AP, "Mondale Assails Grenada Move and a Lack of Security in Beirut," *New York Times*, October 28, 1983, A12.

3   UPI, "Jackson Assails Invasion," *New York Times*, October 28, 1983, A12.

4   R. Emmett Tyrrell, Jr., "A Noble Minority," *Washington Post*, November 30, 1984, A19.

5   AP Archive, "President Ronald Reagan Addresses the Nation to Accept Responsibilities for His Part in the Iran-Contra," YouTube, July 31, 2015.

6   Eric Hoffer, *The Temper of Our Time,* (New York: Harper & Row, 1967), 51.

7   Ethan Bronner, *Battle for Justice: How the Bork Nomination Shook America,* (New York: Union Square Press, 2007), 264.

　　　Linda Greenhouse, "Foes of Bork Gain Majority in Panel; Urge Withdrawal," *New York Times*, October 6, 1987, A1.

8   Paul Lettow, "President Reagan's Legacy and U.S. Nuclear Weapons Policy," Heritage Foundation, July 20, 2006.

9 Times Wire Services, "Anti-Soviet Bloc Targets Arms Pact," *Los Angeles Times*, December 4, 1987, 1.

10 Dinesh D'Souza, *Ronald Reagan: How an Ordinary Man Became an Extraordinary Leader* (New York: A Touchstone Book, 1997), 192.

11 Michael Oakeshott, "On Being Conservative," in *Rationalism in Politics and Other Essays*, (London: Methuen & Co. Ltd., 1962), 169.

Chapter VIII

1 AP, "Transcript of the Bush-Gorbachev News Conference in Malta," *New York Times*, December 4, 1989, A12–A13.

2 R. Emmett Tyrrell, Jr., "Strange Devices," *The American Spectator*, December 1991, 8.

3 "Notable Quotables," Media Research Center, vol. 17, no. 13, June 21, 2004.

4 Anatoly Chernyaev, "Notes from the Politburo Session," George Washington University, National Security Archive, October 8, 1986.

5 Robert C. McFarlane, "Consider What Star Wars Accomplished," *New York Times*, August 24, 1993, A15.

6 Anthony Lewis, "Onward, Christian Soldiers," *New York Times*, March 10, 1983, A27.

7 Richard Cohen, "Convictions," *Washington Post*, May 26, 1983, C1.

8 Bill Peterson, "Reagan's Use of Moral Language to Explain Policies Draws Fire," *Washington Post*, March 23, 1983, A15.

9 Lou Cannon, "President Seeks Futuristic Defense against Missiles," *Washington Post*, March 24, 1983, A1.

10 Lou Cannon, "Reagan Radiated Happiness and Hope," *George*, August 2000, 58.

11 Lou Cannon, *President Reagan: The Role of a Lifetime* (New York: Public Affairs, 2000), 273.

12 Lee Edwards, "CNN Documentary Gets Reagan's Legacy Wrong," *Daily Signal*, September 7, 2017.

13 Personal Diary Note, December 15, 1986.

14 Tom Bethell, "Conservative Bird, Liberal Bush," *The American Spectator*, August 1987, 11.

15 Victor Gold, "Canards of '88 (So Far)," *The American Spectator*, May 1988, 48.

16 Albert R. Hunt, "Now Bush Needs a Mandate Campaign," *Wall Street Journal*, November 11, 1988, A14.

17 "Ideology, Competence and Mr. Bush" *New York Times*, November 10, 1988, A30.

18 Martha Sherrill, "The Conservatives' Menu: For the American Spectator, a Dinner of Brains and Bush," *Washington Post*, January 23, 1990, C1.

19 Tom Bethell, "The Interview Ace," *Wall Street Journal*, March 31, 1989, A14.

20 R. Emmett Tyrrell, Jr., *The Conservative Crack-Up* (New York: Simon & Schuster, 1992), 232.

21 Michael Kinsley, "Greed Gets Most Mileage Out of Airline Credits," *Wall Street Journal,* October 10, 1985, 33.

22 P. J. O'Rourke, "Conspiracy Overload," *New York Times,* October 30, 1997, A31.

23 Personal Diary Note, June 5, 1992.

24 P. J. O'Rourke, "Brickbats and Broomsticks," *The American Spectator,* February 1993, 20.

25 Howard Kurtz, "At American Spectator, a Firing Offense," *Washington Post,* October 20, 1997, C1 & C3.

Chapter IX

1 Lisa Schiffren, "Bill and Hillary at the Trough," *The American Spectator,* August 1993, 22.

2 Daniel Wattenberg, "The Lady Macbeth of Little Rock," *The American Spectator,* August 1992, 25.

3 "Excerpts from Speech by Gore at Convention," *New York Times,* July 17, 1992, A15.

4 Jack W. Germond and Jules Witcover, *Mad as Hell: Revolt at the Ballot Box, 1992* (New York: Warner Books, 1993), 345.

5 William Jefferson Clinton, Speech at the 1992 Democratic National Convention, New York City, July 16, 1992.

6 Recorded in my notebook, which I lost somehow.

7 Charles F. Allen and Jonathan Portis, *The Comeback Kid: The Life and Career of Bill Clinton* (New York: Birch Lane Press, 1992), 202.

8 Ibid.

9 Lisa Schiffren, "Bill and Hillary at the Trough," *The American Spectator,* August 1993, 21.

10 Richard A. Serrano, "Panel Hears Drug History of 36 Clinton Staffers," *Los Angeles Times,* July 18, 1996, A11.

11 Byron York, "Fast Times at White House High," *The American Spectator,* November 1996, 22.

12 David Brock, "Living with the Clintons," *The American Spectator,* January 1994, 21.

13 Ibid., 26.

14 Ibid., 26.

15 Ibid., 27.

16 Ibid., 27.

17 Ibid., 24.

18 Ibid., 25.

19 Ibid., 28.

20 Ibid., 28.

21   Michael Kinsley, "TRB from Washington: F-Troop," *New Republic*, vol. 210, no. 2–3, January 10 & 17, 1994, 4.

      Michael Kinsley, "The Spectator Story: Unbelievable…" *Washington Post*, December 23, 1993, A23.

22   Paul Duke, on "Washington Week in Review," PBS, December 31, 1993.

23   Joe Klein, "The Citizens of Bimboland," *Newsweek*, vol. 123, no. 1, January 3, 1994, 59.

24   Howard Kurtz, "The Spectator's Hard Right Jab," *Washington Post*, December 24, 1993, C1.

25   Andrew Sullivan, "Miami Diarist: Point of View," *New Republic*, vol. 212, no. 12, March 20, 1995, 42.

26   Jeffrey Hart, *The Making of the American Conservative Mind: National Review and Its Times* (Wilmington, Delaware: ISI Books, 2005), 330.

27   William F. Buckley, Jr., "Let Clinton be Clinton," Dallas Morning News, January 6, 1994, 21A.

28   "Splashes and Growth at The American Spectator," *New York Times*, December 27, 1993, D6.

29   John F. Harris and Daniel Lippman, "Can the F-Bomb Save Beto?" *Politico*, September 6, 2019.

30   Alex Caton, "Why Democrats Are Dropping More F-Bombs than Ever," *Politico*, April 24, 2017.

31   Hours after being sworn into Congress in January of 2019, Rashida Tlaib, emphasizing her hatred of Donald Trump, recounted the touching moment when she told her son she intended to "impeach the mother f—er."

32   Steven Nelson, "Jill Biden Said Harris Should 'Go F—k' Herself for Debate Attack on Joe," *New York Post*, May 19, 2021.

33   Patrick J. Buchanan, "The Apologists," *The American Conservative*, January 27, 2003.

34   Byron York, "The Life and Death of *The American Spectator*," *Atlantic*, November 2001.

35   "FBI Memo Reveals Drug Smuggling at Mena Airport in 1980," Associated Press, July 20, 2020.

36   Editorial, "Investigate Mena," *Wall Street Journal*, July 10, 1995, A14.

Chapter X

1   Al Kamen, "Biting the Hand You Feed," *Washington Post*, July 19, 1995, A19.

2   Bob Bartley, "Will Bill Clinton Find Peace?," *Wall Street Journal*, April 8 2002.

3   Howard Kurtz, "At American Spectator, a Firing Offense," *Washington Post*, October 20, 1997, C1:5.

4   John Mintz, "In Arkansas, a Cloud Over Starr Witness," *Washington Post*, April 19, 1998, A01.

5   Neil A. Lewis, "Justice Dept. Wants Inquiry into Anti-Clinton Witness," *New York Times*, April 10, 1998, A16.

6   John Corry, "Presswatch: Salon's Spectator Project," *The American Spectator*, June 1998, 45.

7   Tony Snow, "Weird Diversions…and Yearnings," *Washington Times*, April 17, 1998, A17.

8   David Brock, "Living with the Clintons," *The American Spectator*, January 1994, 28.

9   Stephen Glover, "Where Were These Grand Papers When America Needed Them," *Spectator* (London), September 19, 1998, 34.

10 R. Emmett Tyrrell, Jr., "The Continuing Crisis," *The American Spectator*, September 1999, 8–9.

11 Statement of Special Counsel Michael E. Shaheen, Jr., issued by the Office of the Independent Counsel, July 28, 1999.

12 John F. Harris and Peter Baker, "White House Memo Asserts a Scandal Theory," *Washington Post*, January 10, 1997, A1.

13 Ibid., A14.

14 Ibid., Al4.

15 Mentioned to RET in conversation.

Chapter XI

1   Lucinda Franks, "The Intimate Hillary," *Talk*, September 1999, 174.

2   Ibid.

3   Hélène Carrère d'Encausse, *The Russian Syndrome: One Thousand Years of Political Murder* (New York: Holmes & Meier, 1992), 5–6.

4   Simon Gottschalk, "The Infantilization of Western culture," *Salon*, August 8, 2018.

5   Ibid.

6   Ibid.

7   Kevin Sack and Frank Bruni, "How Gore Stopped Short on His Way to Concede," *New York Times*, November 9, 2000, A1.

8   Charles Krauthammer, "The Delusional Dean," *Washington Post*, December 5, 2003.

9   Richard L. Berke, "From the Outside, Former Presidents Lend the Support of Insiders," *New York Times*, September 28, 2001, B1.

10 David Frum, *The Right Man: The Surprise Presidency of George W. Bush* (New York: Random House, 2003), 275.

11 David Frum, *Comeback: Conservatism That Can Win Again* (New York: Broadway, 2009), 8.

12 Robert Stacy McCain, "Wolfe Praises *Spectator* Reporting," *Washington Times*, November 7, 2007, 4.

13 Personal Diary Note.

14 Ibid.

15 Ibid.

16   Sidney Blumenthal, *The Clinton Wars* (New York: Farrar, Straus and Giroux, 2003), 399.

17   Personal Memorandum from Conrad Black on file at *The American Spectator*.

18   Personal Diary Note from October 22, 2000. Also in this notation, Henry tells me he admires my "courage" in turning down Conrad's offer to purchase *The American Spectator*.

19   Rebecca Hardy, "GB News Is Just a Disaster," *Daily Mail*, September 24, 2021.

Chapter XII

1   Douglas MacKinnon, "Douglas MacKinnon: Don't Bother These Guys with the Facts," *Washington Examiner,* July 25, 2009.

2   Gabriel Sherman, "The Courtship," *New Republic*, August 31, 2009.

3   Sheryl Gay Stolberg and Marjorie Connelly, "Obama Is Nudging Views on Race, a Survey Finds," *New York Times*, April 27, 2009.

4   Giovanni Russonello, "Race Relations Are at Lowest Point in Obama Presidency, Poll Finds," *New York Times*, July 13, 2016.

5   "Cambridge Police Officer to Obama: Butt Out of My Arrest," Fox News, December 24, 2015.

6   Katharine Q. Seelye, "Obama Wades into a Volatile Racial Issue," *New York Times*, July 23, 2009.

7   Byron Tau, "Obama: 'If I Had a Son, He'd Look Like Trayvon,'" *Politico*, March 23, 2012.

8   "Revisiting Obama's Historic 'Race Speech' 12 Years Later," NPR, March 17, 2020.

9   Kenneth T. Walsh, "Obama 'Typical White Person' Comment Delights Clinton Aides," *U.S. News & World Report*, March 21, 2008.

10 Mary Kay Linge, "Why Obama Got a Nobel Peace Prize for Nothing—and Trump Never Will for Anything," *New York Post*, November 2, 2019.

11 Ibid.

Chapter XIII

1   R. Emmett Tyrrell, Jr., "Donald Trump, Carly Fiorina Forces to Be Reckoned With," *Washington Times*, June 23, 2015.

2   Ashley Parker and David E. Sanger, "Donald Trump Calls on Russia to Find Hillary Clinton's Missing Emails," *New York Times*, July 27, 2016.

3   Andrew C. McCarthy, *Ball of Collusion: The Plot to Rig an Election and Destroy a Presidency* (New York: Encounter Books, 2019), 195–196.

4   "Transcript: Donald Trump's Victory Speech," *New York Times*, November 9, 2016.

5   Politico Staff, "Full text: 2017 Donald Trump Inauguration Speech Transcript," *Politico*, January 20, 2017.

6   Ben Smith, "The Old-Time Clinton Hater Who Saw Trump Coming," BuzzFeed, February 10, 2017.

Acknowledgments

I have had a gaudy and grand time of it through all the days of my life. Oh, there were a few slipups along the way, but for the most part, I have been preceded by little girls heaving bouquets. Writing my memoirs has been immensely entertaining and even enlightening—did I really meet Prince Charles, now King Charles III? Did Ronald Reagan listen to the music of Frederick the Great in my living room? Frankly, I would like to do a second volume of memoirs, but that would entail another fifty years of public life and honestly, I am not up to it. The writing I can handle, but the living would be impossible. It is enough to say I am very grateful to have the memories, the friends, and even the enemies, or at least most of the enemies.

Among the friends who are still with us are the Donners, Joe and his son Alex, the gifted bandleader who is working diligently to keep the Great American Songbook alive. Also, there are the Mercers: Bob, who is among other things a gifted line editor, and his daughter, Rebekah, who serves on our board. Of course, I would be remiss if I did not acknowledge the talented staff of *The American Spectator*, who now keep the news and the commentary coming on a daily basis.

Thanks especially to our publisher Melissa Mackenzie and, for more than forty years, to my right-hand man, Wlady Pleszczynski.

Frank Buckley read over my manuscript, as did Wesley Smith and his wife Debra J. Saunders. Paul Kengor, who is at work on a history of the magazine, also read this book in manuscript. He liked it so much that he has become *The American Spectator*'s editor. Our board of directors, led by the incomparable Bob Luddy, has been invaluable, along with the board's ex officio member Hunt Lawrence, the New York City investor. I would like to thank my agent, Alex Hoyt, and my editors, Adam Bellow and Aleigha Kely. Alas, Myrna Larfnik has gone into retirement, but after assisting me with thirteen books, she deserves a rest. Finally, I had as my research assistant one woman who single-handedly outperformed Churchill's gifted team of Oxfordians, Erin McLaughlin, and she is a lot younger than Churchill's team. Special thanks to Erin, and of course to my wife, the irrepressible Jeanne.

RET
May 16, 2023
Old Town
Alexandria, Virginia